Praise for *High on the Hog*

"[A] passionate perspective on the culinary history of the African diaspora." —*Booklist*

"There is more than enough for every taste in [*High on the Hog*]." —*Chicago Tribune*

"Delicious . . . *High on the Hog* [is] as satisfying as a smothered pork chop." —*Cleveland Plain Dealer*

"Harris . . . offer[s] a tremendous cast of characters whose names deserve wider renown." —*New York Times Book Review*

"Our leading historian of African-American cooking continues her quest to trace the multiplicity of ways that American food has been enriched—and in many ways created—by the Africans who were forced to immigrate to North America and their descendents." —**Vogue.com**

"Harris's flavorful writing moves with an effortless voice that you feel could recite most of these pages from loving memory. As much historical document as ethnography of a vital and rich gastronomy, *High on the Hog* is a book to make your mouth water." —*Paste*

"Rejoice, all you lovers of the personal and inimitable voice of Jessica B. Harris. In *High on the Hog*, she has woven her own story into the epic of the African Diaspora, using food to illuminate the intertwined tapestries of Africa, Europe, and America. From General George Washington's black cook Hercules to New Orleans's famed Dooky Chase, she shows how important are the African underpinnings of the American table. Harris's passionate devotion to languages and history, together with her own compassion and wit, resonate with the humanity she espouses in all her books, but especially this one." —**Betty Fussell, author of *Raising Steaks* and *My Kitchen Wars***

HIGH ON THE HOG

A CULINARY JOURNEY

FROM AFRICA TO AMERICA

JESSICA B. HARRIS

BLOOMSBURY
NEW YORK • LONDON • OXFORD • NEW DELHI • SYDNEY

Bloomsbury USA
An imprint of Bloomsbury Publishing Plc

1385 Broadway 50 Bedford Square
New York London
NY 10018 WC1B 3DP
USA UK

www.bloomsbury.com

BLOOMSBURY and the Diana logo are trademarks of
Bloomsbury Publishing Plc

First published 2011
This paperback edition published 2012

ISBN: HB: 978-1-59691-395-0
PB: 978-1-60819-450-6
ePub: 978-1-60819-127-7

Library of Congress Cataloging-in-Publication Data

Harris, Jessica B.
High on the hog : a culinary journey from Africa to America /
Jessica B. Harris.—1st U.S. ed.
p. cm.
Includes index.
ISBN 978-1-59691-395-0 (hardcover)
1. African American cooking—History. 2. African Americans—
Food—History. 3. Food habits—America—History.
4. Food habits—Africa—History. I. Title.
TX715.H29972 2011
641.59'296073—dc22
2010024899

20 19

Designed by Rachel Reiss
Typeset by Westchester Book Group
Printed and bound in the U.S.A. by Thomson-Shore Inc., Dexter, Michigan

To find out more about our authors and books visit www.bloomsbury.com.
Here you will find extracts, author interviews, details of forthcoming
events, and the option to sign up for our newsletters.

First and always to my late parents
Jesse Brown Harris and Rhoda Alease Jones Harris

And

To the Ancestors who slaved, served, survived, and
created a cuisine from a sow's ear
To those past who used that food to nourish families,
grow fortunes, and connect communities

And

To the African American cooks, chefs, and culinary
entrepreneurs now and yet to come
Who honor the food, serve it up proudly, and keep the
circle unbroken.

CONTENTS

FOREWORD

BY MAYA ANGELOU

Jessica Harris, the well-known cook and cookbook author, has taken a great risk. She is already highly respected for the meticulous care she has shown in describing her recipes. She has been reliable in listing her sometimes exotic ingredients and where they can be found. However, in this new book she has offered only twenty recipes. Each is clear and well explained; still, the majority of *High on the Hog* is comprised of stories and essays written in well-chosen prose about food and how it traveled and made its impact on the world.

Harris has chosen African cookery and tracked its influence to the United States, to South America, and to the Caribbean. She shows explicitly how the culinary efforts changed the mores and cultures and people in each place. She has left little room for argument with her findings. I do, however, wonder if Ms. Harris is about to change permanently her ways of producing books.

Because I had written many books and had taught many classes years ago, I thought I was a writer who could teach. When I took the risk of accepting a permanent job teaching, I found I was not a writer who could teach, but a teacher who could write.

If Harris decides that she is more a prose writer than a recipe writer, the world of cookbook users and readers will be poorer for it. However, because she writes so well, all readers will be well serviced.

I will be among that group.

INTRODUCTION

I am an African American. My family comes from here and can trace itself on both sides back over much of the period documented in this book. Therefore I know intimately, and am linked by blood to, the tastes of pig meat and cornmeal that are a part of this country's African American culinary heritage. I've spent more than three decades writing about the food of African Americans and how it connects with other cuisines in the hemisphere and around the world, and so I also know that the food of the African continent and its American diaspora continues to remain a culinary unknown for most folks.

The history of African Americans in this country is a lengthy one that begins virtually at the time of exploration. Our often-hyphenated name, in all of its complexity, hints at the intricate mixings of our past. We are a race that never before existed: a cobbled-together admixture of Africa, Europe, and the Americas. We are like no others before us or after us. Involuntarily taken from a homeland, molded in the crucible of enslavement, forged in the fire of disenfranchisement, and tempered by migration, we all too often remain strangers in the only land that is ours. Despite all this, we have created a culinary tradition that has marked the food of this country more than any other. Our culinary history is fraught with all the associations with slavery, race, and class that the United States has to offer. For this reason, the traditional foodways that derive from the history of enslavement that many of us share are often perceived as unhealthy, inelegant, and hopelessly out of sync with the culinary canons that define healthy eating today.

Yet, for centuries, black hands have tended pots, fed babies, and worked in the kitchens of this country's wealthiest and healthiest. The disrespect for our food and for the people who cook it has been a battle that has raged for decades. *Ebony* magazine's first food editor, Freda DeKnight, wrote about it in the introduction to her 1948 cookbook, *Date with a Dish*: "It is a fallacy, long disproved, that Negro cooks, chefs, caterers, and homemakers can adapt themselves only to the standard Southern dishes, such as fried chicken, greens, corn pone and hot breads." More than a half century after the book's publication, at a period when chefs have become empire builders and media millionaires, that debate still rages. Certainly I will have much to say about slave markets, both those in which my ancestors were sold and others where my ancestors and those like them sold goods that they'd grown and items that they'd prepared. I will speak of scant meals of hog and hominy and of simple folk who became culinary entrepreneurs, like illiterate "Pig Foot" Mary, who created a real estate empire from the food that she cooked on an improvised stove on the back of a baby carriage!

I will also speak of presidential chefs like George Washington's Hercules and Thomas Jefferson's James Hemings and of an alternate African American culinary thread that weaves through the fabric of our food. This parallel thread is a strong one and includes Big House cooks who prepared lavish banquets, caterers who created a culinary co-operative in Philadelphia in the nineteenth century, a legion of black hoteliers and culinary moguls, and a growing black middle and upper class.

My family is a part of that middle class and encapsulates both culinary threads. In 1989, I wrote in *Iron Pots and Wooden Spoons: Africa's Gifts to New World Cooking*, "Fate has placed me at the juncture of two Black culinary traditions: that of the Big House and that of the rural South." The Jones side of the family always held reunions at table. Early childhood memories are filled with images of groaning boards, of "put up" preserved peaches, seckle pears, and watermelon rinds, of "cool drinks" such as minted lemonade, of freshly baked Parker House rolls and yeast breads. The Harris side of the family were no slouches at "chowing down" either. Grandma Harris insisted on fresh produce, and some of my early memories are of her gardening in a small plot where she lived.

Writing about the food of African Americans connects me to my forebearers. On one side of the family was Samuel Philpot, who was born enslaved in Virginia and in his thirties at the time of Emancipation. My mother knew him, and I have several photographs of him, as he lived to be more than one hundred years of age. He was reputed to have been a Big House servant who on one occasion served Abraham Lincoln at supper. He married the daughter of free people of color, settled in Virginia, near Roanoke, and became the progenitor of the Jones side of my family. On the Harris side of the family, my great-grandmother Merendy Anderson had an orchard in the post-Emancipation period where she grew stone fruit—plums, peaches, and more—and sold them to neighbors in her Tennessee town. Closer to me were both of my grandmothers, who embodied the culinary traditions of their families. Grandma Harris cooked little and not particularly well, but she made beaten biscuits and could put a hurtin' on a mess of greens. She read her Bible and wrote poetry, but was plainspoken, a vestige of her struggle with literacy. Grandma Jones was more eloquent on paper; she'd gone to a women's seminary in Virginia in the late nineteenth century and embodied all the elegance that that state claims at table.

As this book is the direct result of my knowing them, I wrote it as if they'd survived to read it. I have deliberately foresworn the traditional academic format that I teach in order to move the odyssey forward. For *High on the Hog* is a journey into the realm of African American food, but makes no claim at being *the* definitive volume (that copiously annotated, weighty opus has yet to appear and will be the work of another). Rather, this is a personal look at the history of African American food that tells the tale in brief compass, introduces a rich and abundant cast of characters, and presents some of the major themes in a discursive narrative.

Each chapter is—like Gaul—divided into three parts. An introduction sets the stage and presents a personal and present-day look at one of the stops on the journey. The main section of each chapter begins with a chronological presentation of the African American history of the period discussed that raises questions, presents a number of glorious participants, and moves the journey forward. Finally, each chapter ends with a coda that adds a closer look at some aspect of the period's food, much like what is called a *lagniappe* in Louisiana. A collection of recipes—some archival, some from my cookbooks—follows, presenting many of the key dishes in the African American culinary repertoire. Finally, there is a list of further reading and brief chronological listing of a selection of African American cookbooks for the questing bibliophile.

This book is at the same time a last and a first, as its writing has led me on an odyssey as well as opened doors in my life, my mind, and my soul that I will be entering and investigating in future years as I too attempt to journey from the hock to the ham and take my own life higher on the hog.

◆◆◆◆◆

Old Master killed about forty or fifty hogs every year. He had John to help him. When he was ready to pay him off he said, "John, here's your pig head, and pig feet, and pig ears." John said, "Thank you, boss."

So, John killed hogs for about five years that way; that's what he got for his pay. Then John moved on back of the place and got himself three hogs. Old Master didn't even know he had a hog. Next winter at hog-killing time Old Master went down after John. Old Master says, "John."

John come to the door—"Yessir." Old Master says, "Be down to the house early in the morning, I want to kill hogs—be there about five-thirty." John asks, "Well, Old Master, what you paying?" "I'll pay you like I always did. I'll give you the head and all the ears, and all the pig's feet and all the tails."

John said, "Well, Old Master, I can't, because I'm eating higher on the hog than that now. I got three hogs of my own an': I eat spareribs, backbone, pork chops, middling, ham, and everything else. I eat high on the hog now!"

CHAPTER 1

OUT OF AFRICA

Foods, Techniques, and Ceremonies
of the Mother Continent

Dan-Tokpa Market, Cotonou, Benin, West Africa—

I visited my first African market with my mother three decades ago. It was a sunny day in Dakar. We had left our hotel, the Croix du Sud, a grand art deco vestige of colonial times, to take a few turns around the European part of the city. Shortly after setting out, we found ourselves in the Marché Kermel, one of the city's many markets. I didn't know it then, but before independence the small bustling market had been designated for use by Europeans. We wandered, looking at the displays, wrinkling our noses at the butchers' stalls. We were fascinated by the flower sellers who jostled each other for position and rather loudly demanded payment for any of the photographs taken. (Indeed they seemed to sell more photographs than bright bouquets of flowers.) Little did I know that my first experience in the Marché Kermel would initiate me into a lifetime of market-love on the African continent and a love of the food that those markets have spawned on both sides of the Atlantic.

I'll never forget that first market visit, but to me the Dan-Tokpa Market in Benin will always be the mother of all African markets. No matter how many visits I make, I am always startled by its vitality and its vibrancy. After years of travel and countless skirts boasting hems stained with market mud from around the African continent, I continue to be amazed at how this large neighborhood market is transformed overnight into a small city of purveyors, each with his own clientele and all trying to hawk their wares.

The Dan-Tokpa Market, or the Tokpa, as it is affectionately known by locals, is a daily market, but every four days it surges into new life and trebles its size to become a *grand marché*. The Tokpa is not solely a food market; everything from brilliantly printed fabric to small and surely incendiary plastic demijohns of gasoline can be purchased. However, the exuberance of the food section and the variety of comestibles sold there speaks to the importance of food on the African continent.

Enormous snails that look like escargots on steroids are piled on mats in one section. In another, the air is pungent with the funk of dried smoked shrimp that are used for seasoning dishes. Bulging burlap sacks overflow with *gari*, or cassava meal, a major local starch. Earthenware cooking pots and calabash bowls are displayed in all sizes and shapes. Familiar leafy greens, tomatoes, and chilies are sold as well, albeit in different varieties and with unfamiliar names. Everywhere the eye glances there is a celebration of the food of West Africa. In terms of variety, the Topka rivals the exoticism of the souks of Marrakesh and the bazaars of the winding alleyways of Mombasa, Kenya. Yet many of the goods sold— okra, black-eyed peas, watermelon, and more—are familiar and remind me of my American home.

The markets of the African continent are timeless. I collect late-nineteenth and early-twentieth-century postcards of African markets and am often amazed and bemused by the similarities of clothing, gesture, and ingredients. Even today, despite the growing proliferation of supermarkets and home freezers among the middle class, there is still a love for the marketplace and the community it creates that will drive even the fanciest West African homemaker to mix with the crowds in search of just the right ingredient.

Over the years, I've also accumulated a mental Rolodex of recipes of West African market food, from the *poisson braisé* (grilled fish) of Benin to the *aloco* (deep-fried bananas) of the Côte d'Ivoire. They include grilled meats that are served up in spicy sauces for busy housewives to carry home in enameled basins and one-pot stews that nourish hungry laborers in from the country. There are also small fried tidbits for after-school snacks and cocktail nibbles for the elite: peanuts roasted on sand-covered griddles, orange-hued fritters dripping with palm oil, and more. The dusty streets of the Topka seem the perfect place to begin this culinary journey. With the food of the African continent on glorious display we can begin to learn how over the course of centuries that food has transformed the cooking and the tastes of the United States.

◆◆◆◆◆

The cooking of Africa has yet to have its moment on the foodie radar. With the exception of the food of the southern Mediterranean coast and of South Africa, it would seem that we're content to remain in the dark about the tastes of the continent. However, those who have tasted *yassa*, the lemon-infused chicken and onion stew served over fluffy white rice, from Senegal, or *kédjenou*, the deep, slow-cooked Ivorian stew of guinea hen, or a freshly caught grilled fish served up with an oniony, tomato-based sauce called *moyau* in Benin know how shortsighted this is. Much African food is tasty indeed. The traditional foods of the African continent may also reflect some of the world's oldest foodways, for, as James L. Newman puts it in *The Peopling of Africa: A Geographic Interpretation*, "all humanity shares a common Africa-forged genetic identity." Some of the continent's food even tastes surprisingly familiar, because, for centuries of forced and voluntary migration, the food of Western Africa has had an influence on the cooking of the world, transforming the taste and the dishes of many nations east and west, few more than the United States.

Current thinking is that the African continent is where man originated. If this is true, it is also where humans first began to forage for food. As early as eighteen thousand years ago, some Nile Valley communities in Upper Egypt made intensive use of vegetable tubers. Later humans began to care for wild grasses as well, but did not establish true cultivation until about the sixth millennium B.C., when people started to domesticate plants and animals and evolved lifestyles that were less nomadic. Many of the crops they cultivated then were native to the continent and are still cultivated today. These include some types of yam, African rice, and cereals such as sorghum and millets. Evidence of early agriculture has even been found within the Sahara, which then had a moister climate. Over time, these peoples migrated south, driven by the increasing desertification of the Sahara. In the western part of the continent, they settled in three different areas, each of which depended on a major grain or foodstuff as the basis for nourishment.

A wide band below the Sahara spanned from Sudan in the east to Senegal in the west and developed around the cultivation of sorghum and several varieties of millet. A coastal area and the Niger Delta region, including what is today Senegal and the Republic of Guinea, depended on rice and *fonio*, a native cereal grass that produces a small mustard-like seed. A third area, also on the coast, ran from today's Côte d'Ivoire through Cameroon and cultivated yams.

These three crucibles—cereals, rice, and yams—also marked three distinct areas from which enslaved Africans were brought to the United States. Each had its own traditional dishes centered on the starch that was its preference. Those from the rice crucible were among some of the earliest transported by the Transatlantic Slave Trade to what would become the United States. They brought with them their knowledge of rice cultivation and their memories of a rice-based cuisine, like that of today's Senegal, where wags say that the Lord's Prayer should be rewritten to say, "Give us this day our daily rice"! Those from the yam crucible arrived later, as the voracious slave trade made its way down the West African coast from Senegal to the Gold Coast, then south to the Bight of Benin and beyond. They saddled the United States with eternal confusion between the New World sweet potato and the Old World tuber whose name it came to bear—the yam. Those from the cereal crucible were inland and therefore not an immediate influence on American tastes until the inception of the slave trade. They depended on millet and on *fonio*, which were traditional, and by the time they were involved in the trade, on large amounts of American corn.

The Western world first began to hear of the food of the sub-Saharan Africa from one who had actually voyaged there in the middle of the fourteenth century. Abdalla Ibn Battuta, a famous Tangerine traveler, left Marrakesh in 1352 to head for Bilad al Sudan (the place of the blacks). He was sent by the sultan of Morocco on a mission to the kingdom of Mali to observe the kingdom that was one of the principle destinations of Berber trade caravans. Like many travelers before and since, he thought of his stomach, wrote often of the food that he encountered on his two-year journey, and became one of the primary recorders of the early foodways of Africa. He reckoned the dates of Sijilmasa in northern Mali some of the sweetest he'd ever encountered and suggested that the dessert was full of truffles (although these were probably some other kind of vegetable fungus). He crossed the Sahara with trade caravans and visited salt mines where the salt came from the earth in huge tablets. He spoke of calabashes decorated with intricate designs that were used as eating and storage vessels. Ibn Battuta's account is of particular interest to those looking at the origins of African American foods and foodways because almost seven hundred years ago he noticed elements of African foodways that are still reflected today in those of the continent's American descendants. He spoke not only of ingredients and storage vessels but also of cooking techniques, a woman-driven marketplace, a tradition of warm hospitality, and the importance of food in ritual.

Ibn Battuta's journey predated Columbus's voyages by almost a century and a half. By the early years of the Transatlantic Slave Trade, another century and a half later, the African continent had come under the influence of what is now known as the Columbian Exchange. Following Columbus's explorations, a New World larder of foods was unleashed. New World crops like tomatoes, corn, chilies, peanuts, and cassava arrived on the African continent and transformed its cuisine and changed its dining habits. Many of the New World additions, especially corn, chilies, and cassava, have become so emblematic of the continent's cuisine that it is almost impossible to imagine its dishes without them.

Not only the foodstuff made its way across the Atlantic; so did the basic cooking techniques. Whether frying, steaming in leaves, grilling, roasting, baking, or boiling, they could be duplicated using the hearth that was the European culinary standard. Cooking was done using flame, charcoal, and ash. There was no sautéing or braising, and most traditional dishes, while possibly elaborate in ingredients or preparation, relied on some form of live fire until fairly recently. From Morocco in the north to South Africa, from Kenya in the east to Cameroon in the west, the continent's traditional dishes tended to be variations on the theme of a soupy stew over a starch or a grilled or fried animal protein accompanied by a vegetable sauce and/or a starch. The starch changed from the couscous described by Ibn Battuta to millet couscous known as *tiéré* in Mali to the banana-leaf-wrapped fermented corn paste known as *kenkey* in Ghana or its pounded plantain variant, *akankye*. It might even be the plain white rice accompaning the yassa in Senegal. The stew might be served over the starch or the starch might be formed into balls, broken into bits, or scooped up with the fingers and dipped or sopped. It has been that way for centuries and remains that way today. Any Southerner who has ever sopped the potlikker from a mess of greens with a piece of cornbread would be right at home.

Our knowledge of early African foodways came not only from

voyagers like Ibn Battuta but also from explorers and missionaries. Mungo Park, the first European to view the headwaters of the Niger, traveled to the continent in the late eighteenth century. Like Ibn Battuta, he was concerned with his stomach and gave a detailed accounting of some of the foods he encountered. By the time that Park made his exploratory journey, American corn had begun to supplant the millet and *fonio* mentioned by Ibn Battuta, but couscous remained a traditional preparation no matter the starch. In his journal, Park described the process for making a corn couscous so precisely that it could be followed as a recipe.

> In preparing their corn for food, the natives use a large wooden mortar called a *paloon*, in which they bruise the seed until it parts with the outer covering, or husk, which is then separated from the clean corn, by exposing it to the wind: nearly in the same manner as wheat is cleared from the chaff in England. The corn thus freed from the husk is returned to the mortar and beaten into meal; which is dressed variously in different countries; but the most common preparation of it among the natives of the Gambia, is a sort of pudding, which they call *kouskous*. It is made by first moistening the flour with water, and then stirring and shaking it about in a large calabash or gourd, till it adheres together in small granules, resembling sago. It is then put into an earthen pot, whose bottom is perforated with a number of small holes; and this pot being placed upon another, the two vessels are luted together either with a paste of meal and water, or with cow's dung, and placed upon the fire. In the lower vessel is commonly some animal food and water, the steam or vapour of which ascends through the perforations in the bottom of the upper vessel, and soften and prepares the *kouskous* which is much esteemed throughout all the countries that I visited.

Park also spoke of rice dishes and of corn puddings and of the fact that there were a wide variety of vegetables. Fowl was abundant and included partridge as well as guinea hens, which are indigenous to the continent.

Like Ibn Battuta, the explorers were amazed by the lavish hospitality that was offered by rich and poor alike to guests and visitors. René Caillé, who traveled overland from Morocco through Mali into Guinea, spoke of the foods he ate in his 1830 travel account. He mentioned a "copious luncheon of rice with chicken and milk," which he ate with delight and which filled the travelers for their journey. He also recounted a meal offered to him by the poor of a village, which consisted of a type of couscous served with a sauce of greens. While Caillé enjoyed his copious meal, his hosts made due with boiled yam with a saltless sauce. Similar prodigious hospitality garnered commentary from virtually all writers. However, some of the more gastronomically inclined French travelers, like Caillé and others, were as astonished by the sophisticated tastes of the food as they were by the generous hospitality. Theophilus Conneau, another Frenchmen, recorded that on December 8, 1827, he ate an excellent supper. It was

> a rich stew which a French cook would call a sauce blanche. I desired a taste which engendered a wish for more. The delicious mess was made of mutton minced with roasted ground nuts [or peanuts] and rolled up into a shape of forced meat balls, which when stewed up with milk butter and a little malaguetta [sic] pepper, is a rich dish if eaten with rice en pilau. Monsieur Fortoni [sic] of Paris might not be ashamed to present a dish of it to his aristocratic gastronomes of the Boulevard des Italiens.

This was high praise indeed from a Frenchman.

Ibn Battuta, Park, Caillé, and others like them also visited the courts of African rulers and commented on the grandeur that attended the sovereigns. Mansa Kankan Musa of Mali, ruler of the region that Battuta visited, was so extravagant in his lifestyle that when he went on a pilgrimage to Mecca, he distributed such quantities of gold that in his wake the Egyptian dinar was devalued by 20 percent. Leaders of the Akan, Fon, Bamiléké, Bamun, and Yoruba peoples and other coastal kingdoms equally impressed early European arrivals with their wealth, the splendor of their courts, and the ceremonies and rituals surrounding food and food service.

Christianized Anna Nzingha, and also known as Dona Ana de

Souza, the seventeenth-century queen of the Ndongo and Matamba kingdoms was an absolute sovereign. A lunch in her court, as recorded in 1687 by João António Cavazzi de Montecúccolo in *Descrição histórica dos três reinos do Congo, Matamba e Angola*, was a finely tuned show of prestige combining African and Westernized customs. The queen, in her usual manner, was seated on a mat surrounded by her ladies and ministers. Her meal was served in vessels of clay, although she owned silver ones. When the food was served, it was piping hot, and the guests ate with their hands, passing the food between their left and right hands until it cooled off. Cavazzi, an Italian priest who was in attendance at court, once counted eighty different dishes being served. When the queen drank, all those present clapped their hands or touched their fingers to their feet to indicate that she should enjoy what she was drinking from her head to her toes. She ate in great pomp, and the leftovers were given to the rest of the court.

The pomp of the African courts amazed the travelers, but they also commented on the elaborate rituals surrounding service. Food has remained an integral part of ritual on the continent, from the milk that is poured into the sea at Gorée, Senegal, to placate Mame Coumba Castel, the spirit of that island, to the mashed yam that is symbolically "fed" to the sacred stools of the Ashanti. In general, traditional holidays on the continent can be divided into two basic types: those that offer thanksgiving and sacrifice to the ancestors and the gods and those that celebrate the new harvest. "Hooting at hunger," or Homowo, among the Ga people of the Accra plains of Ghana, is a thanksgiving festival where the community gathers annually to ridicule hunger and celebrate triumphing over it and vanquishing famine. In Ghana and Nigeria and other countries within the belt where yams are the major starch, traditional yam festivals like Homowo remain common. New yams are propagated from old ones, and so the tuber has come to symbolize the continuity of life. Yam celebrations range from new yam shoots being paraded through the street of the community to ensure prosperity and a fruitful harvest to the elder or communal leader reading yam peelings as an oracle to foretell what the next crop will yield. Many of these celebratory occasions end in a communal meal of pounded yam. Over the centuries, these ceremonies and others like them were transformed by time and place, religion and culture, and they form the basis for many culinary rituals that remain integral parts of African American life: holiday celebrations, church suppers, traditional New Year's meals, and even Kwanzaa.

In Western Africa, the recipes and indeed the festivities changed as the continent increasingly became invaded by the cultures of the outside world. The Dya'ogo dynasty that ruled the kingdom of Tekur in what is today Mali adopted Islam around 850 C.E. From this foothold, the religion began to make further incursions into sub-Saharan Africa. It spread through trade, jihad, and conversion deeper into the Sahel and fanned out toward the coastal regions. It was integrated in the cultures of Mali, Senegal, Niger, Mauretania, Upper Volta, and Guinea by the time of Ibn Battuta's travels and those of the early explorers. Islam brought with it dietary prohibitions, rules about meal service, and a cycle of feasting and fasting, complete with holidays and rituals that melded with those of traditional religions and became a potent cultural force in the western part of the continent by the time of the Transatlantic Slave Trade. The Christianizing of the continent from the fifteenth century onward resulted in Roman Catholic dietary rules and regulations being adopted by its followers. Those who lived in the coastal areas were more rapidly influenced by the Europeans who made increasing incursions into the continent. Coastal dwellers eventually developed a creolized society that mixed African mores with those of the prevailing European colonial powers. Over the centuries, travelers were followed by explorers who became colonizers, and the Portuguese, French, Dutch, British, Belgians, and Germans all brought their dietary habits, religious restrictions, and everyday rituals to the continent, where they became a part of the culinary kaleidoscope that is the western segment of the African continent.

Recipes, religious celebrations, meals, menus, and more from the African continent were a part of the cultural baggage that was brought across the Atlantic by those who would be enslaved. No matter where the individual's origins, direct ties to the mother continent were ruptured and scattered in the upheaval of the Transatlantic Slave Trade. The general notions of ceremony and the tastes of the food of ritual and of daily life, however, remained in memory, atavisms that influenced the taste, cooking techniques, marketing styles, ritual behaviors, and hospitality of their descendants and of the country that would become theirs. The matrix was fixed on the African continent; the transformation from African to African American involved one of the most brutal passages that humans have had to endure: the Middle Passage of the Transatlantic Slave Trade.

OKRA, WATERMELON, AND BLACK-EYED PEAS: AFRICA'S GIFTS TO NEW WORLD COOKING

472. Afrique Occidentale — DAKAR
Un Marché indigène

Collection Générale de l'A.O.F., Fortier, Dakar - Reprod. interd

While millions of Africans were brought in chains to the New World, the botanical connection to the African continent remained relatively small. The list is even smaller in the United States, where the weather did not permit the introduction of such tropical species as ackee, the oil palm, kola, true African yams, and other tubers. The few plants that could survive—okra, watermelon, and black-eyed peas—have, however, remained emblematic of Africans and their descendants in the United States and of the region in which most of them toiled, the American South.

Okra is perhaps the best known and least understood outside African American and Southern households. Prized on the African continent as a thickener, it is the basis for many a soupy stew and is served up in sheets of the slippery mucilage that it exudes. Okra probably was first introduced into the continental United States in the early 1700s, most likely from the Caribbean, where it has a long history. Colonial Americans ate it, and by 1748 the pod was used in Philadelphia, where it is still an ingredient in some variants of the Philadelphia gumbo known as pepperpot. In 1781 Thomas Jefferson commented on it as growing in Virginia, and we know that it was certainly grown in the slave gardens of Monticello. By 1806 the plant was in relatively widespread use, and botanists spoke of several different varieties.

Our American word *okra* comes from the Igbo language of Nigeria, where the plant is referred to as *okuru*. It is the French word for okra, *gombo*, that resonates with the emblematic dishes of southern Louisiana known as gumbo. Although creolized and mutated, the word *gumbo* harks back to the Bantu languages, in which the pod is known as *ochingombo* or *guingombo*. The word clearly has an African antecedent, as do the soupy stews that it describes, which are frequently made with okra.

Watermelon has been so connected with African Americans that it is not surprising to learn that the fruit is believed to have originated on the African continent. Pictures of watermelons appear in Egyptian tomb paintings, and in southern Africa they have been used for centuries by the Khoi and San of the Kalahari. More than 90 percent water, the fruit is useful in areas where water may be unsafe, and it is also especially prized to cool folks down in hot weather.

Watermelons arrived in the continental United States fairly early on in the seventeenth century and were taken to heart and stomach rapidly as new cultivars were developed that were more suitable to the cooler weather. As with okra, watermelon has been indelibly connected to African Americans. Indeed some of the most virulently racist images of African Americans produced in the post–Civil War era involve African Americans and the fruit. Watermelon became so stereotypically African American that black comedian Godfrey Cambridge in the 1960s developed a comedy routine about the travails of an upwardly mobile black man trying to bring home a watermelon without being seen by the neighbors in his upscale white community. He declared that he couldn't wait until a square water-melon was developed that would defy detection. (It has been; in the late twentieth century, the Japanese perfected a square watermelon that could be stacked.) National attitudes toward watermelon have changed, but the fruit and its stereotyped history still remain a hot-button issue for many.

Before Fergie sang with a music group known as the Black Eyed Peas, the vegetable was perhaps best known as an ingredient in the South Carolina *perloo* (or composed rice dish or pilaf) known as Hoppin' John. Legumes are among the world's oldest crops. They have been found in Egyptian tombs and turn up in passages in the Bible. The black-eyed pea, which is actually more of a bean than a pea, was introduced into the West Indies from Central Africa in the early 1700s and journeyed from there into the Carolinas. The pea with the small black dot is considered especially lucky by many cultures in Western Africa. While the pea was certainly not lucky for those who were caught and sold into slavery, the memory of the luck it was supposed to bring in West Africa lingered on among the en-slaved in the southern United States and the Hoppin' John that is still consumed on New Year's Day by black and white Southerners alike is reputed to bring good fortune to all who eat it.

As came okra, watermelons, and black-eyed peas, so came ses-ame and sorghum. The African continent is also responsible for our eternal confusion about yams and sweet potatoes. Some variants of true yams are African in origin. Across the Atlantic, they became confused with the sweet potatoes that were the predominant tubers to which the enslaved in the United States had access. In African American parlance and from there into Southern usage, they re-tained the name of the African tuber that they replaced—yam.

Peanuts are New World in origin, yet they remain connected in many minds with the African continent, because it is likely that they moved into general usage in the United States via the Transat-lantic Slave Trade. They returned to the northern part of their na-tive hemisphere complete with an African name that derived from the Bantu word *nguba*, meaning "groundnut"—goober. So we're all celebrating Africa when we're eating goober peas.

Whether in the slip of okra in a southern Louisiana gumbo, the cooling sweetness of a slice of watermelon on a summer day, or the luck of a New Year's black-eyed pea, the African continent is the origin of many of African American foodways. From its ingredients to its techniques and its hospitality, rituals, and ceremonies, the continent has remained a vivid memory: one that left its mark on its displaced children in the New World.

CHAPTER 2

SEA CHANGES

Enslavement, the Middle Passage,
and the Migrating Tastes of Africa

Gorée Island, Senegal—

Sunday was the day that the small ferries that took travelers back and forth to Gorée from Dakar were most crowded. Then day-trippers headed over to frolic on the tiny island's beaches and stopped for lunch in the local restaurants that caught the sea breezes. Those with more cash splurged on a gourmet luncheon at the Relais d'Espadon, or overnighted at the Chevalier de Boufflers, the small hotel named for one of the island's early-century governors. To those with little knowledge of its past, Gorée was a pleasant place in the 1970s: a picture-book spot where time seemed to have stopped. There were no cars, only sandy streets and alleyways bounded by rosy brick walls festooned with brilliantly colored bougainvillea blossoms. The breezes kept the island relatively cool, and the sight of a woman rounding a corner with her brightly colored robes billowing in the wind was one of the island's joys.

In the early 1970s, I journeyed to Senegal frequently and visited the island occasionally during my stays in Dakar. There, I learned of the calabash of milk that islanders offered annually to the sea to placate its tutelary spirit, Mame Coumba Castel. In those days, the aroma of frying fish turnovers called *pastels* and of meat grilling on the stoves of the small eateries near the ferry dock perfumed the air, and I loved the slip of sand under my feet. I enjoyed the warm greetings of the folks who lived on the outpost and the friends I made there. The most unforgettable thing about Gorée, though, was La Maison des Esclaves.

An unprepossessing building from the street, it looked like any other one, its rosy stucco facade broken by a wooden door that had seen much wear. A hand-lettered sign was the only indication that this house was different from the others surrounding it. It said, simply, LA MAISON DES ESCLAVES: the House of the Slaves. Through the door, one entered a courtyard where the most arresting feature was a curving horseshoe staircase under which a small corridor led to an open doorway to the sea. The brilliance of the sparkling sea on the other side beckoned through the darkness of the hall.

A small office was on one side of the entrance. In it sat the curator cum guide, whose ramrod posture and carefully enunciated French made me think of him as one of the *ancien combattants,* war veterans, who manned such venues throughout Western Africa. Joseph Ndiaye was his name, and on my first visit, he took me, my mother, and our small group of tourists through the former dwelling, detailing how the slave traders lived lavishly upstairs while terrified captives huddled in misery below them. He showed us the room where the women and young children were held, the stygian dungeons that housed the general population of men and boys, and the cramped lockups for the recalcitrant. He pointed out the open doorway to the rocks and sea and called it the Door of No Return. Ndiaye had a pair of iron shackles, which he put on, and as he hobbled around the courtyard, the realities of enslavement became vividly real. In 1972, before Alex Haley penned *Roots* and revised the way that many black Americans thought of their African ancestry, this was transformational. Certainly slavery was not a new concept, but actually standing on one of the spots where Africans had been forced on ships and sent off to the Americas was harrowing and unforgettable.

Gorée was no more than a shadow on the horizon for a few subsequent trips to Dakar until several years later, when I found myself compelled to go there again. By this time, *Roots* had transformed the place, and Ndiaye's demonstration had become more studied, more theatrical, and to me, less moving. The walls were decorated with slips of paper inscribed with quotations from around the world about slavery and its horrors. The crowds were larger; the house, however, remained the same. On this solo journey, without the comfort of my mother or fellow black Americans, the spirit of the place overwhelmed me, and I, like many others before and after me, broke down and began weeping with despair and grief at the thought of history's transgressions. I was in such a state that a newly made Senegalese friend, Yaya MBoup, took it upon herself to find me some African Americans who lived on the island and introduced me to John Franklin and Elaine Charles. That evening, I missed the last ferry from Gorée and spent the night amid new friends and the island's ghosts, listening to the slap of sandals on the sandy lanes, savoring the fragrant chicken *yassa* that had been prepared. That night I began to learn the tale of Gorée and the Transatlantic Slave Trade.

In the fifteenth century, Gorée was settled by the Portuguese as a beachhead of incursion into the African continent. Subsequently, the Dutch, British, and French took over the island in turn and made it their base during their years of slave trading. The transportation and enslavement of millions of Africans and their descendants was not a clear-cut issue but rather the result of much complicity between Europeans and Africans, many of whom had lived together in relative harmony in the coastal areas of the continent for centuries. There, in places like Gorée, they had developed their own culture, one that was creolized and that mixed European and African ways with facility. Historian Ira Berlin has called these people Atlantic Creoles. Up and down the West African coast they created a buffer community between Europeans and Africans and often served as middlemen in the Transatlantic Slave Trade.

In their forays to the Senegalese coast, the French, like their predecessors, developed friendships with local natives and established liaisons with local women who were known as *signares* (from the Portuguese *senhora*). These women, with European names like Caty Louette, Victoria Albir, and Anne Pépin, were members of Gorée's mulatto elite, which had developed from centuries of intermingling between Africans and Europeans. The *signares* bridged the worlds of Africa and Europe and evidenced the best and worst of each. Practiced courtesans, they dressed in European finery, contracted "local marriages" with powerful Europeans, headed their own businesses offering goods to provision ships, provided canoe men to transport the enslaved to the ships, made fortunes as slave traders, worked as go-betweens in the trade, and generally were complicit in the enslavement of many. They dominated the island and were its leading citizens. In 1767 Caty Louette had her own household slaves and owned one of the island's first stone houses. Victoria Albir built the colonnaded domicile that today houses the island's ethnographic museum, and Anne Pépin was the mistress of the chevalier de Boufflers, the island's French governor. She visited him resplendent with jewels and received his guests in lavish European style. For her, he constructed the house that became La Maison des Esclaves. The signares kept European-style households and developed a sumptuous fusion cuisine. The dishes they created for entertaining were designed to impress their French patrons and European guests. One example is the culinary tour de force *dem farci*: fish that is skinned, boned, stuffed with a forcemeat of fish and bread, reconstituted, cooked, and served whole. Their hospitality was as legendary as their beauty and their avidity, and the descendants of the dishes that they served to their French "husbands" are reputed to be some of Senegal's most sophisticated even today.

Goreé Island, which flourished under the French in the eighteenth century, was only one such place along the western coast of Africa where millions of Africans were sent to embark on the harrowing journey to the Americas. As the trade grew, slave depots pockmarked the western coast from Gorée in the north to Luanda and Benguela in Angola in the south. They are etched in infamy, yet, ironically, names like Elmina, Cape Coast, Anécho, Ouidah, Calabar, Bonny, Loango, and Cabinda are largely unknown to the American descendants of those who passed through them. These were the last spots on the African continent on which millions stood in fear, not knowing what would befall them before being loaded onto longboats or canoes, transported to the big ships that sat at anchor, and carried in misery across the ocean to the American future that awaited them. Surely, as they looked back in horror at the coastline ebbing away, they thought of families and loved ones lost, of traditions shared, and of the homes they would see no more. Not all came to the North American colonies; of the Africans who arrived in the hemisphere, only 6 percent came to the continental United States. The others went to Latin America and the Caribbean, with the largest number going to Brazil. No matter where their journeys from Gorée and like spots took them, they brought with them a remembrance of the meals they had eaten on the African continent that transformed the tastes of their new homes.

◆ ◆ ◆ ◆ ◆

Slavery existed in the world for centuries before it came to the shores of the Americas. We get our word *slave* from the Slavic peoples of middle Europe, who were captured and sold at the slave markets in Roman times along with prisoners of war from around the vast empire. Africans also knew slavery long before Europeans arrived on their shores. Enemies, criminals, and debtors all became slaves of those in power. An African slave trade to Europe that presaged the one to the Americas began as a trickle in 1441, when the Portuguese first brought sub-Saharan African slaves to European markets. Once Spain established its American settlements, Nicolás de Ovando, governor of Hispaniola, decreed that only black slaves born in Spain or Portugal could be imported into the colony. Eventually that ruling was abandoned, as those slaves incited the Indians to revolt. Yet, as the Spanish colonies grew in the New World, so did their need for slave labor, and regular slave traffic from Africa to the Americas began in 1519. Then, a century later, in 1619, a captured ship brought nineteen Africans who had been bound for enslavement in Cuba into the Jamestown Colony in Virginia. The original Africans were indentured and not enslaved, but they, like the millions of others who would follow them to the continental United States, had endured the Atlantic transit. They had survived the Middle Passage that was the birth canal of African Americans. It was a voyage that took Africans and transported them through moans, screams, pain, and wrenching separation into life on American shores.

The Middle Passage was the central leg of a complex triangular voyage that offered enormous profit to those whose ships successfully completed all three legs. In the early years, the journeys began in home ports in northern Europe, where captains provisioned their ships with trade goods—rum or brandy, gunpowder, beads, and cloth—and headed out to Africa. Once on the shores of the continent, they purchased slaves and transported them to the New World markets on the middle leg of the journey. The final leg of the tripartite journey was the voyage home, bringing sugar, tobacco, or other agricultural products from the colonies to European or American ports. For a period of more than three hundred years, the ships plied the waters of the Atlantic. It is estimated that during the period of the slave trade there, from 1527 to 1866, there were 27,233 transatlantic trips. The litany of ships and their names seems endless.

On September 13, 1693, the *Hannibal* left Gravesend, England, for the African coast. On January 13, 1698, the sloop *Albion Frigate* sailed from the Downs, on the English Channel, to the African coast. On October 25, 1773, *Adventure* cleared Newport, Rhode Island, for the Atlantic coast. On November 22, 1806, the brig *Tartar*, owned by Frederick Tuell of Charleston, South Carolina, headed out of Rhode Island bound for Rio Pongo in Guinea. The schooner *Nancy* left Charleston for Senegal on June 1, 1807. The trips continued clandestinely after the Transatlantic Slave Trade was outlawed in 1808; in 1845, the *Spitfire* sailed from New Orleans and was captured and found to be transporting 346 individuals. The *Wanderer* left Charleston flying the flag of the New York Yacht Club with false papers claiming it was sailing for Trinidad but in reality set course for the Congo, completed its journey successfully, and returned to the Georgia coast on December 1, 1858. Virtually all the nations of northern Europe engaged in the trade. Eventually they were joined by the northern and southern ports of the colonies that became the United States.

Ships left at all times of the year from Bristol and Liverpool in England; from Nantes, Bordeaux, and La Rochelle in France; from Boston, Providence, Newport, Baltimore, New York, Annapolis, Charleston, and other ports throughout the northern Atlantic. Canny slavers out of the British ports even calculated their sailings with the objective of arriving in South Carolina or Virginia between May and October, during the growing season, when Africans fetched higher prices. No matter what their home port or when they set sail, ships were provisioned with shackles and slaving equipment as well as with some staples that had to last the entire journey. The scale of provisioning ships was such that purchases by British slave traders influenced the cost of everything from the timber that was used to refit the ships' holds once they arrived on the African coast to edible stores.

Slave ships required more food than any of the other vessels trading on the Atlantic. In addition to the rations of the crews, which numbered about thirty individuals, they also had to provide for feeding three hundred or so enslaved Africans, who came from different cultures and had different food preferences. Slave-ship provision lists from Royal African Company records from 1682 to 1683 include such items as stockfish and beef, beans, salt, flour, and brandy, which was both a provision and a trade good. (In later years, the brandy was replaced with rum.) All was boarded for the first leg of the journey to the African coast. Estimating a six- to fifteen-week journey from British ports to the African coast, depending on winds and weather, captains planned on arriving on the West African coast in time for the harvests there, in order to be better able to take on additional supplies.

Once on the West African coast, the ships met up with others with the same mission, and it became a race among them to fill their hold with food and slaves. Captains cajoled and bribed African rulers, traded with middlemen and factors, and bought foodstuffs from locals while they waited for enough slaves to fill the holds, which were like voracious maws gobbling up human lives. Often they remained on the African coast for months at a time, sailing from port to port in search of human cargo; the average time most ships remained on the coast was four months. As the slaves were acquired, they were examined: lips pulled back and mouths probed for missing teeth and sores, eyes examined for ophthalmia and blindness, muscles palpated, genitals fingered—all to determine age and health. If the slaves were deemed sound, the bargaining began. Once the negotiations were concluded, the hapless captives were branded with a company's mark and herded out to the canoes that would take them to the ships that waited at anchor. Many were despondent; others attempted suicide; still others threw themselves overboard and were eaten by the sharks that followed the slave ships, preferring death to an uncertain future. Once on board, they were led belowdecks. Alexander Falconbridge, a ship's doctor who sailed with the slavers in the eighteenth century, observed these conditions:

> The men, on being brought aboard ship, are immediately fastened together, two and two by handcuffs on their wrists and irons rivetted on their legs . . . At the same time they are frequently stowed so close as to admit of no other position than lying on their sides. Nor will the height between decks, unless directly under the grating, allow them to stand; especially where there are platforms on either side, which is generally the case.

The holds in which they were kept were horrifying. Buckets served as latrines, and those too far away were reduced to relieving themselves on themselves and their neighbors. Falconbridge reported that the decks of the slave holds were covered in blood and mucus and concluded that "it is not in the power of the human imagination to picture a situation more dreadful or disgusting."

More compelling still is the testimony of Olaudah Equiano, an African who had experienced the Middle Passage firsthand:

> The stench of the hold while we were on the coast was so intolerably loathsome, that it was dangerous to remain there for any time, and some of us had been permitted to stay on the deck for fresh air; but now that the whole ship's cargo were confined together, it became absolutely pestilential. The closeness of the place, and the heat of the climate, added to the number in the ship, which was so crowded that each scarcely had room to turn himself, almost suffocated us.

The Middle Passage had begun.

Many have told tales of the newly enslaved Africans bringing with them in their hair or their clothing okra and sesame seeds, thereby transplanting them to the New World. The truth is that, with the exception of necklaces and amulets, the beads of which have been found in archaeological digs on this side of the Atlantic, most slaves arrived with no belongings and had little idea of their ultimate fate; some thought that they would be eaten! The arrival of African foodstuffs in this hemisphere during the period of the Transatlantic Slave Trade is the result of a more brutal reality. The economics of slavery were such that slavers needed to feed slaves a diet on which they would survive. Much ink flowed during the period of enslavement on how to feed the slaves inexpensively with foods that they would eat. Therefore the almost-four-century-long period of the Transatlantic Slave Trade was one that was marked by a second trade in the foodstuffs necessary for the enslaved Africans to endure their arduous and unspeakable journey. Their survival was of prime importance to the traders who studied West African cultures and dietary habits and used their knowledge in provisioning the ships that plied the trade. They traded with local peoples for fresh fruits and vegetables, but they were mainly interested in finding sufficient food to feed their captives on the lengthy and unpredictable transatlantic journey.

Three basic food crops were taken on, which corresponded to the three basic food crucibles of the western part of the continent: corn, rice, and yams. Indian corn, or maize, had arrived on the continent with the Columbian Exchange and had become one of the primary foods of the African coast from the Gambia River to Angola by the time of the transatlantic trade. Akan merchants in the Gold Coast region were among the few who offered corn in the enormous amounts the slave ships required; corn was also obtained on the Slave Coast. It was estimated that an adult captive would consume between fifteen and twenty stalks a day, and the journey could take months. Holds had to be filled to ensure slaves' survival. Demand was fierce. Prices fluctuated, and woe unto the trader who arrived during one of the periodic famines or between the twice annual corn harvests. For captives from the Senegambia and rice-growing regions, rice was needed. An African cultivar of rice (*oryza glaberrima*) was grown near the mouths of the Gambia and Senegal rivers and as far as the western extent of the Gold Coast (today's Ghana). While rice from the Carolinas was shipped to England and became a part of the English provisioning of the ships, it often was not adequate and had to be supplemented with bulk quantities of African rice bought on the upper Guinea coast. Captives from the Gulf of Benin required yams, the true yams that are native to the African continent and grown from the Ivory Coast to eastern Cameroon. They were the primary crop for the traders of Calabar and Bonny in present-day Nigeria, where the all-important yam was harvested, beginning in August. Supplies for sale usually lasted through early March. All the newly enslaved Africans were also thought to have a "good stomach for beans." As the trade increased, knowledge of African agriculture and growing seasons was employed by all traders to provision ships. Falconbridge reported:

> In their own country, the Negroes in general live on animal food and fish, with roots, yams and Indian corn. The horse beans and rice, with which they are fed aboard ship, are chiefly brought from Europe. The latter, however, is sometimes purchased on the Coast where it is superior to any other.

Other nationalities provisioned their ships and fed their captives differently, but North American slavers commonly fed their captives rice and corn, both of which could be obtained on the African coast and in America. They also gave them black-eyed peas. Seed rice was brought aboard ships to be winnowed and processed by enslaved women during the journey, then boiled in iron cauldrons: the corn was fried into cakes. British ships fed their captives fava beans, which were known as horse beans. They were brought from England and stored in vats, later to be mixed with lard and turned into a pulpy mash.

On most vessels, the enslaved were given two meals a day. In the morning they were brought on deck, and the hold was sluiced down in an attempt to alleviate illness and keep the notorious stench of the Guineamen, as the slave ships were called, at bay. The first meal was distributed around ten in the morning and usually consisted of rice, corn or yams, depending on the origins of the enslaved, along with water. Following the meal, the bowls, called "crews," and spoons were collected, as they could serve as weapons during mutinies. On some ships, bread was offered to the adults in the afternoon, occasionally with a pipe of tobacco and a tot of brandy. The afternoon meal was more dependent on European stores and might consist of slabber sauce or *dabbadab*. William Richardson recalled in *A Mariner of England*:

> Our slaves had two meals a day, one in the morning consisting of boiled yams and the other in the afternoon of boiled horse-beans and slabber sauce poured over each. This sauce was made of chunks of old Irish beef and rotten salt fish stewed to rags and well seasoned with cayenne pepper.

Others suggest that the infamous and repellently named slabber sauce was a mixture of palm oil, flour, water, and chili. The second concoction, *dabbadab*, was a mixture of rice, salt meat, pepper, and palm oil. The pepper, which was a part of many slave rations, was not the chili of the New World or the black pepper of the Indies but rather one of the pre-Columbian African spices: melegueta, or malagueta, pepper, a relative of cardamom, from which the Grain Coast, or Pepper Coast, got its name. It served as a flavoring agent and also as a medicinal designed to keep down the incidents of "flux and dry belly-ached."

The beverage was water, occasionally flavored with molasses. On some ships the allowance of water was a half pint per meal, unless the ship was put on short rations as punishment or because of the length of the voyage. Some slavers noted a general African taste for the "bite-y" and offered rice wine flavored with cayenne pepper. Usually, though, wine and spirits were only used medicinally or given on a cold day to ward off illness. All ships meals for the enslaved and for the crew were prepared under the direction of the ship's cook.

The cook was an important part of the slave ship operations because his ability to feed the newly enslaved in a manner that allowed them to survive was directly related to the voyage's financial success. Although not originally considered skilled laborers on board, like coopers and navigators, cooks were essential in the slave trading process. Cooks usually came from the ranks of superannuated sailors who could no longer hoist heavy items or climb the riggings. They usually spent their time in the cookhouse or galley of the ship, surrounded by pots, pans, and boilers. Their task of feeding three hundred to four hundred enslaved daily, plus crew and officers, was a daunting one, to say the least. By the eighteenth century in the northern colonies, the profession of ship's cook had become one of the few career paths open to free people of color, and even on slaving vessels this role was increasingly taken by African Americans or by one of the Atlantic Creole sailors. Whatever the cooks' color, they were frequently aided by "guardians," or confidential slaves, who were given positions of power because of their linguistic ability or because they were deemed more tractable. Considered less of a threat to the ship's security, women were often assigned such food preparation tasks as milling corn and husking rice, and as a result, the African hand remained in the cooking pot, evidenced by foods prepared with malagueta pepper and palm oil.

Mealtimes were dangerous times onboard slave ships, as the enslaved were usually brought on deck to eat. There are numerous accounts of mutinies and insurrections where slaves attacked the sailors with bowls and gouged them with spoons. Meals therefore were distributed with armed sailors in attendance at full watch.

Often press-ganged into service or waylaid in seaport taverns, the sailors who guarded the enslaved on board had living conditions only marginally better than those of their captives. These sailors were often flogged by the captain and other crew, and their diet consisted of moldy sea biscuits, weevil-infested grain, and the same beans that were served to the enslaved. If the ships lay becalmed in the horse latitudes, the crew could be put on short rations and their water supply reduced as well. Sailors supplemented their often-meager rations by fishing over the side of the ship. Many an ordinary sailor protested that the slaves were given better rations than the crew, and sailors frequently found themselves in competition with the enslaved for food. As Olaudah Equiano recalled,

> one day they had taken a number of fishes; and when they had killed and satisfied themselves with as many as they thought fit, to our astonishment who were on deck, rather than give any of them to us to eat as we expected, they tossed the remaining fish into the sea again.

White sailors died at a higher rate than their captives, and short-handed crews were occasionally supplemented with the enslaved. Sailors on the slave ships were certainly deemed more expendable then the slaves, and their high mortality rate gave credence to the slavers' saying

> *Beware and take care*
> *Of the Bight of Benin.*
> *For one that comes out*
> *There are forty go in.*

Sailors in the slave or Guinea trade also died of the fevers and diseases that waited on the African coast, as well as from the privations of all three legs of the triangular voyage, where human life was cheap. On the Middle Passage, though, they were also subject to mutinies by the enslaved caused by hunger strikes and other privations.

While they might have ignored the needs of their crew, captains found that correct provisioning and feeding of the captives was crucial: If they were not nourished according to their preferences, the enslaved would quite simply not eat. Even when the food did meet

the cultural dietary guidelines, many of the disoriented, newly enslaved Africans chose to exercise the only power that they had; they
drank only saltwater or simply refused to eat, preferring to waste
away and die rather than to face an uncertain future in an unknown
destination. Alexander Falconbridge wrote:

> Upon the Negroes refusing to take sustenance, I have seen
> coals of fire, glowing hot, put on a shovel, and placed so near
> their lips, as to scorch and burn them. And this has been
> accompanied with threats, of forcing them to swallow the
> coals, if they any longer persisted in refusing to eat. These
> means have generally had the desired effect. I have also
> been credibly informed that a certain captain in the slave
> trade poured melted lead on such of the Negroes as obsti-
> nately refused their food.

Refusal of food occurred in numbers great enough to necessitate
the invention by slavers of the speculum oris, a diabolical three-
pronged screw device designed to force open the mouths of the stub-
born so that they could be force-fed with a funnel. It was used when
the cat-o'-nine-tails was not sufficient to prod the recalcitrant. In
their refusal of food the Africans had unwittingly discovered a first
culinary step in resistance to enslavement: The power of no. This
first step in the resistance would be used again and again throughout the period of enslavement.

Hunger strikes were common occurrences on board the Guineamen. The *Loyal George* witnessed a hunger strike and mass suicide
in 1727; in 1730, a larger hunger strike broke out aboard the *City of
London*. In 1765, on the *Black Joke*, a small child was pitched overboard in front of his mother because she had refused to eat. And in
1787, the enslaved refused food on the *Deux Soeurs* from Nantes
as well. Whether despondent or rebellious, the slaves surely realized that their only remaining power was the control of their own
bodies, and refusal of food imposed their personhood on the brutal system. The battle of wills between the newly enslaved and
their captors was the daily routine for the transatlantic voyage.

Then, after weeks or often months at sea, land was spotted, and
preparations began for landing on American shores and for the

sale. Once in port, rations improved, and the enslaved were given food to bulk them up and give them the appearance of health. They were bathed, shaved, and covered with palm oil to disguise any skin ailments. They were also given cloth to cover themselves. Most were unable to walk after the long journey and the cramped conditions, and their general condition was pitiable. The records are filled with tales of disoriented slaves haltingly leaving the boats with excrement dripping down their legs, blinking at the light of day. Dazed and frightened, they again became despondent and melancholy, and captains often had to find other blacks onshore more acclimatized to enslavement and take them onboard the vessels to allay the fears of the newly arrived.

Their introduction to the new world in which they'd landed was a sale by public auction or a private sale by the more barbarous "scramble." Falconbridge explained:

> The mode of selling them by scramble is most common. Here, all the negroes scrambled for bear an equal price; which is agreed upon between the captain and the purchasers before the sale begins. On a day appointed, the negroes are landed and placed altogether in a large yard belonging to one of the merchants to whom the ship is consigned. As soon as the hour agreed on arrives, the doors of the yard are suddenly thrown open and in rushes a considerable number of purchasers, with all the ferocity of brutes. Some instantly seize such of the negroes as they can conveniently lay hold of with their hands . . . The poor astonished negroes are so much terrified by these proceedings, that several of them, on one occasion, climbed over the walls of the courtyard and ran wild about the town but were soon hunted down and retaken.

Surely, they must have wondered into what hell their fate had brought them. Then, came the rupture of another separation; this time the newly enslaved were torn from their shipmates, who had become a second family. They were taken off by their new owners to the destinies that awaited them in America. The transit was over; the sea change had taken place. They were bound to the fate of a new place.

AN EBOE FROM ESSAKA

Hanging on the walls of the Royal Albert Memorial Museum in Exeter, England, is an eighteenth-century portrait of a black man. The man is dressed in the clothing of the period: a scarlet waistcoat and an immaculate white stock, simply tied. He gazes at the observer from the canvas with a slight smile at the corners of his full mouth. The smile, though, does not reach his eyes, which are filled with sadness. The portrait, attributed to a member of the English school, is titled *Portrait of a Negro Man, Olaudah Equiano*.

Olaudah Equiano, also known as Gustavus Vassa, was the individual who offered the earliest and most detailed account of his capture, enslavement, and journey to America in the Middle Passage. While many slave narratives detailed the lives of the enslaved in the nineteenth century, few portrayed eighteenth-century life, and even fewer still detailed the horrors of capture and the degradation of the Middle Passage. Much of what the world knows about the early period of the slave trade comes from his autobiography, *The Interesting Narrative of the Life of Olaudah Equiano; or, Gustavus Vassa, the African, Written by Himself.* Born an Igbo in what would become Nigeria, Equiano led an extraordinary life. Captured as a child, he was sold to various African masters and eventually found himself in the hands of white slave traders who shipped him to the colonies, where he was taken to Barbados and eventually sold in Virginia to Michael Pascal. His master was a naval captain, and as Pascal's personal servant, Equiano accompanied him and traveled to Europe. With his master he saw action in the Seven Years' War and was given rudimentary naval training. He also performed a variety of military duties aboard ship. During journeys with his master, which took him as far afield as the Mediterranean and Canada, he received an education and learned to read and write.

At the end of the war, however, Equiano did not reap the benefits that had been promised: prize money and freedom. Instead he was sold again, this time in the Caribbean, where travels had taken him. His education made him too valuable for plantation labor, and potential buyers were leery of acquiring a slave who could read and write and who knew how to navigate a ship. He was eventually sold to Robert King, a Quaker merchant from Philadelphia, who allowed Equiano to engage in his own trading activities and promised that he would free him upon payment of forty pounds. By his twenties, Equiano had earned enough through his trading to pay the debt and was a free man. As unscrupulous traders had attempted to re-enslave him during his Philadelphia sojourn, Equiano fully understood the perils of being a free black in federal America and declined King's offer to remain there and become his business partner. Rather, he journeyed to England, where he spent the rest of his life as a public figure.

In 1789, three months before the storming of the Bastille, Equiano self-published his autobiography, *The Interesting Narrative of the Life of Olaudah Equiano.* The book was a runaway bestseller in London, directly influenced British attitudes toward slavery, and fueled the abolitionist cause. Equiano promoted the book assiduously, gave

speeches, and became renowned and wealthy. When he died, eight
years after the book's publication, he left a considerable estate. He
was known to the prince of Wales and numerous dukes as well as
by the leading abolitionist statesmen of the time. Equiano, though,
when he sat down to recall his life, remembered not only the travails
of the Middle Passage, the brutalities of enslavement, and the multiple events of his peripatetic life; he also remembered the tastes of
Africa and recalled the foods eaten in his West African village:

> Our manner of living is entirely plain; for as yet the natives
> are unacquainted with those refinements of cookers which
> debauch the taste: bullocks, goats, and poultry, supply the
> greatest part of their food. These constitute likewise the
> principal wealth of the country, and the chief articles of its
> commerce. The flesh is usually stewed in a pan; to make it
> savoury we sometimes use also pepper, and other spices,
> and we have salt made of wood ashes. Our vegetables are
> mostly plantains, eadas, yams, beans, and Indian corn. . . .
> They are totally unacquainted with strong or spirituous li-
> quors; and their principal beverage is palm wine. This is
> gotten from a tree of that name by tapping it at the top, and
> fastening a large gourd to it; and sometimes one tree will
> yield three or four gallons in a night. When just drawn it is
> of a most delicious sweetness; but in a few days it acquires
> a tartish and more spirituous flavor.

Several scholars today question whether Equiano was as he advertised himself: an Eboe from Essaka. It has been argued that his
autobiography is a composite one made up of the reminiscences of a
number of enslaved or even that it is a work of pure imagination. No
matter what the final verdict, *The Interesting Narrative of the Life of
Olaudah Equiano* remains a moving account of the trade that ripped
millions from their homeland and transported them to another
hemisphere for more than five centuries. Equiano speaks for the millions of individuals who departed captives and arrived enslaved with
no families, no friends, and no possessions—nothing except the fad-
ing memories of their distant homeland and perhaps, like Equiano, a
fleeting memory of the sweetness of palm wine on their tongue.

CHAPTER 3

THE POWER OF THREE

Arrivals, Encounters, and
Culinary Connections

Aquinnah, Martha's Vineyard—

Aquinnah, on the westernmost tip of Martha's Vineyard, used to be called Gay Head until relatively recently, when younger folk became sensitive about the contemporary implications of the name that had referred to the multihued cliffs that are the town's trademark. In years past, excursions down the russet, terra-cotta, and gray clay cliffs were a highpoint of any trip around the island, but the fragile ecology means that they are now closed to the public and the descent is only a thing of memory to islanders of my vintage. Parts of Aquinnah are tribal land, and the area itself is the home of the Wampanoag, the tribe that greeted the Pilgrims when they landed in Plymouth in 1620. On a Wednesday, I received a call from one of my many Up-Island friends asking me to a local event and offering me the thing that is more precious than gold to the nondriving New Yorker that I am—a ride.

As we drove along the twists and turns of the tree-shaded Up-Island roads that I have known for more than fifty years, I stared out of the window. I found myself looking at the tall oaks and the underbrush covered with poison ivy and blueberry bushes as though seeing them for the first time. The forest was dense; the light was dappled as we headed toward the setting sun. I thought back to the Hawthorne that I had to memorize decades ago, and the lines came flooding back:

> *This is the forest primeval.*
> *The murmuring pines and the hemlocks,*
> *Bearded with moss, and in garments green, indistinct*
> *in the twilight,*
> *Stand like Druids of old, with voice sad and prophetic.*

This, though, was not a first-growth forest; this forest was of more recent vintage, but the land was rich with history.

It was curious that after so many years of journeying to the island's tip for sundowner drinks or luncheon stops, I had never really made the historic connections that the island's Wampanoag have. They, though, work hard to retain their culture and create an awareness of their heritage for their children and for the rest of the island since receiving federal recognition in 1987.

As the road entered the town, through the trees I saw a huge stone beehive oven behind a massive pile of firewood. It was part of a new local bakery, where we were all to meet. I was curious about the gathering. It was not a powwow or tribal event; rather, it was a group of local families and their friends coming together for pizza night. Each family brought something to add to the meal—fresh tomatoes, homemade fennel sausage, cheese from one of the island farms, birthday cakes for celebrations, and, of course, wine. (One child even brought candy sprinkles to top his pizza.) Julie Vanderhoop, the daughter of a venerable Indian family, was the baker and had decided to use her oven and her culinary skills to bring the town together. Each Wednesday she provided the dough and made the individual pizzas that became the communal supper. Standing by the oven that she had fired up for her usual round of baking, she tested the heat and fed the round pizzas into the oven's open maw with professional precision. The festive atmosphere of the gathering reminded me of some of the ceremonies and family occasions that I'd attended on the African continent. Mothers watched not only their children but also the offspring of others; all felt free to feed the children, and, when they got too rowdy, to gently discipline them as their own. That fall evening on Martha's Vineyard, I was struck by the seamless way that the assembled folk came together over food—sharing, preparing, celebrating, and for the duration of the evening, melding into an extended family.

The majority of the Indians of the Southeast, the Gulf Coast, and the coastal Northeast—the first American points of European contact—have been either assimilated like the Wampanoag, decimated, or removed to make way for the expansion of the American nation long ago. My night in Aquinnah, however, offered a hint of what a similar community gathering might have been like in the sixteenth or seventeenth century, and I left musing on the many cultural parallels shared by Africans and American Indians.

What did the Native peoples think of the pale folk who disembarked from ships with such different views about land and property and ownership? Equally, what must they have thought when, one day, they discovered others who were of darker hue? We have the European side of the record of first contact with the Indians, but what was the first contact between the peoples of color? Of the Indian and the African sides of the equation, we have little record.

The Massachusetts Wampanoag did not experience African captives early on. Their experience was with the early settlers. Up and down the eastern seaboard, however, there are spots of first encounter. Along the South Carolina–Georgia coastline, there is a sign posted on the highway indicating the turnoff to a place that is known as Ibo Landing. It is one of the other places where Africans, Indians, and Europeans met up in this country for the first time. The topography is not the oak-dimmed thicket of the New England forest on Martha's Vineyard; rather, it is mangrove wetlands with twisting knots of tree roots sticking up out of its slow lapping waters. It's all undulating grasses and deceptively calm waters rife with dangers: snakes, alligators, mosquitoes, fevers, and the unknown. The Indians there met different Africans, who came ashore in first encounters that were repeated from the bayous of Louisiana to the Tidewater of Virginia, the Piedmont of North Carolina, and the Florida coast. At each of these encounters, the African captives met up not only with those of Europe but also with those Native Americans. I like to imagine that on one or more occasions—at a stall on the outskirts of a market, walking along a dusty country road, foraging in the woods at the edge of a thicket—black man would spy red man, red man would spy black man, start, smile, and recognize a kinship.

◆ ◆ ◆ ◆ ◆

After the interminable voyage, after the crossing of the vast ocean that formed the hyphen that is often used between African and American, after the greasing with palm oil to disguise the travails of the trip, came the tentative first steps on the new land. The Africans arrived still tottering uncertainly after the weeks and months at sea. Scramble or auction followed, complete with separation from shipmates. The new life in America had begun. In it, Indian, African, and European formed a tightly wrought tapestry, one so intricately woven that it is often impossible to distinguish which threads belonged to which group. The Africans were landed without regard to their home cultures. European groups, however, each made landfall in a different area of the country; they came on ships that had the fragility of walnut shells for different reasons: some for adventure, others to flee religious persecution, and still others in search of fortunes. Spanish, English, Dutch, and French—the arrival story for each group of settlers was as different as their relationships with the Indians and with the Africans.

The first to arrive were the Spaniards. They had a long familiarity with the African continent from their more-than-seven-hundred-year occupation by North African Moors. They also had a tradition of slavery. African slaves sailed with Columbus and had been in the hemisphere since 1492. Others entered Mexico with Cortés and accompanied the conquistadores throughout the central and southern regions of the hemisphere. African slaves were a part of the ill-fated expedition of Lucas Vásquez de Ayllón to the Carolina coast in 1526. After a wreck, they rebelled, settled among the Native Americans, intermarried, and disappeared with no trace.

A year later, in 1527, the Spanish arrived more permanently on the North American mainland on an Easter Sunday and named the place Pascua Florida in honor of the day. They set out in search of gold and riches, which they hoped would rival those found in Central and South America. With them was the first African known by name to step foot ashore on the North American continent: Estebán Dorantes, the slave of Andrés Dorantes. Estebanico, or Estebancico, as he is sometimes called, was from Azemmour in Morocco and had been a slave in Spain. He followed his master to the New World as part of the 1527 expedition of Pánfilo de Narváez, who landed near Tampa, Florida, with four hundred men bent on conquest. De Narváez, though, was not a good leader. His bad decision to separate his men from the provisioning ships was the first step in a saga of mishaps. His tactical errors were compounded by encounters with hostile Indians. Nature also terrorized the expedition in the form of alligators, mosquitoes, and snakes. Then there was a hurricane. The ships were destroyed, and the survivors were reduced to using what timber they could salvage to build a raft and sail along the Gulf of Mexico in hopes of reaching Mexico. They landed near Galveston, Texas, and there, under the leadership of Álvar Núñez

Cabeza de Vaca, set out to walk to Mexico. Astonishingly, eight years later, four of them actually arrived in Mexico and amazed the viceroy with their tales of the southwestern portion of the country. Estebán Dorantes was one of the four.

After initially being enslaved by some of the Indians, Cabeza de Vaca's group began to move through the country. The four lived on nuts, rabbits, spiders, and the juice of prickly pears and learned to forage in the new land. Times of famine alternated with times of plenty, depending on the terrain and the welcome of the various native peoples that they encountered. During the eight-year odyssey with the Cabeza de Vaca band, Estebanico, the first African seen by the Indians of the interior of the country, became accustomed to the ways of the Indians and was regarded by them with wonder. A remarkable linguist, he rapidly acquired many of the Indian languages and proved to be a leader of the group and a healer. More important, he was a man of exceptional cultural fluidity; it seemed he was able to understand the ways of the Native peoples and adjust to them with more alacrity than his Spanish fellow travelers. As the years progressed, he came to be regarded as a shaman by the Native peoples. In his narrative *La Relación*, first published in 1542 as a report to the Spanish king, Cabeza de Vaca speaks of Esteban as being "constantly in conversation, finding out about routes, towns, and other matters we wished to know."

The group finally arrived in Mexico City and was taken to the astonished Governor Antonio de Mendoza, the first Spanish viceroy of Mexico, who listened to their tale with amazement. The Europeans were rewarded with riches and became heroes. Esteban, however, despite his aid to the expedition, was not freed. Instead, he was purchased by the viceroy and given to a friar, Marcos de Niza, who led a second expedition back into the little-known territory. The new group embarked with Esteban in the lead as translator and expediter. This voyage was not successful. Although the welcome was warm at times, many of the Indians were wary of Europeans and animosities among tribes created contention. Esteban, caught in the tribal conflicts, was killed by Indians in Hawikuh, a settlement just over ten miles southwest of Zuni Pueblo. Esteban's remarkable journey among America's first peoples encapsulates the relationship between black man and red man in early America. It is a saga of admiration and friendship turning to mistrust and hostility that would be repeated over and over again in the country's early years.

The Roman Catholic Spanish were the first European settlers on the American mainland. The other Roman Catholics to establish a foothold on the continent, the French, were last to arrive in what would become the United States, having spent their time battling the British and establishing colonies in the Caribbean and Canada. The French arrived with different attitudes toward race and slavery from the Spanish and often brought the children of their liaisons with Africans enslaved in the Caribbean with them to the mainland. The French were trappers and traders more than settlers, and their society was initially one with few women, therefore liaisons with Native American women were common. Because of their Indian wives, they lived in closer proximity to the Native peoples and learned much about their ways. They were also inveterate chroniclers of things culinary and left some of the best observations of Native American life. They had a rich field for observation, as witnessed by explorer Antoine-Simon Le Page du Pratz, who recorded the annual calendar of the Natchez people of the Lower Mississippi in 1758:

> This nation begins its year in the month of March, as was the practice for a long time in Europe, and divides it into 13 months . . . At every new moon they celebrate a feast, which takes its name from the principal fruits gathered in the preceding moon, or from the animals usually hunted then . . .
>
> The first moon is that of the Deer. The renewal of the year spreads universal joy . . . The second moon, which corresponds to our month of April, is that of strawberries.

The third moon was little corn; the fourth, watermelons; the fifth, peaches; the sixth, mulberries; the seventh, great corn; the eighth, turkeys; the ninth, bison; the tenth, bears; the eleventh, cold meal; and the twelfth, chestnuts. The thirteenth month was also nuts, which were broken then mixed with cornmeal to make bread in winter, when famine was always a possibility. As reported by the

French explorers, the year unfolded in an ever-changing celebration of foodstuffs.

The months were shifted somewhat by other travelers to the Lower Mississippi region, but available food and game were the organizing principles behind the monthly divisions of most tribes. Each month began with a feast. In times of plenty, they were lavish; in times of want, there was less, but there was always an acknowledgment of the changing foodstuff. The feasts were celebrations of the first fruits, and they would have been understood by those from the African littoral, as they paralleled traditional agricultural festivals that continue to be held throughout the continent. For Native Americans, as for Africans, the celebrations were designed to ensure continuing supplies of food and to bring health and prosperity.

When there was abundance, a repertoire of recipes could be made; there were pumpkin preparations and multiple uses for corn. There were stews thickened with pounded sassafras leaves, an addition that is still used and known as filé in some of Louisiana's gumbos. The slippery stews must have had a familiar mouthfeel to those raised on the okra-based gumbos of Senegambia and the Bight of Benin. Early explorers even mention a dish of chestnuts and corn that was pounded, kneaded, wrapped in "green corn blades," and boiled, which may be the first indication of something like tamales in the delta! The dish was also much like the fermented-corn *akassa* of the Bight of Benin and other West African dishes wrapped in leaves, like the *dukonoo* of the Twi of Ghana.

As the French presence grew, so did the number of Africans and their descendants. Many did not come directly into the region from the continent but arrived via the Caribbean colonies held by the French. By 1750, 20 percent of the population in the Illinois French settlements was black, and that number almost doubled by the 1770s. One of those arriving from the French colonies in the Caribbean was Jean Baptiste Point du Sable, the son of an African woman and a white sailor from St. Domingue. He arrived in the Louisiana Territory in the latter third of the eighteenth century. He made his way up the Mississippi River, purchased a homestead and land in Old Peoria, Illinois, and married a woman of the Potawatomi Indian Nation, joining the tribe in order to do so. Du Sable displayed the same cultural fluidity as Estebanico and was reputed to have

spoken several Indian languages as well as English, Spanish, and
his native French. By the mid-1770s, he'd created the first permanent settlement in an area that was known by the Indian name
of Eschikagou, which meant "stinky place" or "swampland." In 1782,
he built up a trading post in the area, which became the main supply source for French trappers and local Indians. The post was successful and grew in scope with du Sable "wholesaling" food items to
other trading posts in Detroit and as far away as Canada. At its apo-
gee, du Sable's trading post had a mill, bakery, dairy, poultry house,
and smokehouse. There were also workshops, two barns, and stables. Du Sable's trading post flourished, and he operated it for two
decades, until 1800, when he retired and moved to Peoria and then
to Missouri. He sold the post to Jean La Lime for six thousand livres
(about $1,110) and left the area that is now Chicago as a rich man.
By the time du Sable sold his trading post, blacks in the French Illinois colonies made up 39 percent of the total population, and elsewhere in the nascent nation, African faces became a part of the
daily experience of settlers and Indians alike.

The Dutch arrived in New York state and New Jersey in 1609
when Henry Hudson sailed by what is now Manhattan Island. In
the Dutch colonies, Africans worked on plantations like Philipsburg
Manor, in the Tarrytown, New York, area, growing and preparing
provisions that were then exported to other locations throughout
the colonies. The butter that was churned by slaves on this plantation was sent as far south as the Caribbean in a north-to-south commerce route that linked the northern colonies of the mainland to the
more prosperous Caribbean ones. Many plantation owners in the
northern colonies became wealthy by provisioning their Caribbean
counterparts, who lived on islands where most of the land was given
over to the more lucrative cultivation of sugarcane. At Philipsburg
and other northern plantations, therefore, enslaved blacks grew
food not only for their masters' tables and to provision themselves;
they also raised foodstuffs that would be exported to feed their Caribbean counterparts and the islands' plantation owners.

Blacks enslaved by the Dutch in rural areas also worked in the
grist mills and taverns and performed domestic chores. At Philipsburg Manor and other grand houses throughout the colonies, enslaved blacks also worked in the kitchens and served Brueghelian

burghers' feasts that would be written about by Washington Irving a century later—tables filled to overflowing with ripe melons, hearty roasts, juicy stuffed birds, and an array of cookies and cakes that harked back to the delights of the Netherlands. Afro-Dutch kitchens in New York and New Jersey served *ollycakes* (doughnuts), *koolsla* (cole slaw), and *koekjes* (cookies), and enslaved blacks observed holidays like Pinkster Day (the Dutch Protestant celebration of Pentecost) with gingerbread and rum. Some of these traditions lasted among the Afro-Dutch descendants of New York and New Jersey well into the twentieth century.

It was not all *koekjes*, gingerbread, and rum for blacks in Dutch New Amsterdam. The African American population, whose burial ground wasn't discovered in lower Manhattan until centuries later, was worked literally to death. Forensic evidence from the skeletal remains in the African Burial Ground shows necks snapped from carrying large loads, teeth eroded from insufficient nourishment, and other injuries sustained from heavy lifting. Death, no doubt a relief, came at a young age; the median age of the remains is forty. Some sustained their fatal injuries while toiling as day laborers and dockworkers. Others worked as servers and cooks in the taverns and eating houses around the docks. Still others sold goods on the street in a manner that must have reminded them faintly of haggling and huckstering on the African continent. The African presence transformed the dusty streets of the nascent New York City into a marketplace ringing with the cries of women selling foodstuffs, from fresh vegetables and fruits to savories and sweets that they'd prepared, from baskets and trays on their head.

Florida reflected Spain's racial history, with its centuries of contact with the African continent. The French, who controlled the middle of the continent, had a more liberal attitude to race and intermarriage. The Dutch had a brief tenure in New York and New Jersey. However, the European nation that established the prevailing racial and cultural attitudes for the thirteen colonies that would become the United States was England.

The British had attempted to establish American colonies early on in the sixteenth century in direct competition with the king of Spain. Their contacts with the Native peoples in the Roanoke Colony were well documented by artists like John White and diarists like Thomas Hariot. The expedition failed, however, and the British did not establish a permanent foothold on mainland America until the seventeenth century, with the founding of the Jamestown Colony. There, in late August 1619, a ship entered port. John Rolfe (of Pocahontas fame), the colony's outgoing recorder, wrote to the London-based sponsor of the colony, the Virginia Company, that "a Dutch man of war . . . brought not anything but 20 odd Negroes which the Governor and Capt. Merchant brought for victualle." The captured slaves were traded to the Jamestown colonists in exchange for food, including a chest of Indian maize. Rolfe, though, was inaccurate in his recording of the arrival of the original Africans in British America. In fact, the ship, the *White Lion*, may not have been a Dutch man-of-war, as Rolfe claimed, but instead an English corsair ship, carrying expired Dutch letters of marque, that had been on a raid in the Caribbean, where it had captured a Spanish vessel with African slaves bound for Mexican silver mines.

The Africans who arrived in the Jamestown Colony were from Angola ports, in southwestern Africa, where traditionally Bantu women were farmers and Bantu men tended cattle. The Africans entered the British colony not as slaves but as bound laborers. In the first half of the seventeenth century, there was no general regulation about the status of Africans, and enslavement was not necessarily hereditary. Many of the laborers in the colonies, black and white, were indentured and had signed themselves up to work for a limited time period. Indentured servitude was seen by some as a way of paying off debts or of gaining a foothold in the new colony. The race-based chattel slavery that would mark the country for centuries became the rule of law only later in the seventeenth century. The first Africans used their agricultural know-how to create their own fortunes. Angolan-born Antonio, one of the original group, served his indenture for fourteen years, then married a slave working in the same household, took the name Anthony Johnson, and became a farmer and substantial landowner in eastern Virginia. Others engaged in diverse occupations, but more than one of the group became a link in the food chain of the fledgling colony in one way or another, whether working in the fields or serving in a tavern.

There are no written remembrances of the arriving Africans' first encounters with the Native peoples of the region, but if John White's amazing watercolors of North Carolina Algonquians are to be believed, they found many cultural similarities between the lives they knew on the African continent and the Native American ways of life that they found. On the African continent, while each tribe or group has its own culinary specificities, there are generalities among the culinary habits of the Ashanti, the Yoruba, the Mande, the Wolof, and the Bantu peoples. The same can be said of the foodways of the Choctaw, the Chitimacha, Tunica, and Algonquian peoples and other eastern seacoast tribes. Africans and Indians both shared a common culture of farming supplemented by hunting and gathering. Equally shared was the notion of foraging for food. Both groups also knew the frightening privations of periodic famines while waiting for crops to mature or when the crops failed.

As in many agricultural societies, daily life was organized around the hunting and gathering of food, especially in the months before crops were ready for harvest. From February to May, the Algonquians, who lived in the Virginia area, were dependent on the sea, and its bounty was nothing short of miraculous. The coastal regions offered fish in great variety and abundance. Captain Smith reported from Virginia in 1608 that he saw a massive school of fish "lying so thicke with their heads above the water" that his boat could scarcely get through. Hariot recorded sturgeon, herring, trout, alewife, mullet, and abundant shellfish. The fishing seasons were different, and the species certainly differed from those on the West African coast, but the Africans from the continent's coastal areas certainly knew of fishing and of sun-drying and smoking fish and shellfish—and those culinary techniques continue to be used even today by coastal and river peoples.

The Algonquians were also dependent on hunting in the early months of the year, as their crops of corn were planted in late winter and early spring and not ready for harvesting until later in the year. Game was abundant; Hariot recorded eighty-six different types of fowl. The careful observation of prey and the use of decoys were common points shared by African and Indian alike. The Seminole used homemade wild-turkey calls, and many groups used the skins of animals to create decoys for hunting. The Choctaw and Chickasaw of Alabama and Mississippi were also recorded as using different types of disguises, and their methods were sophisticated indeed. In 1753, Dumont de Montigny spoke of deer decoys used by the Natchez of the Mississippi Valley in *Mémoires historiques sur la Louisiane.*

> When a savage has succeeded in killing a deer, he first cuts off the head as far down as the shoulders. Then he skins the neck without cutting the skin and having removed the bones and flesh from it, he draws out all the brains from the head. After this operation, he replaces the bones of the neck very neatly and fixes them in place with the aid of a wooden hoop and some little sticks . . . He carries it with him hung to his belt when he goes hunting, and as soon as he perceives a bison or deer, he passes his right hand into the neck of this deer, with which he conceals his face, and begins to make the same kind of movements the living animal would make.

Once caught, meat was dressed and cooked immediately or dried in some form of pemmican. The resulting jerky would have been familiar to Mande peoples, who knew the sun-dried *khilichili* of the area that would become Niger.

While Africans might have found many of the Native American agricultural methods familiar, European settlers marveled at the harvests. The early bounty of the New World was described by Thomas Hariot, a member of Sir Walter Raleigh's Roanoke expedition in 1585. He wrote of corn in *A True and Briefe Report of the New Found Land of Virginia*: "*Pagatowr,* a kinde of graine so called by the inhabitants, the same in the West Indies is called *Mayze.* Englishmen call it *Guinney wheat* or *Turkie wheate.*" He went on to detail that the kernels were of "divers colours: some white, some red, some yellow, and some blew. All of them yeelde a very white and sweet fouwre which maketh a very good bread. Wee made of the same in the countrey some mault, whereof was brued as good ale as was to bee desired." (Hariot's use of the term *Guinney* [for Guinea] indicated that corn was already well identified with the African continent. It became a major food crop there following the Columbian Exchange and would have been familiar to many West Africans.)

In the English colonies, corn, beans, and pumpkins or squash were grown in symbiotic harmony by the native peoples. The system—called a *conuco* in the Caribbean—consisted of seed corn planted in a circle in small hillocks in rows. (The corn was grown so that there were three annual crops of it.) The beans were planted along with the cornstalks and used them as bean poles to climb. The leaves of the pumpkins or squashes provided shade for the young plants. The Iroquois (or Haudenosaunee) of the Northeast called this Indian agricultural triad the Three Sisters. In Virginia, Hariot noted the efficiency of the system and especially that of the Native way of planting with single seeds carefully sown. He remarked that Native agriculture netted about two hundred English bushels an acre, as opposed to the prevailing European system of scattering seeds at random, which produced about only forty bushels an acre. Again the Native peoples and Africans shared similar knowledge, for the Africans were also familiar with the careful planting of crops, and in general compass, neither group used the scattered-seed method in practice in Western Europe.

John White's illustrations are invaluable to researchers, as they show other early Indian practices that offer additional cultural parallels. One depicts an Indian man and woman eating; their use of their hands and the manner in which they are hunkered on a mat around a communal bowl might have brought a nod of recognition from African arrivals. Earthenware cooking vessels and fish cooked on a grill of sticks—two other shared traditions—also appear in White's watercolors.

While they cannot be discerned in White's detailed drawings, tastes were also similar. African and Indian both evidenced a taste for the soured and the fermented. Dishes like *sofk* (a Creek watery maize gruel prepared from water, corn, and ashes that was slowly cooked until thick and then allowed to sour for three days) would have had a familiar tang to those who had eaten West African dishes such as the leaf-wrapped and fermented *akassa* and *ablo* of the Republic of Benin, the granular *attiéké* of the Ivory Coast, and the buttermilk-like *lar* and *tchiakri* of Senegambia. One-pot boiled soupy stews like Cherokee succotash (from the Narragansett *sukquttahash*), with beans, corn, and pumpkin, would have been reminiscent of the one-pot stews that abound throughout the African continent. The coarsely ground corn porridge known as *samp* by the English and *sagamité* by the French might have been recognized by Africans as a cousin of couscous, pounded millet, plantain and yam mashes, and corn porridges that were used to scoop up their own one-pot soupy stews. Indeed the poorer Europeans would have also noted similarities with their own porridges and pottages.

The division of labor was another tradition shared by Native peoples and African captives. Europeans, especially those in Virginia, with its patrician progenitors, were appalled to see the hard labor done by the Native American women. While Europeans were used to seeing indentured and, later, enslaved women toil in the fields, European women did not work outdoors, and it seemed to them to indicate laziness on the part of Indian men. This was not so to the Africans, who were used to gender-specific roles within the agricultural realm, with the women having tasks as well as the men.

As a result of these and myriad other culinary confluences and cultural communalities, relationships between Native Americans and Africans began with a sense of a common bond. Seventeenth- and eighteenth-century accounts are rife with mentions of escaping Africans finding refuge with Native Americans. Africans had interacted with Native Americans since the arrival of the Spanish in the sixteenth century, and the welcome that Estebán Dorantes initially received was mirrored multifold. Most of the Africans who arrived early on mainland America were culturally fluid and used to existence on their multicultural and multilingual home continent. They were attuned to nuance in ways that Europeans, for the most part, were not. Their future and often their lives depended on an ability to intuit meaning and interpret language and gesture. For this reason, they were often appointed as linguists aboard ships (even slave ships) and as translators of language and manners, like Estabán was. Equally, Native Americans would have been predisposed to acknowledge arriving Africans without the prejudices that were inherent in the European worldview of the period. Intermarriage and sheltering of escaped slaves by Native Americans was common in early years of settlement, though this all changed as the number of blacks increased and race-based chattel slavery became the law of the land.

Africans and their descendants in the English colonies that would become the thirteen original states grew in number throughout the seventeenth century as the trickle of African slaves became a tidal wave. In 1675, there were only five thousand African slaves in the British North American colonies compared with one hundred thousand in the British West Indies. But the numbers grew, and as early as 1708, black slaves in the Carolinas outnumbered whites, both free and bonded, for the first time.

However, as Africans and Native Americans began to see their common cause, Europeans realized that their joining together threatened European sovereignty. Indians had freedom. Africans had knowledge of European ways and could give Indians not only military knowledge but also information about the day-to-day workings of the colonies. The wedge of distrust placed by the Europeans split the groups asunder. Africans were demonized to Native Americans, and slave-catching bounties were paid to those Indians who returned Africans to European masters. Yet, despite centuries of calculated division and incited mistrust, a bond somehow remained. It is witnessed by the numerous black branches of eastern tribes and the high percentage of African Americans who boast Native American blood in their veins. It is seen even today at powwows and gatherings. When seated around communal tables piled high with dishes that share our many common tastes, the descendants of the Africans and those of the Wampanoag, the Cherokee, Creek, Choctaw, Seminole, and others can finally sit back, relax, and share a complicit smile.

❖❖❖❖❖❖❖

MAROON FOODS:
FROM CIMARRÓN TO SEMINOLE

Jamaicans celebrate the Maroons, and Nanny of the Maroons is a national hero. Afro-Brazilians thrill to thoughts of the Quilombo of Palmares and of Ganga Zumba and Zumbi, its leaders. And Cubans research the palenques and the life of Estebán Montejo. The Surinamese have the Djuka, and there are black Carib groups in Dominica and on the Mosquito Coast. African Americans in the United States, though, know little of our own Maroon communities. The term "Maroon" comes from the Spanish word *cimarrón*, which is defined as a "wild savage" and itself comes from the Spanish word *cimarra*, meaning "wild place." In the Caribbean, "Maroon" has come to mean any of the descendants of those slaves who freed themselves by escape or guerrilla fighting and established isolated communities that survived in the mountains or forest country.

Some groups of the Seminole Indians are prime examples of Maroon communities in the United States. The Seminole are a Native American people originally from Florida, and they get their name from the Creek word *simano-li,* an adaptation of the Spanish word *cimarrón.* The Seminole tribe was formed in the eighteenth century of many different elements, including Lower Creeks from Georgia, Mikasuji-speaking Muskogees, and escaped African American slaves

from South Carolina and Georgia, who banded together in the
Florida Everglades. During the removal, some three thousand Seminoles were moved to Oklahoma and established a second, western
branch of the tribe. The Seminoles of Oklahoma are divided into
fourteen bands, including two "Freedman Bands," also known as
the Black Seminoles, since they are descended from escaped slaves.

In the mid-1990s, the western group was the subject of one of the
Smithsonian Institution's Folklife Festivals, and representatives of
the Oklahoma Seminoles brought their food with them to the Mall
in Washington, D.C. The food was an enduring witness to the conjoining of African and Native American culinary aesthetics. On the
tables around the Mall were dishes like *tetta poon*, a sweet potato
pone prepared with grated sweet potatoes, brown sugar, allspice,
and the addition of the North African/Hispanic flavoring cumin.
The word *pone* comes from the Algonquian *apan*. There was *sufkee*,
a hominy dish in which the kernels are soaked overnight, then
boiled and crushed in a mortar (or on the Mexican metate) and
served hot, topped with cinnamon and sugar. There was also *tolie*,
a variation of the cornmeal gruel that is universally known. It's
called *cococoo* in Barbados, *amala* in Nigeria, and *polenta* in Italy.
There was also a dish of pinto beans, cooked long, low, and slow
with salt pork, that would certainly have been a mainstay in many
an African American household in centuries past and is still right
at home on the table today.

Maroon foods like *tetta poon*, *sufkee*, *tolie*, and even the pinto
beans combine the tastes of Africans and Native Americans. They
make good use of the techniques of cooking on live fire that both
Africans and Indian peoples shared: grilling, roasting, boiling, baking in the ashes. They also share methods of seasoning, such as the
use of smoked meats and fish as ingredients in stews for added flavor. These techniques and methods point to parallel culinary
threads that still unite the two groups over time and across history.
At the Smithsonian Folklife Festival on the Mall, the complicit smile
survived, and its story of connection and respect is a tale that continues to be told on the plate.

CHAPTER 4

THE TIGHTENING VICE

Indenture to Enslavement
and the African Hand in the
Food of Colonial America

Lower Manhattan, New York—

Dusk is my favorite time to wander in downtown New York. On late fall days, I love the way that the dying light softens the bustle of traffic and mutes the twenty-first century into something quieter and more evocative of earlier times. Peeking up at windows through myopic eyes, I imagine lamps being lit and dinner being spread on finely polished mahogany tables, and I wonder who lived in these houses in the eighteenth century and who served them. On these strolls, I am invariably struck by how young a country America is. In Europe, the eighteenth century barely gets a nod next to buildings that hark back to the Middle Ages, aqueducts that go back to Roman times, and Minoan palaces. But in New York, where skyscrapers sprout like mushrooms and a landscape can be transformed in two months, it is miraculous to be able to catch a glimpse of the past amid the expansion of the present. I am always thrilled by it. The pale vermilion bricks, the limestone stoops, the dormer windows on the upper floors, the austerity of the red-painted front doors, and the neatness of the shutters all speak of a more organized time.

By the end of the seventeenth century, New York City had a larger black population than any other North American city and was one of the largest slave-trading centers in the colony. In the eighteenth century, New York City was second only to Charleston, South Carolina, in the number of slaves it held. And many of them lived in Lower Manhattan, in what is now Soho and Tribeca. Before then, they lived within and on the farms just outside the walls of the original settlement at the lower end of Manhattan Island. In 1991, construction of a federal building in downtown brought the early African presence in the city vividly to life. Builders discovered an African burial ground that dated to the city's early years. The burial ground was created in the early 1700s, when Trinity Church banned all Africans from burial in its cemetery. By the early nineteenth century it was built over and forgotten. Its rediscovery was galvanizing; construction stopped and archaeologists took over excavating the site, which proved that Africans had been very much involved in all aspects of the city's life. They slept in attics and worked as day laborers and as domestic workers as well as farmers and on the docks of the bustling port. They were assistants to craftsmen and sold goods on the streets. They also worked in the taverns of the developing metropolis, like the one owned by Samuel Fraunces.

Fraunces Tavern remains a fixture in downtown Manhattan even today, and in one of my downtown peregrinations, I wandered in. I knew a bit about the history of the place, which had been the most popular tavern of its day. It was the site where Washington bid farewell to the officers of the Continental Army and the meeting place of the Sons of Liberty. After Washington's inauguration, when the city was the nation's first capital, the tavern rented space to the new government and housed the offices of the Departments of War, Treasury, and Foreign Affairs. Many debated whether or not the tavern's owner, Samuel Fraunces, was of African descent. Recent research suggests that he was born in the French West Indies of African and French extraction. The steward of George Washington's New York house, Fraunces was variously described in texts of the time as Negro, colored, Haitian Negro, and mulatto.

The tavern can be a bit of a tourist trap, but it is an inviting place nonetheless, one where history comes alive and where it is easy to understand the conviviality of taverns of the period, so aptly described in a 1704 poem.

> The days are short, the weather's cold
> By tavern fires tales are told.
> Some ask for dram when first come in
> Others with flip and bounce begin.

The dining room beckoned me that day, with polished brasses, pewter tankards, and scarred wooden tables, but before settling in for a meal, I visited the upstairs museum, where a display on hearth cooking caught my eye. The massive fireplace, which I could almost stand up in, was empty of flame, but an assortment of andirons, hanging cast-iron cauldrons, hooks, and three-legged frying pans called "spiders" were all arrayed in the hearth's vast maw. Next to it were weighted pails designed to give the modern museumgoers an idea of the weight of the kitchen implements and a suggestion of what cooking in the hearth would actually be like.

I'd had some experience with antique cooking. I'd plucked chickens, singed off their pinfeathers, and cooked over a flame at a Candomblé house in Brazil, and I'd watched hearth-cooking demonstrations at the Hermann Grima House in New Orleans. I'd even attended a seminar in Old Salem, North Carolina, where participants from historic properties around the country prepared dishes in the hearths there. But hearth cooking for fun and instruction in jeans is a very different prospect from cooking daily in eighteenth-century conditions. I'd never really thought about the weight of the utensils and the danger involved in cooking near open fire while wearing highly flammable ground-dragging garments. The museum brought the heat, the smoke, the lack of ventilation, and the sheer physical strength needed to haul water and wood vividly to life for one used to piped-in water and electric lights. It was a revelation, a small moment that transformed my ideas about the joys of hearth cooking forever.

For most of the early history of the country, whether in Big House kitchens, on small farms, or in the colonial taverns and alehouses, all cooks worked in dangerous conditions that are inconceivable to the modern cook. That peril was multiplied when the cook was enslaved and subject not only to the physical hazards but also to the whims and fits of temper of mistresses and owners. Yet throughout the colonial history of the country, many of the hands that turned the spits in the massive hearths and brought the tankards filled with ale to the lusty patriots and founding fathers were black. Their fortitude under the extraordinary pressure of the developing slave system that was turning their dreams of freedom and progress into ashes, like those in the hearths they tended, was nothing short of amazing.

◆ ◆ ◆ ◆ ◆

Being black became unmitigated hell in the final years of the seventeenth century in the fledgling colonies. Blacks in the northern colonies that would become the United States lived a long, tortuous slide from can to can't as the slave system became entrenched and the colony increased its dependence on slave labor. In the early years of settlement, a system of indentured work with a view to eventual freedom offered the hope of being able to build a life in the new land to blacks and whites alike. People signed up for a limited time of servitude, and when it was up, they were free to begin their lives anew. However, by the end of the 1600s, for most of those of African descent that hope had died. Indenture gradually evolved into enslavement, and by the end of the century, virtually all of the enslaved were black or Native American. The horrors of race-based slavery became entrenched as the American way of life, and soon it was extended to include unborn children and all future generations.

Color had become the key for enslavement in the American colonies, which were expanding their southern boundaries beyond Virginia and the Chesapeake. As new settlers arrived from the more established British Caribbean colonies to create virtual fiefdoms for themselves in the Carolinas, they brought their enslaved Africans. Soon, a darker skin came to mean a slave. Reverend Morgan Godwyn could decry in 1680 that "these two words, *Negro* and *Slave*" have "by custom grown Homogeneous and Convertible." More blacks kept arriving. Many of the new black slaves came via the Caribbean, however an increasing number were "saltwater slaves"—a term designating those who came directly from the African continent and who had survived the Middle Passage. Both would become the backbone of the Northern American colonies' workforce. Their labor was evident everywhere, from the taverns and eateries of Williamsburg and other colonial towns to, increasingly, the agriculture of the colonies. Soon, north and south, no self-respecting persons of means were without a workforce of black slaves who toiled for their benefit.

At no time was colonial life monolithic. In their early years, the American colonies by no means resembled the map of the thirteen colonies that we envision today. Then, the eastern seaboard of the United States was divided between the British in New England, the Dutch in what would become New York and New Jersey, the British again from Pennsylvania through the Carolinas, the Spanish in Florida, and the French in the Louisiana Territory. The European colonizers brought their own cultures with them. The one thing that they all agreed on was enslavement of Africans.

By the time the British took over New Amsterdam from the Dutch in 1641 and named it New York, 10 percent of the population was black; by 1737, one in five people in the growing metropolis was black. For much of the eighteenth century, the city was second only to Charleston in the ratio of enslaved to white in an urban setting. For the British, enslavement was a hemispheric social order with no distinction between northern and southern (Caribbean) colonies. In addition to trading with the mother country, England, there was a lively north-south trade with ships plying the Atlantic coast maintaining the colonial commercial connections. The northern ones sent livestock, horses, and wood (for barrels) to the plantations of the Caribbean colonies, which returned the barrels filled with molasses to be transformed into rum for the Guinea trade, which bartered molasses, beads, and other goods in exchange for more Africans to be enslaved on the plantations and in the towns north and south. Foodstuffs took the journey as well: flour, dried fish, corn, potatoes, onions, and cattle produced and bred in Connecticut, New York, and New Jersey made the journey from those colonies to the Caribbean to provision plantations there. Wethersfield, Connecticut, became famous for its onions and as late as 1800 sent ten thousand five-pound ropes of the slave-grown globes to the West Indies. Rhode Island developed plantations in the Narragansett area to supply the West Indian trade, and in the area that would become the Bronx, Lewis Morris, a signer of the Declaration of Independence, had a nineteen-hundred-acre plantation producing wheat, corn, and livestock for the trade to the islands. As did Morris, so did the Van Cortlandts and numerous other large and small landholders in Long Island, Westchester, and New Jersey.

The slave system tightened its hold, and the colonies developed ways of housing and handling the forced laborers. Initially, there were more male slaves than female, and on large landholdings the enslaved were housed in barracks, where families were billeted together without regard for kinship. Later, as more women arrived, individual housing of some sort became more common. The plantation system, initially developed in Brazil and fine-tuned in the Caribbean, became the way of the land for large landholders. On plantations north and south, slaves labored under an unrelenting annual round of chores and duties. Tasks were divided between those who worked in the Big House and those who worked in the fields and on the farms.

Those who worked in the fields had more liberty of their thoughts, if not their actions or deeds, but they were subjected to a seasonal round of tasks that kept the plantation productive. In winter the men and women killed the hogs, hauled the grain, filled the ice-house, worked the new ground, threshed the wheat and rye, shelled the corn, and beat out hominy. Spring and summer would find them plowing and harrowing, digging holes for fence poles, making hills for sweet potatoes, and sowing carrots, cabbage, wheat, and flax. There were melons to be planted and fields to be fertilized. Fall brought harvest and its chores: gathering in the crops, preserving them, and preparing the land for the upcoming winter. None were too young or too decrepit to have a task. Some children and older women weeded gardens and gathered cornstalks; others saved seeds and wove clothing. The year was a never-ending round of seasonal agrarian activities.

Those who worked in the Big House were tasked with the daily maintenance of the house and caring for the creature comforts of its inhabitants. The relentless chores went from morning—including drawing and heating water for ablutions, preparing breakfast, aid-ing with dressing, emptying chamber pots, and making beds—right through until the master and family were bedded down for the night, and then began anew the next day. In some cases the house slaves even slept in the master's room or on a pallet outside the door in case he or his family should require services of any sort during the night. House servants were usually better clothed than their field counterparts, as they became representations to the outside world of the plantation's order and wealth. Regarded by some as slavery's elite, they often had the ear of the master or mistress and could petition and inveigle favors. They also were often members of one family and occasionally related to the master as well. They were usually given more privileges and occasionally better food. However, the favors came at a high price: lack of privacy of any sort and constant unrelenting service. Subject to the whims and person-ality foibles of the master and his family, they, in many cases, suf-fered as much as field hands, as they were at the beck and call of the master's family all day and all night.

The slave community within the Big House itself had its own pecking order. Scullions and those who slept outside but worked in the house during the day were on the bottom of a pyramid that extended upward, depending on the size and "greatness" of the plantation, through maids and houseboys to butlers, culminating at the pinnacle of the Big House cook. The planter class took meals very seriously, and the Big House cook was tasked with preparing the meals for the members of the family, and depending on the size of the plantation, with preparing and overseeing meals for other slaves as well. On the more affluent plantations, the slave cook would command a battalion of underlings and produce meals the equal of any chef of the time. Often the cooks were male, because it was thought that men could withstand the searing heat of hearth cooking better than women.

Kitchens were primitive affairs; they were usually located in outbuildings to protect the main house from the fires that occasionally arose and also to keep the heat of the open fires from the main house in the summer. Floors were frequently brick or stone, so that they could be easily washed down, and there were few built-in cupboards or pantries. Dressers, open shelves, barrels, and chests held the ingredients used to prepare the meals, and other items were brought in as needed from the smokehouse, the icehouse, or other outbuildings. The dominant feature in every kitchen was the fireplace, in which most of the cooking was done. It was equipped with iron cranes and chimney bars from which a variety of pots and cauldrons were hung. Roasts were turned on spits by clockwork jacks, and pots were raised and lowered in the fireplace to adjust the cooking temperatures in a never-ending ballet. Three-legged frying pans and Dutch ovens offered added opportunities to use all the hearth's heat, and a head cook had to be aware of the progress of each and every pot on the fire at all times to avoid ruining a meal.

The plantation system, with its dichotomy between field hands and house slaves, became the rural face of the developing colonies. This new way of life thrived in the marshy coastal areas of South Carolina. South Carolina's settlers created a colony that in a brief time became a colonial jewel in the crown, with planters living a lavish lifestyle of luxury and profligacy that was equaled only in the Caribbean, from whence many of them hailed. Indeed Charleston

itself had a Caribbean aspect, as reported by J. S. Buckingham in
Journey Through the Slave States of North America.

> It more resembles a West Indian than an American city—
> from the number of wooden buildings painted white, the
> large verandas and porticoes of the more stately mansions
> of brick, and the universal prevalence of broad verandas,
> green Venetian blinds, and other provisions to secure shade
> and coolness.

The Carolina colonists' lives of unparalleled luxury depended on
the labor of their slaves. Most boasted well-appointed houses in the
city of Charleston as well as lavish rural plantations that were virtual mini fiefdoms and enjoyed a seasonal lifestyle that swung between the two. They lived in a colony that in the 1700s had a black
majority, which it would maintain until the 1850s. One traveler observed that the capital of Charleston looked more like an African
village than a European town. Another remarked that he "met five
negroes as often as one white person."

Charleston may have had an African aspect, but it was the wealthiest city in British North America in the late eighteenth century, and
nothing was too rich or outré for the wealthy. European taste prevailed in the city's drawing rooms, which were painted in fantastic
hues that mirrored the latest styles in London and Paris. Dinner
tables of mirror-shined mahogany were laden with blue and white
China trade tureens and French porcelain platters filled to overflowing with the bounty of the region. But on each table, there was always a bowl of the fluffy grain that created the colony's wealth and
an ornate silver spoon with which to serve it. No fine Lowcountry
table was fully set without rice, for the good planters understood
that rice was their gold. As one former slave put it, "Rice been
money, them day and time." Charleston's planters knew that they
owed their wealth to the agricultural know-how of their slaves.
Beyond Charleston's in-town houses on King and Church and Bay
streets, where planters dined nightly on oyster soup and shrimp and
venison from the land, out in the lagoons and inlets of the marshy
coastal area known as the Lowcountry, out on the Sea Islands, Afri-

can knowledge took over and reigned supreme—its power so all-pervasive that the masters depended on it.

South Carolina legend states that rice first arrived in the colony on a ship from Madagascar; the story may be apocryphal, as others suspect that the grain that created the colony's enormous wealth was actually *oryza glaberrima*, from the West African area that is today known as Senegambia. No matter where its African origin, in South Carolina, rice was produced by a uniquely African system of agriculture. From the flooded alluvial plains where it was grown, to the system of dikes and sluiceways, to the system of assigning specific production-calibrated jobs (known as "tasks") to workers, Africa shows its hand in Carolina's rice cultivation. Africans whose names rang with the sonorities of Senegambia and the Grain Coast brought this knowledge with them in the holds of slave ships to the Charleston docks, where it was sold at a premium in the slave marts that flourished in the small area bounded by Broad, East Bay, Queen, and Meeting streets on the peninsula. There, Charlestonians vied for the pricey slaves from the Windward Coast whose heads and hands had the expertise that would grow and maintain the colony's wealth.

In the kitchens, African hands also prevailed, and for generations, whether in plantation kitchens or in-town backyards, they turned the wooden spoons in the pots. Along with the roasts of Sir Loin and Baron Beef that turned up on grand tables, they began to feed the colonists a creolized diet that placed the emphasis on the rice that was the source of their wealth. Rich rice-based dishes like Hoppin' John (the black-eyed peas and rice dish) and the emblematic Charleston red rice maintained strong culinary connections to Senegambia; there, the former is called *thiébou niébé*, and the latter is similar to Senegal's national dish, *thiébou dienn*.

These and other rice dishes entered the Lowcountry culinary repertoire and made the transition smoothly from West Africa to slave cabin to Big House kitchen. This transition was aided in no small measure by the fact that many of the original settlers in the region boasted plantations in the Caribbean as well, and there they may have already become acclimatized to a more African palate, with its taste for the spicy and its use of rice and beans and okra and the like. Over time, the culinary omnivores that were the South

Carolina plantocracy came to claim African-inspired dishes like Hoppin' John, red rice, and roux-less Charleston gumbo as their own.

If Charleston had a northern counterpart in style, it was Philadelphia. In the colonial period, Philadelphia was known for its food and its cosmopolitan lifestyle. It was the city of the Continental Congresses, the home of the Declaration of Independence, and the second capital of the United States. In 1780, the city numbered 2,150 blacks among its citizens. The city's Quaker background and its location—in the North, but near the slaveholding South—gave it special significance for African Americans. In the same year, Pennsylvania took its first step toward gradually abolishing slavery, an act that transformed the city into a veritable mecca for blacks, freedmen and enslaved alike. By the 1790s, Philadelphia was a city of promise for blacks and numbered more free blacks among its citizens than did Northern cities like New York and Boston or Southern ones like Baltimore, Charleston, and New Orleans. The city was home to such notable blacks as Richard Allen and Absalom Jones, former slaves who had purchased their freedom and were critical to the founding of the African Methodist Episcopal denomination and the Free African Society. Black churches and a lively abolitionist movement among the free black community were a part of the city's daily life.

Like many cities of the fledgling nation, Philadelphia had an African underpinning that came from the bustling port, where ships arrived daily from the Caribbean and from Africa bringing foods, goods, and slaves and giving the city a lively creole feel. The docks and seaport areas of Philadelphia and other northern maritime cities were riddled with warehouses that were Ali Baba's caves of ingredients fresh off the boats; plantains and mangoes, while not common, were known among the well-to-do, as were pineapples, a delicacy of Caribbean origin, which became the symbol of hospitality.

Some of the more exotic ingredients would have been familiar to the "saltwater slaves." Caribbean blacks also knew their uses and no doubt demonstrated them to their mistresses. Women wandered the streets with trays selling their own version of a West African okra-based gumbo complete with *foufou* dumplings (pounded plantain or other vegetable starch) that would become renowned as Philadelphia's pepperpot. The spicy dish, prepared from inexpensive cuts of meat and vegetables, was sold for pennies by hucksters of West Indian origin. Although pepperpot certainly had West Indian origins, the good hearty soup of meat and greens also had African American antecedents. In 1778, one soldier from the Revolutionary War recalled that a free black woman, "having received two hard dollars for washing, and hearing of the distress of our prisoners in the gaol, went to market and bought some neck beef and two heads with some green[s], and made a pot of as good broth as she could." It became a Philadelphia classic, and the street vendors' cry "Pepper pot, smoking hot" is even illustrated in the 1810 pamphlet *Cries of Philadelphia*. The city would be a proving ground for African Americans in food for more than three centuries.

Two black chefs would come to prominence in creolized eighteenth-century Philadelphia. They worked in a city where Caribbean and colonial combined and where a group of free blacks created black cultural institutions such as churches and abolitionist organizations early on. Each was from Virginia, and although they had very different paths, they both became culinary stars of the era and attained levels of the culinary profession that remain unequaled to this day. Each worked for one of America's founding fathers.

In the twenty-first century, it is difficult to conceive that, at the time of the first Continental Congress, all the original thirteen colonies were slaveholding. Indeed, no signer of the Declaration of Independence was without the taint of slavery. Even if the individual was not a slaveholder himself, all the districts represented by the signers were slaveholding. It was the norm, therefore, that the father of the country was a slaveholder, not the exception. George Washington's plantation, Mount Vernon, comprised eight thousand acres and was divided into five separate farms on which the enslaved worked. At Mount Vernon, and later in New York and in Philadelphia, Washington's kitchen was manned by enslaved blacks overseen by a slave Big House cook. At Mount Vernon, this person was named Hercules.

Described as a "celebrated artiste" and an "accomplished master of the culinary arts" by his contemporaries, Hercules had begun his life in the kitchen at Mount Vernon, probably as a member of a house servant's family. Little is known about him. Like many of the young boys who worked around Big Houses in the South, he was no doubt first tasked with hauling water and bringing in logs, removing ashes, and other menial jobs, and then he worked his way up the pecking order. It is known that he was named chief cook at Mount Vernon by 1786. Hercules was brought to New York when his master, George Washington, was displeased with the presidential fare there, and in 1790, when the capital moved to Philadelphia, Hercules moved there with Washington. He won accolades and was noted for his exacting efficiency and the flawless working of his kitchen at 190 High Street. Martha Washington's grandson, George Washington Parke Custis, called him "as highly accomplished and [as] proficient in the culinary art as could be found in the United States." Another observer was more eloquent:

> Iron discipline, woe to his underlings if speck or spot could be discovered on the table . . . or if the utensils did not shine like polished silver . . . His underlings flew in all directions to execute his orders while he, the great master-spirit, seemed to possess the power of ubiquity, and to be everywhere at the same time.

Hercules' duties extended beyond simply cooking; he also oversaw the smooth running of Washington's kitchens, which at one point contained a German cook and two French ones. He managed their work. No recipes attributed to Hercules have been found, but he certainly must have been adept at preparing the steak and kidney pie and trifle that were known to be among Washington's favorite dishes. Hercules was charged not only with overseeing all family meals, from the preparation to the service, but also with personally preparing the more formal Thursday dinners and congressional repasts. The latter were served up to the founding fathers with style and aplomb atop white linen and accompanied by glittering crystal, fine porcelain, and highly polished silver.

Although the food was closer to that of Britain, meals were served in what was called *service à la française*, or French service. The table was completely set with multiple dishes to tempt the diners. The number of dishes offered in each course had to be the same. Featured dishes occupied top, bottom, and central positions on the table and were large roasts, including a turkey and an entire pig. They were surrounded by arranged side dishes, making the entire tablescape a symmetrical array of china. The master and mistress would carve and serve the dishes, and the others would be served by those closest to them. At the conclusion of the first course, the dishes and napery were removed, revealing a new tablecloth underneath, which was then set for the second course—usually a dessert course of cakes, cookies, pies, and jellies in vast array. House slaves in service at the table would place the platters on it, bring fresh glasses and dishes as required, and serve drinks and the additional dishes that were displayed on the sideboards. At extremely formal occasions, the second tablecloth would be removed to reveal the mahogany table underneath, preserved fruits and nuts would be served along with beverages, and a series of toasts would be made.

This then was dinner; it was usually served between two and four P.M. Supper was served before bedtime and might be proceeded by tea in the early evening. Breakfast began the day at eight or nine in the morning and was similar to a continental breakfast of hot breads with the occasional addition of the previous day's leftovers in the form of sliced ham or a meat hash. Hercules oversaw it all. Respected by his peers, feared by his underlings (who dreaded his exactitude and iron discipline), and renowned in Philadelphia as the president's chef, Hercules was known as a dandy. Although enslaved, he, like many free chefs of the period, was able to sell leftover food and tallow; his perquisites from the kitchen garnered him the tidy sum of almost two hundred dollars a year. Following the service of the presidential meals, he would step out into the streets of Philadelphia immaculately attired—linen, silk shorts, a waistcoat, a velvet-collared frock coat, silver-buckled shoes, and a cocked hat—and brandishing a gold-headed cane, to head forth to meet with other fashionable black dandies of the time. The city was full of black notables; Hercules was one of them, and he was certainly aware of the others.

However, despite his princely income, his fame, and his relative freedom of movement, Hercules was not content with his lot. He wanted his freedom. He yearned for it and planned for it and escaped when he could. Tobias Lear, Washington's longtime personal secretary recorded his escape:

It is sad to relate that Uncle Harkless was so captivated with the delights of Philadelphia that in 1797, on the day Washington left the city to retire to private life at the end of his second term, he ran away rather than return to Mount Vernon. Although diligent inquiries were made for him, he was never apprehended.

His escape troubled the Washington family. "The running off of my cook has been a most inconvenient thing to this family," wrote Washington, who spared no expense in attempting to find him. No doubt finding it difficult to understand why one such favored slave would leave, Washington charged Frederick Kitt, his former household steward in Philadelphia, with finding Hercules and returning his property to him, noting, "but little doubt remains in my mind of his having gone to Philadelphia, and may yet be found there, if proper measures were employed to discover (unsuspectedly so as not to alarm him) where his haunts are." Several weeks later, Washington renewed his request to Kitt, stating that any expenses incurred in finding Hercules and returning him to Mount Vernon would be paid by Colonel Clement Biddle, but it was to no avail. Hercules had slipped off into the night. His six-year-old daughter, who remained enslaved at Mount Vernon, expressed thoughts that were probably more representative of those of Uncle Harkless himself. When asked by a guest at Mount Vernon if she were upset to never see her father again, she replied, "O! sir, I am very glad, because he is free now." Despite our lack of knowledge of him or his dishes, Hercules, the chef who doesn't even have a last name for history, was more than a grace note to the history of African American chefs. He was the first black chef for the country's first chief executive.

Washington, though, was not alone in savoring food prepared by enslaved hands. Throughout the country, south and north, whites reveled in the foods that blacks cooked. The smooth running of many of the founding fathers' households rested on the strong black backs of the enslaved. It resided in the firm grasp of the laundresses who starched and ironed tablecloths and the scullions who scrubbed out pots both iron and copper. It depended on the young children who weeded the gardens and flicked flies from foodstuffs at the tables and on the serving men and women who walked briskly along the "biscuit express," bringing the food from the kitchen outbuildings to the main dining rooms. It was there in the sound agricultural judgment of the farmers as well as in the capable hands of not only the chefs but also the kitchen staff. The enslaved grew the squashes and tomatoes, prepared the broiled shad and macaroni pie, set the tables, served the food, and cleaned up afterward. The first chief executive may have set the bar with his black chef, but the preeminent *bec fin* of the founding fathers was undeniably Thomas Jefferson.

The man from Monticello and his culinary contributions to the American menu are legion. Less well known is the fact that Jefferson was also responsible for the inclusion of many African foodstuffs in the diet of Virginians. Furthermore he promoted African American chefs and cooks to the highest levels of their profession. The world now knows of Jefferson's liaison with Sally Hemings, the enslaved half sister of his wife. Yet little is known about another member of the Hemings family: James Hemings, Sally's brother, who was also one of the slaves on the farms that made up Jefferson's estates. In the kitchens at Monticello, James Hemings mastered hearth cooking and knew the functions of clockwork-turned spit jacks that roasted the joints of meat and how to wield the long-handled "spider" skillets to cook the food evenly. He had felt the heavy weight of the filled cast iron pots and endured the scorched arms and burned clothing that were occupational hazards for any eighteenth-century cook. Hemings excelled in the culinary realm and was singled out for his industry and his talent. On July 5, 1784, at Jefferson's request, he set sail from Boston Harbor on the *Ceres*. By the end of the month, he was in Le Havre, and by August 6, he arrived in Paris to join Jefferson there and be apprenticed to French chefs.

The Paris that James Hemings arrived in was a city in transition. Revolution was in the air, and the events that were going on in the capital's streets and cafes would transform the world in the five years of Jefferson's Parisian sojourn as America's minister plenipotentiary. Hemings lived through the American Revolution; in Paris he would witness the beginning of the French one! The city in the dying years of the ancien régime must have been an astonishing place for a young visitor from America. Paris was a formal capital with a history rooted in monarchy, where Jefferson, lord and master to Hemings, was regarded as ill-clothed and lacking in manners—a provincial. Despite that, Jefferson was much admired and received great adulation, but the world of the French aristocrats into which Hemings had been plunged was far removed from that of Tidewater Virginia.

Paris was also abuzz with the revolutionary thoughts of liberty, which could only have been galvanizing for the enslaved young man from Virginia. Hemings was in the city at a crucial time in modern French history. He surely had many a stroll through the Palais Royal, as Jefferson's Parisian residence, at the Hôtel de Langeac on the Champs-Élysées, was not far away. The popular spot was a favorite of the city's increasingly strident revolutionaries and also of the growing American contingent. On his daily walks he might have heard Camille Desmoulins exhort his countrymen to revolution at a Palais Royale café. Hemings was also in the city on July 14, 1789, as crowds massed to head westward to storm the Bastille. As he went about his daily business for the Jefferson household, he was a witness to a world in transition.

Paris was surely a culinary wonderland to Hemings, whose prior experience was defined by what he'd learned in the kitchens of Monticello. The city was filled with cafes and the newly established eating venues known as restaurants, which were created by law only two years prior, in 1782. A revolution was taking place at the tables of the French capital as well, as the entrenched formality of court dining yielded to a more democratic type of cuisine, with the new eateries offering the public dishes previously unavailable outside royal palaces. The new restaurants offered menus that tempted the capital's diners with an embarrassment of riches. Some offered as many as twelve soups, twenty-four hors d'oeuvres, twenty main dishes each of beef, lamb, poultry, veal, and seafood, and a choice of fifty desserts. The whole was washed down with copious quantities of wines from France and Europe and an array of liqueurs and mixtures, like punches, syllabubs, and the beverage of the moment, coffee. The refined fare was served in a sophisticated atmosphere unlike that of the more rustic inns and traditional taverns. Chefs began to be known for their specialties, like Chef Baleine of the Rocher de Cancale on the rue Montorgueil, who was famous for his delicate hand with fish dishes; and Chef Beauvilliers, who expertly paired fine wines with his fare.

Hemings, as one enslaved, was certainly aware of the underpinnings of poverty that upheld the lives of the French aristocracy. He apprenticed in their kitchens and worked alongside their impoverished help. But he also served in a diplomatic household where the elite of the time gathered and no doubt heard Franklin and Jefferson and Adams debate the relative merits of the American and French systems of government. French laws regarding slavery were a labyrinth of confusion. Once he landed in France, Hemings fell under the "Freedom Principle," which held that slaves were free on French soil, as French slavery was usually confined to its colonies. However, the laws were complex and often contradictory and slaves did exist in the capital, having been brought from the colonies by their wealthy masters. Their numbers were small, however. Indeed, the French were concerned with the growing presence of slaves in the country and tried to regulate their length of stay.

At the time, Paris numbered among its citizens only one thousand blacks and people of mixed blood, a small number when compared with the black inhabitants of London of the period or the large black populations in developing American cities like Charleston, Philadelphia, and New York. The free Parisian blacks were the manumitted sons and daughters of colonial plantation owners. The city though was comparatively open and even had its black elite. There was the mulatto Chevalier de Saint-Georges, son of a former governor of Guadeloupe and a black woman; he was the best swordsman in Europe, a Freemason, and a composer whose name alternated on concert bills with that of Mozart. Mixed-race Thomas-Alexandre "Dumas" Davy de la Pailleterie, the father of writer Alexandre Dumas, was a noted solider and another honored swordsman. Both were leaders of the elite black community. Hemings would have known of these other blacks and their stature in the city. Although enslaved, he was paid wages by Jefferson during his Paris sojourn and had relative freedom of movement.

Hemings was initially apprenticed with the caterer who provisioned Jefferson's Parisian household, Monsieur Combeaux. From him, he is certain to have learned the basics of French cuisine and how to create the multiple dishes that were required for the classic *service à la française*, which offered multiple dishes set out on crisp napery that was de rigueur in the best houses of Virginia. Hemings also mastered the European *potager*, or stew stove, a brick and plaster assemblage complete with wood-fired burner holes, which was the precursor of today's modern stoves. The new stove granted the cook the ability to control the flame and the temperature in ways that were unimaginable in hearth cooking and allowed for the creation of the more subtle dishes. Jefferson was so taken with the novelty that he had a stew stove built in a kitchen of Monticello in later years, one of the few in the United States. In France, Hemings came to know the wide array of copper cookware that was essential for the preparation of meals in the French manner: *turbotières* (lozenge-shape pans for cooking fish), braising pans, roasting pans, boilers, molds, and more. Costlier than cast iron, but better able to conduct heat, the copper cookware was an integral part of the culinary equation that produced the fine dishes to be served on Jefferson's cornflower-sprigged blue-painted china, newly acquired from the royal porcelain factories.

Hemings's work under the tutelage of Monsieur Combeaux was only the beginning of his Parisian apprenticeship. He was also sent for periodic training sessions with a variety of the city's notable chefs, including a pastry chef and a cook in the household of the prince de Condé. His Virginia repertoire of simple country fare was expanded with the addition of dishes made with à la mode ingredients like crawfish, truffles, and the newly adopted potato, all washed down or even seasoned with champagne and cognac. The entire French culinary world was undoubtedly quite an eye-opener for the young Hemings, who worked assiduously for his first three years in Paris, going from apprenticeship to apprenticeship. By 1788, he was considered accomplished enough to be placed in charge of Jefferson's kitchens at his residence on the Champs-Élysées. There he oversaw the meals that were served to the notables of Europe; it was a far cry from the kitchens at Monticello, where the lifestyle, although lavish, was closer to that of an English country squire than of a French prince of the blood.

Much about Hemings, though, remains an enigma. He could have declared his freedom while on French soil. He was literate, had used his wages to hire a French tutor, and given his culinary training, was highly employable in Paris or elsewhere in Europe. Yet, unlike Washington's Hercules, Hemings elected to remain enslaved.

Perhaps because of his attachment to his sister, he chose, instead, to return to America with Jefferson. There he served as his chef in both Monticello and in Philadelphia when Jefferson became secretary of state of the fledgling republic under George Washington. No doubt Hemings knew the other black chefs in Philadelphia. Washington's residence, presided over by Hercules, was only three blocks away from his own.

Hemings clearly chafed under the bonds of slavery, and witnessing the fires of liberty in France surely made him fixed in his resolve. In 1793, four years after his return from Paris and four years before Hercules' escape, he petitioned Jefferson for his freedom. Jefferson granted his request, but his manumission was contingent on his training another slave to take his place. In a letter that had no legal force, but that placed him on his honor to free Hemings, Jefferson wrote:

> Having been at great expence [sic] in having James Hemings taught the art of cookery, desiring to befriend him and to require from him as little as possible, I do hereby promise & declare, that if the said James shall go with me to Monticello in the course of the ensuing winter, when I go to reside there myself, and shall there continue until he shall have taught such person as I shall place under him for that purpose to be a good cook this previous condition being performed, he shall be thereupon made free, and I will thereupon execute the proper instruments to make him free. Given under my hand and seal in the county of Philadelphia and the state of Pennsylvania this 15th day of September one thousand seven hundred and ninety three.

Characteristically for the period, where Big House privileges were carefully guarded familial perquisites, the person selected to be trained by James Hemings was his brother, Peter. With Peter's selection, the Hemings culinary dynasty continued its hold on the kitchens of Monticello. Peter continued the work begun by his brother and ultimately added brewing to his culinary portfolio, having studied the art under the tutelage of an English brewer. James and Peter were not the only Hemings to take on the role of Monticello chef;

other relatives also labored in the kitchens of the Virginia plantation, where the family became a parallel sepia culinary dynasty.

On February 26, 1796, Hemings left for Philadelphia with thirty
dollars from Jefferson "to bear" his expenses. He was free. He was
also restless. He lived in Philadelphia, then traveled—probably to
Spain—and finally settled in Baltimore, where in 1801 Jefferson con-
tacted him again. Following his election as the nation's third president, Jefferson chose for his chef the emancipated James Hemings,
who initially accepted the position. However, a wrangle over
Hemings's request for a formal letter of confirmation of his duties
from Jefferson ensued. Communication through third parties and
Jefferson's refusal to send such a letter resulted in Hemings declining the post, thereby depriving the country of its first official black
White House chef.

The job went instead to a Frenchmen, Honoré Julien, but slaves
from Monticello worked under him and tended the pots in the kitchens of America's first house. The wooden spoons and turning forks
passed to another generation of cooks from the extended Hemings
family. Later in 1801, Hemings did return to Monticello and was hired
as chef, but he never assumed the post. That fall, word reached the
plantation on the hill that Hemings had taken his own life.

The Jefferson-Randolph family cookbooks contain two recipes
known to have originated with James Hemings: chocolate cream
and snow eggs, both European desserts. Other recipes in the cookbooks display the culinary traditions of the enslaved, who brought
their ways into the kitchen of the founding fathers and helped create such uniquely American dishes as catfish soup, peanut soup,
and Virginia gumbo. It is to known chefs like Hercules and James
Hemings and to the thousands of unnamed and unheralded others
like them throughout the original thirteen colonies that the United
States of America owes the fleeting tastes of Africa that mixed and
mingled with those of Europe in the burnished copper pots and the
porcelain serving bowls of the founding fathers.

❖❖❖❖❖❖❖

TO MARKET TO MARKET

It is a tribute to the indomitable spirit of blacks in this country and to the human need for self-betterment that the slaves made time for themselves when all of their time belonged to someone else, but they did. They carved minutes from tasks by doing them more rapidly, by helping one another, and by taking shortcuts. Having a minute's respite, they stayed up and toiled on their own projects after night fell and they returned to their cabins. In the cracks and quiet times that they created in their harassed lives, they found a way to make a world. Many worked for themselves and their own benefit. Some saved and foraged seeds and tended gardens by moonlight or fished and hunted nocturnal animals like possum; others raised yard fowl for their eggs or hogs for their meat. Still others wove rugs and quilted blankets from scraps using home-made lamps that burned tallow. They assembled brooms and created other myriad goods that could be traded or sold.

Masters knew of this industriousness; some even found that it was easier to distribute seeds and allow the enslaved to supplement rations by growing the vegetables that they preferred on their own time. Many of the plants—okra, watermelon, eggplant, and gourds—that appeared in the slave gardens harked back to distantly remembered African tastes. Others spoke of American adaptations: European collard greens were used instead of African ones, and sweet potatoes replaced the African yams, while New World hot chilies had become important ingredients on both sides of the Atlantic. Their production was such that in many cases throughout the South, masters often purchased surplus goods from their own slaves' gardens, paying them with cash, trade goods, or bartered privileges like passes to visit relatives—a commercial symbiosis between master and enslaved that seemingly contradicted the conditions of enslavement. Thomas Jefferson bought cucumbers, sweet potatoes, and squash from his slaves. George Washington purchased hunted game and fish. In this manner, they and others like them acknowledged that these were indeed items that the enslaved had grown or made on time that was their own and, as such, had to be purchased.

In Natchez, Mississippi, Samuel Chase, a slave on a local plantation, raised hogs and poultry and grew potatoes and corn on his own time. With his mistresses' knowledge, he sold them to folks in the surrounding area from a wagon that was described as a virtual grocery on wheels. More important, he was allowed to keep the monies earned for his own benefit.

Chase's activities and those of others like him redefine our current ideas of enslavement. Even more surprising is the notion of markets maintained and patronized by slaves. Yet such markets existed throughout the Upper and Lower South during the period of enslavement, with the knowledge, if not the total approval, of masters. The slave-run markets were places where slaves would gather to barter or purchase the foodstuffs and goods they had acquired.

(Masters worried that markets of this type encouraged pilfering and poaching, but there is scant evidence of this.)

None was better known than the slave-run market in Alexandria, Virginia. This informal market was held on Sunday, a day on which many slaves were given a measure of leisure time on some plantations. It took place very early in the morning and all commercial activity was over by nine A.M. Slaves stayed up all night and walked for hours to reach it to trade their goods. Like all markets, the slave-run markets were more than simple commercial gathering places; they were also places for meeting and for exchange of news and information. Slaves traded not only eggs and chickens but also snippets of information that aided their survival. They learned which master might be selling off slaves, which plantation had a runaway, and even when the Underground Railroad was passing through. There was also news about friends and family members on neighboring plantations and time to savor communion with other blacks, both enslaved and free, from the surrounding area and the city of Alexandria itself. Witnesses describe the scene of slaves sitting under shade trees with baskets of berries that had been foraged or with chickens or eggs. It must have seemed an African scene transported to the New World, an atavism of a now-forgotten homeland: men in their homespun trousers and women dressed in their Sunday best with their neatly braided hair tied up in fresh head ties.

The market provided not only a place for garnering a few coins to pay for additional food or a bit of tobacco or something else to alleviate the monotonous drudgery of enslavement; it was also a place where folks could smile and court and even listen to music if someone had brought along a fiddle. It was a spot where for a few brief moments, the yoke of enslavement was lifted, and blacks could be themselves among themselves.

CHAPTER 5

IN SORROW'S
KITCHEN

Old Fashioned Cabin, Chimney built of Sticks and Mud, Florida

Hog Meat, Hominy,
and the Africanizing of the
Palate of the South

River Road, Louisiana—

As you fly into New Orleans, you can occasionally see, depending on the approach, Louisiana's River Road, surrounded by neat pie slices of acreage running from the Mississippi River inland. From the air, the slices make a lush green tapestry, with the dwellings raised like crochet knots. I'd been to the South many times before I came there with my mother for the first time. I'd seen the row of brick slave cabins that marched parallel to the mighty live oaks at Boone Hall outside Charleston and listened intently as docents at Drayton Hall verbally brought to life the look of the back of the house where slave and master lived out their lives in proximate and intertwined worlds. Middleton Place plantation had been another stop on my Southern journeys; there I'd explored the farmyard, watching the docents exhibit their skills with the intensity of one trying to recapture a lost thread. I knew that the hands that made the wrought iron work in Charleston and New Orleans had been black and recognized the high, small windows on ground-floor locations that signaled a slave depot. I once startled newly made friends in New Orleans by informing them of their home's history as a slave-trading location. I'd investigated hearth cooking and run my hands over the walls of kitchens that had been manned by slave cooks and surreptitiously taken off my shoes to feel under my feet the dirt of the plantation yards that stretched beyond the Big House. I'd seen the slave cabin at Tullie Smith Farm at the Atlanta History Center and reproductions of others in museum exhibits around the South. I'd read much about the antebellum period and as a Northerner, born and raised, I had tried to understand the culture of enslavement and the people who created it and willed myself to form a mental link with my own ancestors who had been transformed by it. I could rattle off dates, facts, and anecdotes with fair facility. Nothing, however, brought home the depersonalizing realities of enslavement to me like my mother's reaction on her visit to Louisiana's River Road.

My mother, who died in 2000, was also a Northerner. Born and raised in New Jersey, she spent her entire life in the Northeast, except for a brief tenure as dietitian at Bennett College in Greensboro, North Carolina, where she was miserable; she left rapidly, claiming to have gained nothing except a love for grits and the knowledge of how to cook them properly. While my own tendencies ran to the study of the African continent and its diaspora, my mother, though always a willing traveler, was more intrigued by the cathedrals of Europe than the Candomblé houses of Brazil. I was astonished, therefore, when our affinities coincided in New Orleans. In 1998, when I bought a home there, she immediately understood the city's magic and visited frequently. She set about making herself a part of the lives of my friends in that town, which is a noteworthy conjoining of Africa and Europe. Her early training as a dietitian left her with a lifelong love of food, and in New Orleans, with its vibrant food culture, many memorable meals were shared with the new friends who became our adopted family. With her questing mind and her artistic talents, she quickly became everyone's surrogate mother and delighted in her new role.

One of my friends, discovering that neither my mother nor I had visited the River Road, decided to drive us to see the glories of the state's plantation past. Taking off to explore tourist-like, neither of us had any idea of the impact the trip would have. The first stop was Laura Plantation, a French Creole dwelling that was nothing like the Tara-esque images that my mother had envisioned. More like a raised country house, it had none of the majesty and presence expected by one whose images of the plantation South had been formed by *Gone with the Wind* (the film not the book!). We were intrigued by its similarity to homes that we'd seen in the French Caribbean, but caught up in the myth of white pillars and sweeping lawns, it did not visually define a slaveholding past for us. However, the slave cabins on the grounds were a harbinger of things to come.

At Evergreen Plantation, there were more slave cabins. While they were certainly depressing, in truth, many looked like the wooden shacks that we'd seen dotting some of the secondary roads—and some even seemed to be in better shape. The double row of cabins, though, coupled with the knowledge that 103 enslaved people lived on the plantation in 1860, brought the realities of enslavement closer to home, but we didn't tarry there.

The next stop was Tezcuco Plantation, which has since burned down. It was then home to a fledgling African American museum, and as we walked through the small museum, I could see my mother's demeanor change. As we read the captions and examined the potbellied stove and the other meager artifacts lovingly displayed, she began to have that pensive look I knew too well. Lunch was at Tezcuco with our friends and the museum's founder, Kathe Hambrick Jackson. There, over Southern food that was nowhere as good as Mom's, we talked about Hambrick Jackson's plans for expanding the museum. I noticed that Mom's conversation had become "careful." We'd have much to talk about when we returned to New Orleans. The friends we were riding with (who were white) were unaware of my mother's inner turmoil, but I was attuned to her every move.

Ever polite, she soldiered on to the next stop, Houmas House, where we were greeted by a hoop-skirt-clad docent who regaled us with tales of the architecture and also of the home's owners; in deference to the PC times, a word or two *was* given to those enslaved on the plantation as well. This plantation fit the profile; it had high white columns and a vast alley of venerable live oaks that ran down to the river. Majestic and monumental, it was a Palladian-style fantasy of power. My mother took me aside and whispered, "Who built this house?" I replied that I didn't know but that probably much of the work had been done by the people enslaved on the plantation. She thought for a moment and then said, "What artistry. What beauty they created for people who thought we were nothing but goods, not even human beings!"

It was an affirmation of something that she had seen in the white columns and the carefully restored rooms. Where others might see only the degradation and pain of enslavement, she also saw triumph, transcendence, and art. No doubt she saw the pain. After all, she was a woman who had known her grandfather, who had been a house slave in Virginia and whose mother was sold South when he was two years old. No one I knew had a more intimate connection to enslavement than she did. My mother, who, like me, carried his blood in her veins, looked through the pain and the misery and the suffering and saw talent and artistry and ability and industry and amazing grace. Certainly she saw the enslaved—her grandfather, field hands, house servants, Big House cooks, and others—as victims of a horrific system, but she also saw them standing tall and proud in the dignity of their work.

No myth is more pervasive in the history of the United States than the myth of the plantation South—one that is celebrated by some and decried by others. In present-day consciousness our mental images hover somewhere between the happy tractable darkies of *Gone with the Wind* and the more embittered brethren of *Roots*. In the decades since the publication of *Roots* opened the floodgates of interest and historical exploration, the discoveries of new information and new ways at looking at chattel slavery in the United States seem to multiply daily.

Race-based chattel slavery is a keloid on the face of the United States, a thick scar that is our national birthmark. But like those that are tribal markings and symbols of rank on the African continent, America's scar has deep meaning and signals a past that must be carefully examined. It must be looked at in all its horror and degradation, complicity and confusion, for it tells us where and what we have come from. What my mother showed me as she sat in a chair on the veranda of Houmas House is that it must also be examined in light of the creativity and talent and grace expressed by the enslaved under situations that ranged from the unpleasant to the unspeakable. The American ways with music, dance, gesture, language, and, yes, food all bear witness to that inheritance.

◆ ◆ ◆ ◆ ◆

Slavery's duration in the North did not equal its longevity in the South. During the colonial period, blacks made up 61 percent of the population of South Carolina and 31 percent of that of Georgia. But at the time of the American Revolution, fewer than 10 percent of the total population of enslaved in the United States lived in the North. Their numbers, however, continued to grow in the South. In 1680, slaves made up a tenth of the Southern population; by 1790, they made up a third of the population. Following the American Revolution, the slave population exploded in the South, and between 1790 and 1810 the population of enslaved almost doubled. By the late seventeenth century, however, attitudes were changing in the North. Slave labor, which had been largely involved in agriculture in the North, was being eliminated as inefficient in the rapidly industrializing area.

Vermont outlawed slavery in 1777. Pennsylvania banned it in 1780, and it was outlawed in Massachusetts in 1783. Gradual emancipation began in Rhode Island, a former leader in the slave trade, in 1784. New York state began to abolish slavery in 1799, although the process did not end until July 4, 1827. New Hampshire became the last of the Northern states to end enslavement, in 1857. The Southern states were left with the "peculiar institution"—an economic system that increasingly put them at odds with the world and with their former slaveholding countrymen in the North. The slave system, though, continued to grow and prosper in the South.

Most Americans today base their ideas of the antebellum South on images created in popular culture that have little to do with the realities of history. Despite a national tendency to generalize slaveholding into North and South, there was no monolithic South even in the antebellum period. The region was divided into upland and coastal, and then subdivided further into the Up South, the Carolinas and Georgia, the Deep South, and the Gulf South. The mountainous spine of the Appalachians further bisected the region and was an area in which slaveholding was minimal. Each area had a unique experience with enslavement. Our blue-versus-gray vision of slavery is further complicated by popular imagery of white-columned plantation houses manned by a flotilla of enslaved blacks hauling and toting and doing the bidding of Massa and Miz Ann. In fact, even in slaveholding areas, in many cases hard-pressed whites had only a few hapless slaves; and in more than a few cases, owners were apt to be working in the fields alongside their one or two slaves. Less than one quarter of white Southerners held slaves, and half of those held fewer than five. Only 1 percent of Southerners owned more than one hundred, and a minuscule number owned more than five hundred and had the large spreads that we imagine; they lived mainly in South Carolina, Georgia, and Louisiana. In 1860, the average number of slaves residing together was about ten. These realities, though, in no way mitigate the horror of enslavement. "Plantation," in most cases in the South, was just a fancy word for the farm on which slaves toiled for their masters.

The work done by the enslaved was mainly agricultural and varied from locale to locale. Different crops—tobacco, rice, indigo, cotton, and sugar—produced different working environments, and the enslaveds' daily tasks and degree of autonomy varied from crop to crop. In Virginia and the Upper South the crop tended to be tobacco or the Tidewater triad of corn, wheat, and tobacco. Coastal South Carolina and Georgia had rice-based economies where slaves had a particular task to perform, and once it was completed, their time was their own. As slavery progressed from North to South and onward toward the West, it became even more arduous. J. S. Buckingham, an Englishman who journeyed through the slave states of the South in 1839, recounted,

> All the slaves have a great horror of being sent to the south
> or the west,—for the farther they go in either of these directions, the harder they are worked, and the worse they
> are used.

The cotton kingdoms of the Deep South were the ones that have provided us with most of our mental images. The sugar empires of the Gulf Coast offered different systems based on Caribbean models, in which life was cheap and the enslaved were often simply worked to death then replaced. Whatever the crop or the system, all were horrific in that the enslaved, whether under a beneficent or a harsh master, had no control over their own destinies. A gambling debt to be paid, a wedding in the master's family, a bequest given, or something as simple as an argument or a whim could result in a slave family being broken up forever.

Slaves, whatever their number in a household, were omnipresent, and they were dependent on their master for the essentials of life: housing, clothing, and especially food. Throughout the period of enslavement, discussion raged about how to feed the slaves. As the agricultural backbone of the region, the slaves not only produced the cash crops; they also were tasked with growing and processing most of the food that was consumed by all on the plantations, whether white or black. Feeding the enslaved, however, had of necessity to be an economically viable process. Rations had to be sufficiently nourishing to allow the enslaved to perform their tasks but could not be so lavish as to be unprofitable. In some cases, however, rations were so parsimonious as to be tantamount to starvation. On plantations of some size, there were basically two different systems of food distribution: one in which the enslaved were fed from a centralized kitchen somewhere on the plantation, and another wherein the enslaved were given their rations on a schedule and allowed to prepare them in their own cabins or within whatever communities they might have created for themselves. The former system was more common in the early years of enslavement, when the enslaved were often housed in dormitories and lived communally. Distributing rations became more common as the slave populations grew.

In almost all cases, the enslaved supplemented their rations by hunting and trapping. The nocturnal habits of the opossum made it a prime target for the enslaved, who had to hunt after the work of their daylight hours. There was also fishing for catfish, porgies, mullet, and other denizens of the creeks and rivers to supplement the rations. Foraging in nearby woods allowed the enslaved to add wild greens like watercress to their diets, as well as such items as ramps, chives, and wild garlic. In more than a few cases, there was also pilfering and poaching from their master or the masters of others. Theft from masters' fields was so prevalent that the enslaved on one Mississippi plantation even created a song about it.

> Some folks say dat a nigger won't steal,
> I caught two in my own corn field,
> one had a bushel,
> one had a peck
> an' one had rosenears [roasting ears]
> strung round his neck.

On some plantations that followed a more Caribbean model, the slaves were given provision grounds to raise their own crops, including vegetables like okra, chili peppers, and eggplant, which harked back to an African past. The slave gardeners were so successful that they occasionally sold produce back to their masters. At Monticello, Jefferson purchased items from his slaves and duly noted them down in his account books. Slave gardeners raised plants that they liked to eat and items they knew would sell, so it is telling to find on the listings of things grown in the provision grounds such crops as watermelon, cabbage, and greens—foods that even today remain totemic in the cooking of African Americans. They also raised cucumbers, white potatoes, and squash. Gardening was done in the little free time that the enslaved had after their daily work of running the plantation had been completed. This free time was usually on Sunday—a day of little work—or on weekdays after the sun went down. The oral history record suggests that animal fat and tallow were burned in old iron cooking pots to illuminate the gardens and enable the slaves to work after their day's labor. Alternately, they worked by the light of the moon. The quest for food, and enough of it, was a daily obsession for many of the enslaved, if the numerous mentions of food and eating found in the slave narratives of the antebellum period are to be believed. Slave rations were never fixed by national law in the United States, as they were in the French territories, where, the Code Noir (Black Code) of 1685 legislated the amount of cassava meal, beef, or fish to be given to all adult slaves over eighteen years of age. The lack of such uniformity in the United States meant that amounts were often established by individuals who were more interested in controlling costs than providing nourishment. George Washington, deemed a benign if not beneficent master, fed his slaves adequately. However, during the 1790s, after the revolution, he reduced their rations and estimated that eleven pounds of corn, two pounds of fish, and a pound and a half of meat were sufficient weekly rations for each of the twenty-three slaves on one of his farms. Not a lot when compared with those rations remembered by John Thompson, who had been enslaved on a plantation in Maryland: "The provision for each slave, per week, was a peck of corn, two dozens of herrings, and about four pounds of meat."

Even these amounts were lowered by the antebellum period on some plantations. James W. C. Pennington, enslaved to a wheat planter in Washington County, on Maryland's western shore, gave a more detailed account of his rations in his 1849 narrative:

The slaves are generally fed upon salt pork, herrings, and Indian corn.

The manner of dealing it out to them is as follows—Each working man, on Monday morning goes to the cellar of the master where the provisions are kept, and where the overseer takes this stand with someone to assist him, when he, with a pair of steel yards, weighs out to every man the amount of three-and-a-half pounds to last him till the ensuing Monday—allowing him just half a pound per day. Once in a few weeks, a change is made, by which, instead of the three-and-a half-pounds of pork, each man receives twelve herrings allowing two a day. The only bread kind the slaves have is that made of Indian meal. In some of the low counties, the masters usually have to give their slaves the corn by the ear; and they have to grind it for themselves by night at hand-mills. But my master had a quantity sent to the grist mill at a time, to be ground into coarse meal, and kept in a large chest in his cellar, where the woman who cooked for the boys could get it daily. This was baked into large loaves called "steel poun bread." Sometime as a change it was made into "Johnny Cake," and then at others into mush.

The slaves had no butter, coffee, tea, or sugar; occasionally they were allowed milk, but not statedly; the only exception to this statement was the "harvest provisions." In harvest, when cutting the grain, which lasted for two to three weeks in the heat of summer, they were allowed some fresh meat, rice, sugar, and coffee; also their allowance of whiskey.

Solomon Northup, a free black who had been illegally captured in New York City and sold in the South in 1841, bitterly recalled that all that was allowed the slaves on the Louisiana plantation where he was enslaved for twelve years was

corn and bacon, which is given out at the corn-crib and smoke-house every Sunday morning. Each one receives, as his weekly allowance, three and a half pounds of bacon, and corn enough to make a peck of meal. This is all—no tea, coffee, sugar and with the exception of a very scanty sprinkling now and then, no salt. I can say from a ten year's residence with Master Epps, that no slave of his is ever likely to suffer from the gout, superinduced by excessive high living.

Unlike Pennington's plantation, where the master distributed cornmeal already ground, on the Epps plantation, where Northup was enslaved, the corn was given by the ear. So the slaves had to process it, shell it, and grind it into meal on their own time, which added to their already overburdened schedules. Northup's account gives a sense of the never-ending, bone-numbing labor slaves did day in and day out. He notes that after the work in the fields was over, the slaves still had to attend to their other chores—feeding the animals, cutting wood, and the like—before they could finally go to their own cabins to build their own fire, grind the corn, and then prepare their meager suppers as well as the midday meal to take to the fields the next day. This midday meal was usually a form of corn ash cake with bacon. By the time all this was accomplished, he states simply, "it is usually midnight." The dreaded horn or the equally hated bell, depending on the plantation, rang before daybreak, calling them back to the fields for another day's toil. On the Epps plantation and many others, being caught in the quarters after daybreak was cause for flogging.

The midday meal was often taken to the fields and eaten there or was distributed by others so the rhythm of the fieldwork wasn't interrupted. Often superannuated slaves who could no longer do hard labor were selected to distribute meals. John Brown, who had been a slave in Virginia in the first half of the nineteenth century, noted that the first full meal at the plantation on which he was enslaved was served in the field at noon after the cotton was weighed. It was a soup made from cornmeal and potatoes, called "lob-lolly" or "stirt-about." A pint of it was served into a tin pan that each slave carried at his waist, and, as Brown remembered, "the distribution and disposal of the mess did not take long."

Young children were usually fed communally. They were given a mash of cornmeal and milk in a communal kitchen by women who were too old or too infirm to be otherwise useful. Fannie Moore of

South Carolina remembered the midday meal in a 1930s account recorded by the Works Progress Administration (WPA):

> My granny cooked for us chillums, while our mammy away in the fiel'. Dey warn't much cookin' to do. Jes' make co'n pone an' bring in de milk. She hab a big bowl wif enough wooden spoons tro go 'roun'. She put milk in de bowl an' break it [the cornbread] upp. Den she put de bowl in the middle of de flo' an' all de chilluln grab a spoon.

Slave narratives generally agree that the location for eating evening meals was the slave quarters. Many recalled that after the labor on the plantation was finished, the yard that was common ground in the quarters would begin to hum with life as individuals and families began to prepare evening meals, socialized, and savored what few minutes of private time they had. The chimneys in the slave cabins, although frequently made of daub and wattle and not stone, served for heating and cooking, which was done indoors in the winter when fires were necessary for warmth. In the summer, when the additional heat would be oppressive, cooking was done outdoors over a fire of some sort in the plantation yard.

Fanny Kemble was the reluctant mistress of a Southern plantation. A British actress, she met and married Pearce Mease Butler, scion of an illustrious South Carolina family with plantations in the Sea Islands, following a successful American tour. Her visit to the plantations and the journal that she kept during her almost fifteen-week stay offers a view of the meals of the enslaved from the other side of the social spectrum. The meals on her plantation were distributed from a communal kitchen.

> The second meal in the day is at night, after their labor is over, having worked, at the *very least*, six hours without intermission of rest or refreshment since their noonday meal (properly so-called, for 'tis *meal* and nothing else). Those that I passed today sitting on their doorsteps, or on the ground round them eating were the people employed at the mill and threshing floor. As these are near to the settlement, they had time to get their food from the cookshop.

Chairs, tables, plates, knives, forks, they had none; they sat, as I said, on the earth or doorsteps, and ate either out of their little cedar tubs or in an iron pot, some few with broken iron spoons, more with pieces of wood, and all the children with their fingers. A more complete sample of savage feeding I never beheld.

All the enslaved were not in the miserable conditions Kemble describes. On some plantations, they were assigned their own tin pans or were able to barter for wooden utensils. Archaeologists began to look intensely at the remains of slave quarters for the first time in the 1960s, and they have been a remarkable source of information. In the slave quarters at Mount Vernon they have found items ranging from white and brown glazed stoneware to Chinese porcelain to Rhenish stoneware that must have come from the Big House—possibly they'd been cracked or broken. Of the pieces found, slipware and white salt-glazed stoneware seem to predominate, but the most intriguing sherds are those called colonoware. These pieces of hand-thrown, low-fired, unglazed earthenware were once thought to be Native American pottery, but increasingly evidence has pointed to the creation of colonoware by African Americans potters as well. More interesting, the African American forms of colonoware seem to resemble pottery still made in parts of Western Africa and used in cooking and serving food there. Many of the pieces found in both Virginia and South Carolina are from bowls that would have been used to hold the African-inspired one-pot soupy stews and porridgelike mashes that were the enslaved's daily fare.

The cooking of the slave yard inadvertently allowed the enslaved to maintain an African tradition of one-pot meals sopped with starches and stews of leafy greens seasoned with smoked or pickled ingredients. Ingenuity was called upon to relieve the forced monotony of the slave diet and inspired whatever creativity could be wrung from a peck of corn and three pounds of salt pork. Hunting by slave women and men after their hours of plantation labor allowed them to add new meats such as possum, turkey, raccoon, and rabbit to the pot.

Foraging and gardening in provision grounds produced greens and foodstuffs with the taste of Africa, like okra, eggplant, and chilies. The culinary monotony would change only at holiday time, most notably at Christmas, and occasionally at family weddings and harvest time. Then all but the most miserly master allowed the enslaved some modicum of feasting. Solomon Northup writes:

> The table is spread in the open air, and loaded with varieties of meat and piles of vegetables. Bacon and cornmeal at such times are dispensed with. Sometimes cooking is performed in the kitchen on the plantation, at others in the shade of wide branching trees. In the latter case, a ditch is dug in the ground, and wood laid and burned until it is filled with glowing coals, over which chickens, ducks, turkeys, pigs, and not unfrequently the body of an entire wild ox, are roasted. They are furnished also with flour, of which biscuits are made, and often with peach and other preserves, with tarts, and every manner and description of pies . . . Only the slave who has lived all the years on his scanty allowance of meal and bacon, can appreciate such suppers. White people in great numbers assemble to witness the gastronomical enjoyments.

The feasting was followed by general merriment including dances, and on some plantations the enslaved were given hard cider or whiskey as well.

Harriet Jacobs, the first female slave to write a narrative, in 1858, describes the Johnkannus, bands of slaves masquerading in rags who played music on an instrument known as a "gumbo box." In an African parallel to European caroling, they would go from plantation to plantation, begging for Christmas donations, which they received in the form of money or liquor.

> Christmas is a day of feasting, both white and colored people. Slaves who are lucky to have a few shillings, are sure to spend them for good eating; and many a turkey or pig is captured without saying, "By your leave, sir." Those who cannot obtain these, cook a 'possum, or a raccoon, from which savory dishes can be made. My grandmother raised poultry and pigs for sale; and it was her established custom

to have both a turkey and a pig roasted for Christmas dinner.

Other occasions of relative feasting for the enslaved were harvest time or corn-shucking time. At these times and generally when there were guests or celebrations like birthdays, weddings, or other large gatherings at the Big House, there might be barbecues. The cooks for these events were black men, who used their talents to create the iconic Afro-Southern dish.

> Night befo' dem barbecues, I used to stay up all night a-cooking and basting de meats with barbecue sass. It was made of vinegar, black and red pepper, salt, butter, a little sage, coriander, basil, onion, and garlic. Some folks drop a little sugar in it. On a long pronged stick, I wraps a soft rag or cotton for a swab, and all de night long, I swabs de meat til it drip into de fire. Dem drippings change de smoke into seasoned fumes dat smoke de meat. We turn de meat over and swab it dat way allnight long til it ooze seasoning and bake all through.

The Christmas holiday, which might last as long as a week, was a welcome respite. When the holidays were over and the festivities ended, it was back to the work routine of up before the dawn bell, back after dusk, and meals that rang in all possible changes on monotonous rations of corn and hog with whatever additions could be found, foraged, or filched. The world of plenty, however, was never far away. It existed in the Big House, where the master and his guests dined nightly on foods raised, processed, prepared, served, and cleaned up by the enslaved. The Big House kitchen was where the tastes of Africa truly began to colonize those of Europe.

The Big House kitchen was one of the centers of power during the antebellum period in the South; from it, the cook, solo or in conjunction with the mistress of the house, fed the master's family and often oversaw the feeding of all on the plantation. At some of the loftier plantations there could be twenty or more guests to dinner every evening. By the early eighteenth century, it had become custom in the South for the kitchens at plantation houses to be placed in a building that was separate from the main house. John Michael Vlach, a specialist in the architecture of the Southern plantation, suggests that "the detached kitchen was an important emblem of hardening social boundaries and the everyday society created by slaveholders that increasingly demanded clearer definitions of status, position, and authority." Other reasons were more practical. If the kitchen was removed from the house, any kitchen fire would not endanger the Big House complex.

The Big House kitchens were the epicenter of food preparation on the plantation. They were equipped with massive hearths, complete with turning spits and an array of pots and pans and the people to tend them. Mariah Robinson, who must have had intimate knowledge of hearth cooking, recalled these kitchens in the 1930s WPA slave narratives:

> Dere wuzn't any stoves long slavery times. An de chimbleys wuz made special to cook an'warm by dem. Dey built dem out of rock or stick an'dirt. Ledges wuz lef' on each side an' a long heavy green pole wuz put 'cross from one ledge to another. Dis wuz high up in the chimbley to keep it from burning in de flames. On dis rod wuz hooks and chains to hang pots an' things to cook with. Dey call dese pot hooks, pot hangers, pot claws, and crooks. Dey wuz hung at different lengths so as to cook hot or jes warm. Effen dey wuzn't careful, dis long log would burn through an' spill everything an' bend or break de cooking vessels. Sometimes dey would burn a person when dey spilled.
>
> Some of the pots and kettles had legs an' de skillets an' sauce pans had slim legs, so dat day could be placed wid deir food on little beds of coals which had been raked to one side of the hearth. Dere was a trivet to set skillets and pots on over the coals. Dese trivets had [three] legs, some shot to put de pot right on de fire to cook quick, an' some had long legs so dat de food would jes keep warm and not cook much.

The hearth cooking that went on in these kitchens was an arduous endeavor punctuated by lifting heavy cast-iron pots and spiders, bending and arranging and maintaining flame levels, and hauling buckets of ash and used charcoal. In addition, there was always the omnipresent fear that the women's long skirts would sweep up a spark and catch fire. All this was accomplished under the watchful eye of the mistress, who, on any plantation of size, did none of the heavy lifting.

Usually, this world was presided over by a slave cook, who was under the direction of the mistress and in charge of all food preparation. The Big House slave cook was a trusted individual who was given the allowance of ingredients for the meals to prepare and made responsible not only for their preparation but also for overseeing the folks required to do it. The role was one of favor, as house servants occasionally had access to more food. However, the position of Big House cook as one to be envied was not always the case, as remembered by Harriet Jacobs. She recalled the eagle eye with which her mistress, the dyspeptic and aptly named Mrs. Flint, watched over her provisions. The raw materials that were allotted to her grandmother for the preparations of the household's food were "weighed out by the pound and ounce, three times a day. I can assure you she gave them no chance to eat wheatbread from her flour barrel. She knew how many biscuits a quart of flour would make, and exactly what size they ought to be." Jacobs reminded that Mrs. Flint would "station herself in the kitchen and wait till [the meal] was dished, and then spit in all the kettles and pans that had been used for cooking. She did this to prevent the cook and her children from eking out their meager fare with the remains of gravy and other scrapings." Other narratives confirmed that such meanspiritedness on the part of a mistress was not an isolated act.

The Big House cooks wielded a fair amount of power. They were usually women, except on some very large plantations. (In southern Louisiana near New Orleans, however, there was a Gallic tendency to give the word *chef* a masculine article and more male chefs were found there.) They ruled their domains with iron discipline and often garnered praise for their culinary expertise from white visitors. R. Q. Mallard of Georgia wrote of one plantation kitchen where "French cooks are completely outdistanced in the production of wholesome, dainty and appetizing food; for if there is any one thing for which the African female intellect has a natural genius, it is for cooking." Male or female, the results that came from Big House kitchens were overwhelmingly praised by whites. Stereotypes of the time suggested that, to whites, blacks were born cooks, and several even suggested that it was a racial talent. Louisianan Charles Gayarré echoed the prevailing sentiment of the time in an article in an 1880 issue of *Harper's* magazine: "The Negro is a born cook. He could neither read nor write, and therefore he could not learn from books. He was simply inspired; the god of the spit and the saucepan had breathed into him; that was enough." Throughout the period of enslavement, black cooks gradually had their way with their masters' palates, and dishes that had the mark of the cabin and of Africa, whether through ingredients or method, became an established part of the Southern culinary lexicon.

In 1824, when Mary Randolph published *The Virginia House-wife*, she was certainly unaware that the ingredients that she called for, such as field peas, eggplant, and okra, arrived in this country from the African continent. Yet in her book there are recipes aplenty using what must have been new ingredients. They include fried eggplant, a field pea (black-eyed pea) cake fried in lard and garnished with thin bits of bacon, and a simple dish of boiled okra called "Gumbs—A West India Dish," which she pronounces, "very nutricious [sic] and easy to the digestion." Her "ochra" soup—requiring okra, onions, lima beans, squash, chicken (or veal knuckle), bacon, and peeled tomatoes and thickened with a flour and butter roux—could pass for a form of chicken andouille gumbo anywhere in southern Louisiana. She even suggests it be served with an accompaniment of boiled rice. There's also a recipe for young greens. All are culinary refinements of dishes that certainly came from the slave quarters and were transformed in the hands of Big House cooks.

The 1839 *Kentucky Housewife*, by Letice Byran, continues the pattern and includes a recipe for boiled field peas to be eaten with baked or boiled pork. There is also one for stewed eggplant that seems to be a variant of Randolph's recipe and an early recipe for watermelon-rind pickles. There is another okra soup recipe; this one calling for beef, veal, or chicken broth as a base into which thinly sliced okra and tomatoes are placed. The whole is heated, and when ready, it is sieved and seasoned with cayenne pepper. Finally it's served over toast in a tureen.

Sarah Rutledge's 1847 *The Carolina Housewife* includes another of the seemingly ubiquitous okra soups. This one, though, is roux-less and similar to the roux-less Charleston gumbo that is still served today. A groundnut soup seasoned with a "seed pepper" and a bennie soup prepared from sesame seeds using the same method also have a decidedly African feel. Rutledge's recipes are wider ranging than the other two collections and include dishes like groundnut cheesecakes, a confection of ground peanuts and puff pastry topped with grated sugar. There's a Guinea squash recipe for baked eggplant, a New Orleans gumbo thickened with filé, and a Seminole soup of squirrel and hickory nuts served with filé, or the tender top of a pine tree, which "gives a very aromatic flavor to the soup." The book offers the first hints of the elaborate rice kitchen that had been developed in the Lowcountry under the watchful eye of African Big House cooks who had experience with the grain. There is also a selection of recipes for rice cakes, rice breads, rice confections, and other dishes.

The sieved-okra soup of *The Kentucky Housewife*, the delicate roux-less gumbo of *The Carolina Housewife*, and the simple boiled okra of *The Virginia House-wife* all point to the ubiquity of okra dishes on the developing Southern table. Others calling for ingredients such as field peas, benne (sesame), greens, and eggplant hint at a cross-pollination of culinary cultures. These dishes and others like them most certainly made an appearance in other less-sophisticated guises in the quarters before gracing the masters' tables. Seasonings changed in African hands as well, and Southerners developed a taste for more highly seasoned food, as indicated by the frequent use of "seed pepper" and cayenne. The Big House kitchens were slowly having Africa's way with the tastebuds of the South in what historian Eugene Genovese called "the culinary despotism of the slave cabin over the Big House." The Africanizing of the Southern palate outlasted the reign of Baron Tobacco, King Cotton, and Empress Sugar and defined the taste of the American South.

◆◆◆◆◆◆◆

MIND YOUR MANNERS

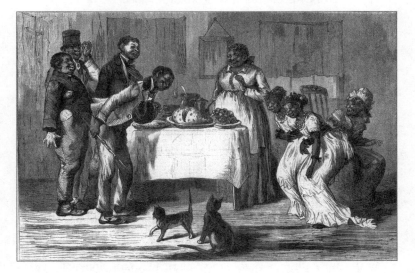

By the early nineteenth century, most of those enslaved in the Southern states knew of Africa only from grandparents or distant relatives. Yet Africa remained. It remained in the shapes of the ceramic ware that was used on tables. It appeared in the foods that were on their plates and, more subtly but perhaps even more pervasively, it appeared in their ways of being in the world: in their manners.

The West African way of being in the world, in general compass, was as filled with dos and don'ts as elsewhere, but they were situated in a tradition of hospitality and of welcome that was mirrored in the U.S. South as nowhere else in the country. The traditions of hospitality go so far back that they were remarked on by explorers and conquerors, travelers, and even slave traders.

Theophilus Conneau, a slaveship captain, even comments on it in his 1853 *A Slaver's Log Book; or, 20 Years Residence in Africa*. He arrived in a Sousou village in Senegambia and was accorded a welcome by the chief, who gave him lodging and sent a crier out to inform the town that there was a white visitor in the village.

In a short time the hut was visited by all the matrons or female heads of families, one bringing a small quantity of rice, another two or three roots of cassava, this one a few spoons of palm oil, the other a handful of peppers or a little more rice. The oldest lady made herself important by presenting me with a fine capon fowl . . . The contribution was not forced but voluntary.

Conneau, impressed by this abundant hospitality, muses, "I found that even when a poor Black stranger demanded hospitality everyone in the town shared in the charity." He concludes with great irony, "Why then, civilize this people and teach them Christian selfishness!" Indeed, hospitality was and remains an especial virtue in some countries of western Africa, where it is a religious as well as a civic and a personal duty to take in and feed the traveler and the stranger. It's called *teranga* in Senegal among the Wolof and *diarama* among Mandinka. These notions of hospitality and propriety crossed the ocean with the enslaved Africans as well.

The film *Gone with the Wind* has influenced a generation's ideas about the antebellum period in the American South. Some of the history is skewed and more representative of the time when the movie was made than the time it was to have taken place. The scenarist got one thing right, though. In the early section of the film, showing Tara before the war, Scarlett is confronted by Mammy, who admonishes her by saying "You can tell a lady by the way she eats in front of folks like a bird!" The notion of eating at home before going to another's house to eat is African in origin. The practice was still common among blacks in the North and South in the 1950s and remains a tenet of Southern belles. The rationale was the same. It was considered well-bred to pick at food. Equally, overeating at the home of another was taken to mean that there was not sufficient food at home.

The African-influenced world of the enslaved retained a notion of hierarchy that was filled with honorifics given to members of the extended family, such as the "Aunt" or "Uncle" bestowed on those who were older and could not be called by first name. A beverage, even if it is only water, is still offered to guests in many African American households. The list goes on, and remains equally the list of dos and don'ts held by many a well-raised white Southerner. Tara, in the film version, shows the reason, but Judith Martin (Miss Manners) defined it in *Star-Spangled Manners*:

> More subtly, so much so that they failed to notice it themselves, southerners were learning to practice African manners. It is not from the British that what came to be known as southern graciousness was developed, with its open, easygoing style, its familial use of honorifics, and its "y'all come see us" hospitality. The higher the southern family's pretensions, the more likely the children were to be receiving daily etiquette instruction from someone whose strict sense of the fitting came from her own cultural background— the house slave who occupied the position known as Mammy.

The rule of the quarters over the Big House therefore extended not only to taste and ingredients and cooking methods, but also to behavior. It manifested itself in ways of being that characterize Southern manners, black and white, through the twentieth century and into the twenty-first. Mammy would have loved it.

CHAPTER 6

CITY FOOD, SOUTH AND NORTH

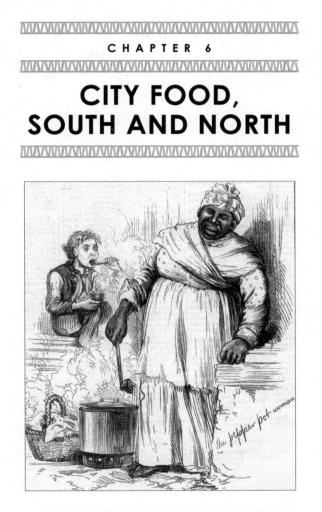

The pepper pot woman

Caterers, *Cala* Vendors,
and the Continuing of
African Culinary Traditions

New Orleans, Louisiana—

It seems as though New Orleans and I were simply destined to meet and bond. My first trip there was in the late 1970s when, as travel editor of *Essence* magazine, I accompanied a team of editors heading to the city to create a college issue that was to feature Dillard University, one of the two historically black colleges in the city. I remember at that time looking forward to the trip with anticipation, as the Crescent City on the Mississippi was a place that had long fascinated me. Seemingly more Caribbean or European than American, with a French and Spanish history, it proved worthy of my fascination. The white-columned buildings of Dillard's campus were astonishing, as was the feeling of pride in being at a black-run institution with a history going back to the days just following Emancipation. Plus the city itself was captivating; I remember staring in amazement at the buildings in the French Quarter, where I was able to sneak away from the group for a quick peruse. I also discovered a wonderful Creole restaurant, Dooky Chase, and its culinary guiding force, Leah Chase. After tasting her cooking, I fell in love with the city.

I returned to New Orleans more than a decade later to participate in a Modern Language Association conference. On that trip, I was aided by a shopping article in *Town and Country* magazine and must have poked my head into every store in the French Quarter. I was hooked: I gazed at the jewelry on Royal Street, gobbled down beignets at the Café du Monde, found my way into the line for Galatoire's Restaurant, and discovered the delights of a culinary antique shop named Lucullus—a shop that not only landed me my first absinthe glass but also gave me a group of lifelong friends who would eventually lead me to a home in the city as well.

The next trip sealed the deal. I was invited to participate in a symposium given by the Hermann Grima House, a historic French Quarter dwelling that showed the grand front parlors of the rich as well as opened its kitchen to the public. Docents gave instruction on the stew-hole stove, called a *potager* in French, and about the hearth cooking that took place there. The symposium cemented my love of the city and created friendships with many ladies who were connected with the Grima. It also allowed me to have an inside look at the house and got me thinking about urban enslavement in the American South and North.

On my periodic trips back to New Orleans, I became entranced by that city's urban landscape and by the outbuildings found behind many of the large French Quarter homes. Many were kitchens, situated away from the main houses to protect it from fire. There were also *garçonnières*, where the young man of the house took up residence after reaching an age when he might be counted on to sow some wild oats. In one notable building in the Faubourg Marigny neighborhood, there is even a *pigeonnier*—a pigeon roost where birds were kept to provide squab for the table. A large number of the outbuildings that dot the skyline of the French Quarter, however, have a more somber history. They are slave quarters— buildings where the urban enslaved lived and worked in close proximity to their masters. It was their labor that underpinned the grand lifestyle of those who dwelled in the front parlors.

Like those of many Americans, my mental images of the physical landscape of slavery had been confined to rows of cabins on plantations that grew cotton or rice, tobacco or indigo. They did not include small bedrooms above hot kitchens in back of brick-fronted town houses in major urban areas. My continuing visits to New Orleans and subsequent trips to Charleston, Savannah, and other cities made me think about the phenomenon of urban enslavement both in the South and in the North. In New Orleans, I heard the tales of one harsh mistress who kept her slaves chained in the attic, where they were discovered only after a fire broke out, and climbed up numerous rickety wooden stairs to the small outbuilding rooms. I also listened to docents describe the kitchen work while gazing into the massive hearth in the outbuilding kitchen in Charleston, South Carolina's Heywood-Washington House and saw the brass and tin badges that slaves had to wear when they went off to work for hire. The small yards and the outbuildings and the differently shaped metal badges are another side of the tale of enslavement in the country, one that is being rediscovered daily and told anew.

While rural plantations provided some distance between the master and the majority of the enslaved in the pursuit of their daily lives, there was no such cordon sanitaire in urban slavery. Master and slave lived proximate lives in towns and cities, which were beginning to grow into the urban landscape that we know in our historic towns today. It's been more than two decades since I first saw the small rooms over the kitchen in the Hermann Grima House, and while the urban landscape remains the same, the world has changed. Today the slave quarters over the Grima House kitchen remain, but the upstairs rooms are open to the public and also interpreted by docents, along with the tale of the enslaved who manned the stoves, hauled the water, tended the gardens, fed wood into the oven and the *potager*, served the meals, and cleaned up afterward. Today, their story is told alongside that of their owners. Their story of urban enslavement is the other side of the black-white diptych of life in America's growing urban areas. It adds another facet of pain to the story of enslavement in the U.S. North and South.

❖ ❖ ❖ ❖ ❖

Even as the South and North grew increasingly divided over the institution of slavery, they shared a strange communality in the proximity of the lives of blacks and whites in urban areas. Most urban slaves were the city equivalent of house slaves on the rural plantation and were responsible not only for preparing the meals and serving them but also for all the household chores. Other urban slaves worked both within and outside the master's home. Many of them had daily jobs to which they hurried each morning and from which they returned in the evening to finish other chores. They dwelled in the small cramped quarters above kitchens and in outbuildings in towns large and small. This phenomenon was not unique to the South but was as old as the country itself. Indeed, urban enslavement was a part of the cultural landscape of the South and North from the nation's beginning. For those raised on the conventional discussion of African enslavement meted out by twentieth-century history books, the South bears the brunt of the blame for slavery. Increasingly in the twenty-first century, this is being revisited, and the North and its participation in the history of enslavement is coming into clearer focus.

From its inception, urban enslavement in the North was no different from its Southern counterpart. Despite curfews and strict laws governing their presence on the streets and in the marketplace, those enslaved in towns and cities began to make their presence felt in the business of food. They became workers in taverns and eateries and sold prepared foodstuffs, vegetables, and other goods on the streets, usually at the bidding of their masters. Indeed many foreign visitors commented on the number of people of African descent on the streets and on their raucous behavior. It seemed that they treated the thoroughfares as their own assembly areas and did not hesitate to be insubordinate and unruly. After emancipation in the North, many former slaves continued to run taverns, eateries, and other dining establishments. On the upper end of the culinary spectrum, they served whites, set trends, and created fortunes from their labor. In both the South and the North, on the more humble end, blacks both free and enslaved and their descendants continued a tradition of street vending which had its roots in the African continent and displayed an entrepreneurial spirit that even enslavement couldn't tamp down. Food provided a path to independence for many blacks, especially in the port towns on the Atlantic and Gulf coasts.

In the early 1800s, most African Americans were emancipated in the North, and many got work in taverns and alehouses, finding more opportunity in those realms than in others. In the North, free people of color occupied a sizable spot in the food market, but the tale of African Americans' finding fortune and fame in the kitchen began even earlier, before the nation was declared. In Providence, Rhode Island, Emmanuel "Manna" Bernoon, a free black, opened that city's first oyster and alehouse, in 1736, the year of his emancipation. He would later own a catering business and a tavern. The state also gives us the story of Charity "Duchess" Quamino, who was born on the African continent—the sonorities of her name indicate that she may have been from the area today called Ghana. Captured at age fifteen, she was brought to the United States in 1753 and became the property of John Channing of Newport, Rhode Island. There she was put to work in the kitchen, where she remained for more than four decades, cooking for not only Channing but his son as well. In her free time, she began to cook for others. She established a catering business and became known as the best pastry chef in the prosperous town; her frosted plum cakes were renowned. Throughout this time she remained a slave, working under the aegis of her owners. She received her freedom only in the later years of her life. Bernoon and Quamino are examples of the possibilities of culinary entrepreneurship evidenced by both enslaved and free.

By the early years of the nineteen century, the African American presence was diminishing in northern cities like New York, where the population of blacks dwindled from 10 percent in the 1800s and 1810s to 7 percent in the '20s and '30s and continued downward. As the cities grew, the proportion of blacks in the urban mix decreased: African Americans were being subsumed by the increasing wave of northern European immigrants. Nevertheless, they continued to dominate the street commerce and still remained major players in the culinary industries of the republic.

Philadelphia was a pivotal city for the growth of African Americans in the food-service industry. Blacks in culinary service had long been the norm there. It was, after all, a city that had seen the culinary likes of Washington's Hercules and Jefferson's James Hemings. Pre–Civil War Philadelphia was a port city that depended on the money, shipping, and patronage of Southerners. Many from the Old South wintered in the city and enjoyed its cultural attractions. In the early years of the nineteenth century, Philadelphia was also a place that beckoned to African Americans; its Quaker heritage made it a potential safe haven for those fleeing from the South. The city continued to maintain connections with the Caribbean, and following the Haitian Revolution of 1804, it received an increase of immigrants from that island, both white and black, free and enslaved, many of whom joined the blacks working in the food-service industries of their adopted city. In 1810 it was estimated that there were eleven thousand free blacks living in Philadelphia and at least another four thousand fugitive slaves seeking asylum in various ways. The city's black community grew by more than 30 percent in the decade between 1820 and 1830 alone. But by the 1830s, the conditions were not as welcoming: The free black community was at odds with the city fathers about political and social rights, though a growing abolitionist community mitigated some of the difficulties. Food and significant African American success in the service industry also helped smooth the way.

In Philadelphia, it was said, "if you're in catering, you're in the swim; if not, you're in the soup." This was because of a group of individuals who saw a niche in the market and filled it. In the North, with no slaves to staff midsize or bachelor households, a public butler, often a free person of color, was frequently engaged by those too small or too frugal to have their own servants. Unlike a private butler employed by a single family, a public butler organized meals and waited on a number of different households. Robert Bogle created the role of the caterer from that of the public butler, although the term "caterer" did not come into wide usage until the mid-nineteenth century. Bogle worked as such a butler and also as an undertaker. On occasion, he could be found presiding over a funeral during the day and a party later that evening with equal aplomb. Bogle also functioned as a waiter, and possibly purveyed meals, and provided staff as required for household events. From these multiple occupations and with his diverse talents, Bogle became the first of Philadelphia's major black caterers. Soon black caterers became the norm in the city. They formed a union that was, in the words of sociologist W. E. B. Du Bois, "as remarkable a trade guild as ever ruled a medieval city. [The caterers] took complete leadership of a bewildered group of Negroes, and led them steadily to a degree of affluence, culture, and respect such as has probably never been surpassed in the history of the Negro in America." Bogle opened a catering establishment on Eighth Street in Philadelphia. According to Du Bois, he was "the butler of the smart set, and his taste and eye and palate set the fashion for the day."

Bogle became so famous that, in 1829, Nicholas Biddle, a prominent white Philadelphian, penned a multi-stanza ode titled "Biddle's Ode to Bogle." It began:

> Hail may'st thou, Bogle, for thy reign
> Extends o'er Nature's wide domain,
> Begins before our earliest breath,
> Nor ceases with the hour of death;

> *Scarce seems the blushing maiden wed,*
> *Unless thy care the supper spread;*
> *Half christened only were that boy*
> *Whose heathen squalls our ears annoy.*
> *If, service finished, cakes and wine*
> *Were given by any hand but thine,*
> *And Christian burial e'en were scant*
> *Unless his aid the Bogle grant.*

Bogle's origins are unclear, but he is listed in the 1810 census as living in Philadelphia's South Ward, where most of the city's African Americans then resided. When he died, in 1848, he was a beloved figure among Philadelphia's elite, known for his able handling of all social situations—from weddings, christenings, and banquets to funerals—as well as for the meat pies that he sold at his restaurant.

Bogle set the groundwork, but the catering fame of Philadelphia also resulted from the expertise of the French West Indian immigrants who arrived in the City of Brotherly Love following the Haitian Revolution and were trained in the French culinary arts and service. One of them was Peter Augustin (sometimes given as Peter Augustine). His additions to Bogle's basics put Philadelphia caterers on the map of high-society families throughout the country. Augustin established a restaurant on Walnut Street after he arrived in the city from Haiti. He and his family not only provided dining facilities but also warehoused materials—chairs, linens, and other service items—that could be used for various catering events. They also trained waiters, as had Bogle, to work at various venues. The Augustins were joined by the Baptistes, another Haitian family with catering and restaurant businesses. The families intermarried and soon established an enterprise of such renown that they purchased a railroad car with a kitchen that dispatched waiters and goods up and down the East Coast. Tastemakers for the upper classes, the Augustin family and its staff were noted for their sophisticated cuisine and served dishes like creamed terrapin and oyster fritters to prominent families as far away as New York and Boston. The Augustin family enterprises continued to grow throughout the nineteenth century; by the late 1870s one of the restaurants was reputed to be the "Delmonico's of Philadelphia." The Augustins continued to intermarry with others from Haitian catering families, like the Dutrieuilles, and their catering business continued until 1967 as the oldest continuously managed black family business in that city.

Bogle and the Augustin family were the first generation of what would become a tidal wave of African American caterers, who had a lock on Philadelphia's entertaining in the second half of the nineteenth century. Their inheritors banded together in enterprise to share resources and facilities and to consolidate their buying power, purchasing ingredients in bulk and sharing the cost of equipment. They not only catered private affairs in the homes of wealthy clients, providing food, waiters, crystal, silver, napery, and more; they also opened dining rooms that functioned as restaurants and catering halls. The caterers, adept at business and with finely honed social skills, became the black elite of the city. While many of the catering families were of Haitian origin, the most renowned Philadelphia caterer of the nineteenth century was undoubtedly Thomas Dorsey, a former slave.

Dorsey was born on a plantation in Maryland in the early decades of the nineteenth century and escaped to Philadelphia in adulthood. He was captured and returned to his owner, but during his brief sojourn in Philadelphia he had made friends among the free blacks and abolitionists who were able to raise the sum necessary to purchase his freedom, and he was able to return to the city a free man in the late 1830s. Like many of the newly arrived blacks from the South, he apprenticed at a trade and is listed as a shoemaker in the *Register of Trades of the Colored People in the City of Philadelphia and Districts,* a pamphlet published by the Philadelphia Abolition Society in 1838. The privately published *Philadelphia City Directory,* which appeared annually between 1793 and 1940, lists him for the first time as a waiter in 1844 and it seems that he rotated among several different eating establishments in the city until 1860. He made his first appearance in the listing as a caterer in 1862. And by the middle half of the nineteenth century, Dorsey was well established as one of the pillars of the catering network that provided the food, servants, and accoutrements for the upper-class soirees and dinner parties in Philadelphia. Dorsey served only the upper crust and had a reputation for excellent fare. At one meal, served on December 27, 1860, the menu included such delicacies as oysters on the half shell, *filet de boeuf piqué*, canvasback duck, charlotte russe, ladyfingers, and champagne jelly! Other dishes that formed the edible display at prominent Philadelphia banquets included lobster salad, deviled crabs, terrapin, and chicken croquettes. Dorsey and his fellow caterers, like those who followed them in later decades, based their reputation on serving excellent European-style food. They set culinary standards and were powerful arbiters of style, with enough clout to launch modes and fads.

Although born enslaved, Dorsey was revered. Twenty-one years after his death, a commentator who went under the sobriquet "Megargee" wrote in the Philadelphia *Times* that he "possessed a naturally refined instinct that led him to surround himself with both men and things of an elevating character." He prided himself on having hosted such notables of the period as abolitionist William Lloyd Garrison and prominent blacks like Frederick Douglass. When Dorsey died in 1875, the *Philadelphia Press* referred to him as "the negro feast furnisher . . . who spread the tables for the marriage supper, or the ball, or the reception; he . . . gave character to any entertainment, and [his] presence was more essential than the honored guests."

The caterers of Philadelphia had such societal preeminence that they became leaders of the city's African American community, creating jobs for black waiters, cooks, and others within their enterprises and generally working to raise the standard of living among the newly freed who arrived in the city following the Civil War. At a time when the entrepreneurial advances of African Americans were being threatened and more often than not thwarted by increasing numbers of immigrants from Europe, the catering business arose from what Du Bois termed "an evolution shrewdly, persistently and tastefully directed, [which] transformed the Negro cook and waiter into the public caterer and restaurateur, and raised a crowd of underpaid menials to become a set of self-reliant, original business men, who amassed fortunes for themselves and won general respect for their people." The caterers proved that blacks had not only the culinary talents but also the business acumen to produce wealth. It was a lesson that would be proven over and over again in the North.

While Philadelphia was the nexus of the phenomenon, other

northern cities also had their black culinary entrepreneurs. Joshua Bowen Smith was a Boston-based caterer who served meals at Harvard and catered for the state of Massachusetts; James Wormley was a caterer, restaurateur, and hotel owner in Washington, D.C. New York, too, had its black culinary elite. The city, after all, was for decades home to the second-largest black population in the country (after Charleston, South Carolina) and had received a number of Haitian immigrants. Culinary business leaders there included Henry Scott, whose pickle establishment did business with many of the vessels sailing out of the port of New York, and restaurateurs like the Van Rensselaers, George Bell, and George Alexander, whose eating establishments served all rungs of the social spectrum. In the early part of the nineteenth century, the African American culinary entrepreneur who was as renowned as Philadelphia's caterers was Thomas Downing, one of New York's black leading citizens.

Downing was the son of free people of color, born in the last decade of the eighteenth century in Chincoteaque, Virginia. He, like many African Americans from the Virginia and Maryland shore, grew up with an intimate knowledge of the region's fauna and flora. Terrapin, clams, crabs, and oysters held no mystery for the young Downing, and when he arrived in New York City in 1819, he discovered that this knowledge was his most marketable skill. At the time, New York was indulging in a citywide oyster obsession—the consumption of oysters was a virtual pastime. In 1810, the city directory listed twenty-seven oystermen, of whom, notably, sixteen were people of color. The oyster trade offered a range of job possibilities. At the lower end of the spectrum, oyster luggers offered their wares at watering holes that served free people of color and to the roustabouts who lived in the notorious Five Points area of the city. Others sold the mollusks on the streets to those who gulped them down on the run.

Although not an oysterman, Downing aimed even higher. He began by renting space on Pell Street in downtown Manhattan and searched for his own oyster beds. According to a biographical sketch written about him by his son, he would get up at two A.M. and, by the light of a lantern, make his way by boat to the New Jersey oyster fields to harvest fresh oysters daily to offer to his customers. His hard work paid off, and by the time the 1823 city directory was published, he was able to number himself among the city's oystermen. His establishment continued to grow and prosper. By 1825, he opened an oyster "refectory" at 5 Broad Street, at the corner of Wall Street, where he offered raw oysters on the half shell as well as roasted oysters that were cooked over a fire of oak shavings. His eatery grew in popularity and began to lure the elite with its fare. Downing's was one of the few places considered acceptable for women who arrived with their husbands or with their chaperones. Soon, as described by his son

> it was fashionable for ladies and gentlemen, whole families—the most respected of the city—to . . . enjoy a repast which would cause their sons and daughters . . . to long for frequent repetitions. Ladies and gentlemen with towel in hand, and an English oyster knife made for the purpose, would open their own oysters, drop into the burning hot concaved shell a lump of sweet butter and other seasonings, and partake of a treat. Yes, there was a taste imparted by the saline and lime substances in which the juice of the oyster reached boiling heat that made it a delicate morsel. Truly, one worthy to be borne to the lips that sipped from the shell the nectareous mite.

By 1827, Downing constructed an oyster vault: a holding space in which the bivalves could be stored in saltwater. His business had grown so large that he could no longer supply his own oyster needs, and so he became a major client of the city's other oystermen, earning their respect for his fairness in dealing and his knowledge of the product. Unlike many other oyster refectories, Downing's was upscale and considered "the model of comfort and prosperity, with its mirrored arcades, damask curtains, dine carpet and chandelier," according to a review. Downing catered to the elite, and the crème de la crème came. Newspapermen and financiers were regulars. Charles Dickens dined at Downing's, as did the earl of Carlisle and Philip Hone, who was New York City's mayor from 1825 to 1826. Downing's refectory offered more than just raw oysters; it served the mollusks in many forms: scalloped oysters, poached turkey stuffed with oysters, fish in oyster sauce, and oyster pie, among other delicacies.

In 1842, New Yorkers were oyster mad and consumed about six million dollars' worth of them. Downing grew richer. Along with owning the restaurant, he became a prosperous caterer and was the man to call for government and society events. He was so well thought of that he was asked to cater the Boz Ball, at which Dickens and his wife were presented to New York's aristocracy. For this event alone he was paid the royal sum of $2,200. Downing shipped oysters to Paris, shipped pickled oysters to the West Indies, and even shipped some of his finest to Queen Victoria.

Even though he had been born free in Virginia and was a prosperous businessman, Downing was what would later be called a "race man." Mindful of the fate of his enslaved brethren, he was an ardent abolitionist. In 1836 he helped found the all-black United Anti-Slavery Society of the City of New York and served on its executive committee for three years. He was also a trustee for the New York Society for the Promotion of Education Among Colored Children, which started two elementary schools for black children. He worked on voting rights campaigns in an effort to guarantee equal suffrage for African Americans.

Downing was succeeded by his son, George Thomas Downing, who continued the culinary legacy and opened his own restaurant in New York in 1842. In 1846 he established a branch of the family business in Newport, Rhode Island, where in 1854 he opened the crowning glory of his culinary empire, the Sea Girt Hotel. Ironically, but representative of the times, the five-story building was restricted to a white clientele. The hotel also included Downing's residence, a restaurant, a confectionery, and a branch of his catering business. A fire on December 15, 1860, destroyed the building, causing him to suffer an estimated loss of forty thousand dollars. The son's career did not end there. A "race man" like his father, he was keenly interested in the treatment of African Americans, especially Civil War soldiers. This concern led him to Washington, where he became the manager of the dining room of the House of Representatives, a position that he held for twelve years, during which time he worked for the passage of public accommodations laws in the capital city.

When Thomas Downing, the father, died in 1866, the oyster craze was still going strong. New Yorkers consumed fifteen thousand dollars' worth of them daily, and more than one thousand boats plied the waterways in search of the bivalves. In 1855, the *New York Evening Post* wrote of Downing, "His private character is above reproach; he has made a large fortune as the keeper of a refectory, which is frequented daily by throngs of the principal bankers and merchants of Wall and Broad streets and their vicinity." Through his skill as an oysterman and his acumen as a businessman, Downing became the elder statesman of black New York in the first half of the nineteenth century. Like the Philadelphia caterers, he understood the value of catering to the white elite in his career and used his position to create his personal fortune as well as to provide jobs for other blacks.

With their understanding of the formality of service and their mastery of the manners of others, the caterers—whether in Philadelphia, New York, or elsewhere—in serving a white upper class, demonstrated the same cultural fluidity that had been evidenced by African Americans since their entry into the country. Their ability to seamlessly flow between several class and cultural levels was a testimonial not only to their culinary abilities and their good taste but also to their finely honed social instincts and their well-developed survival skills. That they used these talents to contribute to the growth and uplifting of the entire African American community of their period is testimony to their humanity.

Most African Americans in the North were free by the time that Bogle, the Augustins, Dorsey, and the Downings were operating in Philadelphia and New York. Their enslaved urban brethren in the South may have demonstrated the same culinary skills, but they garnered little or no pay for their labors. While caterers in cities in the Northeast oversaw lavish entertainments and created personal wealth, in cities in the South gala events were directed by house slaves who were unacknowledged and unpaid. Free blacks did occasionally work in catering, but with houses staffed by unpaid slaves, there was scant money to be made in the field. Money could be earned by blacks vending fresh produce and prepared goods in the street. It was a track that blacks had used for decades in the North.

As early on as the colonial period, women of African descent had cornered the street-food market, selling goods that they'd created from homegrown ingredients; a black woman sitting on a small stool selling sweetmeats or savories was a ubiquitous sight. Free, they worked for themselves; enslaved, they worked for their masters and mistresses and were occasionally allowed to keep a small portion of their earnings. More often than not, slaves were hired out by their masters, who were paid for their services; they received little or no remuneration, hence the term "slave wages." Blacks, both free and enslaved, dominated street vending until newly arriving European immigrants made inroads in the mid-nineteenth century. African Americans street vending in both the North and South gave the fledgling city streets an African air, as vendors hawked their wares with loud cries designed to lure customers.

As early as the late eighteenth century, "Humanitas," a social commentator in the New York press, complained of the nuisance created by noisy street vendors, or hucksterers. He grumbled that the oyster stands and numerous tables of eatables made walking down the streets all but impossible. Indeed, in certain areas of the city, from early morning until late at night, cries such as "He-e-e-e-e-e-ere's your fine Rocka-a-way clams" and "H-a-u-r-t Ca-irrne" [hot corn] were common and created a distinctively African American soundscape.

Throughout the country, newspaper articles criticized the auditory nuisance of the black vendors. Nowhere was this criticism livelier than in Charleston, South Carolina, where street vendors had been a fixture in neighborhoods since the city's inception. African American vendors approached their task with a cacophonous zeal and were often argumentative, insubordinate, and rude. On March 26, 1823, a letter to the editors of Charleston's *Post and Courier*, signed by "A Warning Voice," noted:

> The public cries should be regulated. The negro should be taught to announce what he has to sell and to suppress his wit. A decency and humility of conduct should pervade all ranks of our colored population.

For centuries, Charlestonians' victuals came to them from street vendors, who brought their wares in baskets that they carried on their heads or over their arms. Indeed, each vendor had a specific cry that extolled his or her wares, like the cries so evocatively captured in the twentieth century by George and Ira Gershwin in their folk opera *Porgy and Bess* at the beginning of act 3:

> Oh dey's so fresh an' fine
> An dey's just off the vine
> Strawberry, strawberry, strawberry.

Street cries were typical in most major cities in the eighteenth and nineteenth centuries. Old etchings show various Parisian street vendors like the chocolate seller, the chestnut vendor, and the notions peddler, who had their distinct cries—as did Ireland's Molly Malone, who sold her "cockles and mussels, alive, alive, oh!" Charleston's street cries, like those in New York, offered an African twist on an Old World theme. In regions of the continent's West Coast, market women have long had not only the power of the purse but have wielded considerable political power as well. In earlier times, they were the region's economic foundation. It is certain that their verbally challenging manner of vending arrived in Charleston, where the majority of street vendors were of African descent. Freedmen, the newly emancipated, and the enslaved all brought with them a wit, a verve, and an aggression to marketing their wares that was all their own. By the end of the seventeenth century, a visitor commented on the city's African appearance and the fact that blacks outnumbered whites:

> How strange the aspect of this city! Every Street corner and door sill filled with blacks; blacks driving t[he] drays & carriages, blacks carrying burdens, blacks tending children & vending articles on t[he] sidewalks, blacks doing all.

The cultivation of the Lowcountry's major agricultural products—rice, indigo, and cotton—was based on a task system, allowing the enslaved to use the time after their tasks were accomplished as they wished. Many of the enslaved raised vegetables on small plots of land to supplement their rations and to trade with their masters for privileges and even cash. By 1800, the Charleston city council had ordinances on the books regulating the age of slave vendors (they couldn't be under thirty years of age) and the goods sold ("milk, grain, fruit, victuals, or provision of any kind"). Although slaves worked out of their master's home in urban areas throughout the South, in Charleston, slaves who were hired out wore a metal badge at all times. The square piece of copper, brass, zinc, or tin was inscribed with a number and the slave's profession and signaled the legality of his or her presence and served as a license to sell goods and services. By 1806, the annual badge fee for sellers of fruits, cakes, and other items was a whopping fifteen dollars, higher than the cost of a badge for fishermen, washerwomen, and even porters. The higher fee was designed to strictly regulate fruit vendors, as they had more freedom of movement and could carry money. (The fee was reduced to five dollars in 1813.) Owners had to register their slaves, and the city kept track of the master's name, address, and the number of slaves hired out, as well as each slave's age and job.

Charleston's vending system was not unique. In New Orleans and other port cities, slaves were hired out by their masters to work in building trades, as cooks and seamstresses, and as vegetable sellers. In July 1846, the New Orleans *Daily Picayune* mentioned "Green Sass Men" who traveled through the neighborhoods selling small quantities of figs, melons, and other produce from used champagne baskets balanced on top of their heads. They were older slaves who had been sent into the city by their masters to sell surplus produce from outlying farms. This peddling was strictly regulated. In an 1822 ruling, the Conseil de Ville (Town Council) required that peddlers have licenses from the mayor in order to sell merchandise on public squares or streets. Slaves could not be given licenses, but free people of color could purchase them and specify a slave to do the actual selling. The record books are filled with licenses for vendors and journeymen butchers, including the name of the license holder and that of the slave who actually did the work, as well as the street for which the license was granted. Peddlers of bread, vegetables, milk products, and fodder were, however, exempted from the provisions of the law.

Further regulations in 1831 continued the ban on slaves' selling items without the written permission of their owners specifying the articles to be sold. Anyone caught disobeying the law was subject to "twenty stripes for the first offense and forty stripes for the second, or any subsequent offence." Etienne de Boré, a large sugar planter whose plantation was in the area that's now Audubon Park, purchased licenses for his slaves, and in return made thousands of extra dollars. (One year, de Boré made more than six thousand dollars from his vendors.) It is not recorded if the slaves received any part of this money for their work.

In New Orleans, street vendors became so typical of the city that they became archetypes: the praline seller, the *cala* vendor, and others. They were drawn by visiting artists and featured in newspaper articles of the day. Artist Léon Frémaux was one of the first to capture the images of the peddlers. His drawings and watercolors, made as early as the mid-1850s, depict those who would become representatives of the city. In one, a vendor sells vanilla ice cream from a freezer balanced on his head. Another depicts a *cala* (rice fritter) seller with her fritter batter and her bowl precariously perched atop her *tignon* (head tie). She carries a small brazier and a cloth-covered basket of the final product, which Frémaux opines are "coarse and greasy."

The *cala* is a classic New Orleans dish. It was sold on the streets, but especially in front of St. Louis Cathedral, where those leaving Mass, in the days when Communion was only taken after fasting, could purchase a nibble to tide them over until they could have a more substantial meal. The cries of the *cala* vendors are recorded in the classic collection of Louisiana folk tales *Gumbo Ya-Ya*, by Lyle Saxon, Robert Tallant, and Edward Dryer, who also state that *cala* could be found in two versions: a rice version and a cowpea version. Both have their origins in Western Africa: the rice version in Liberia and the black-eyed pea version among the Yoruba people of southwestern Nigeria. Both versions point to the intriguing fact that the street foods sold by African American vendors often had culinary connections harking back to a continent long forgotten by those who sold them.

While the enslaved black hands in the Big House kitchens of the rural antebellum South helped to Africanize the palates of whites, the street vendors in the country's Northern and Southern urban areas kept some of the cultural and culinary connections alive as well, by purveying snack foods and fried tidbits that were New World variants on classic African culinary atavisms.

Whether at the upper end of the social scale, like the caterers of the North, or more humble, like the *cala* sellers and street hawkers of the South, blacks in urban areas, North and South, both free and enslaved, kept alive traditions of manners and of vending that originated on a continent that they neither knew or claimed. Increasingly, whether free people or those with a view toward freedom, they were Americans moving toward dreams of full citizenship who had become a major force in the urban food-disbursement chain.

❖❖❖❖❖❖❖

A GENTLEMAN'S GENTLEMAN

Now my young friends, you must consider that to live in a gentleman's family as a house servant is a station that will seem wholly different from anything, I presume, that ever you have been acquainted with; this station of life comprises comforts, privileges, and pleasures which are to be found in but few other stations in which you may enter; and on the other hand many difficulties, trials of temper &c, more perhaps than any other station in which you might enter in a different state of life.

So writes Robert Roberts in the introduction to his book, *The House Servant's Directory; or, A Monitor for Private Families: Comprising Hints on the Arrangement and Performance of Servants' Work.*

Published in 1827, it is one of the first books by an African American to be issued by a commercial press. Today, Roberts may seem to be a conundrum: a free man in the early part of the nineteenth century extolling the virtues of a life in domestic servitude. However, he was a man of his time. His pioneering book and the world that it reveals document the lifestyle and traditions of African Americans in domestic service in both the North and the South.

It is not known whether Roberts was born slave or free, but it seems that he was born in Charleston in the late 1700s. He arrived in New England in 1812 as a free man with the ability to read and write and with the skills at keeping house that would bring him great wealth and renown. It is thought that he arrived in Boston in the employ of Nathan Appleton, a Boston merchant and politician who'd visited Charleston from 1802 to 1804. Shortly after Roberts's arrival in Boston, he met and married Dorothy Hall, the daughter of a black Revolutionary War hero from Exeter. Although Roberts was listed in 1820s Boston city directories as a stevedore, that may be an error, for during that decade and earlier, he had worked as a butler for Appleton and for Kirk Boott, a Massachusetts industrialist. Some scholars believe that Roberts may have gone abroad with Appleton between 1810 and 1812 and met Boott in England; in his book, Roberts states that he had served some of the finest families of France, England, and the United States.

Roberts's fame as a butler came between 1825 and 1827, when he worked for Christopher Gore, a former Massachusetts governor. Roberts worked in the British tradition of the trusted majordomo and ran the well-to-do household with Gore's supervision. The first edition of *The House Servant's Directory*, published shortly after Gore's death, includes a posthumous note from the ex-governor: "I have read the work attentively, and think it may be of much use."

Roberts's directory is written in the style of English household manuals of the time but distinguished itself by being written to two hypothetical butlers in training, Joseph and David. Roberts is candid in his discussion about the travails of being in service and advises his imaginary disciples to be accommodating at all times and to observe and understand the temperament of their employers. He also admonishes the young men to "be very cautious of what company you keep." *The House Servant's Directory* instructions for carving roasts, placing dishes on the table, and setting out the sideboard may seem dated today. However, one piece of advice Roberts gives to Joseph and David rings as true almost two hundred years later as it must have in 1827: "Remember my young friends, that your character is your whole fortune through life; therefore you must watch over it incessantly, to keep it from blemish or stain."

O FREEDOM!

Jubilee Jubilations

On Friday, April 12, 1861, the world changed for all residents of the United States, enslaved and free. Before sunrise, shots were fired on Fort Sumter in the harbor of Charleston, South Carolina, from the Secessionist batteries. The Civil War had begun. During the four years of battle, brother fought brother, families were disrupted, and more Americans died than in any war before or since. The War freed the enslaved, but it also rent the country asunder and divided North and South in ways still felt more than a century later. It was a time of trial on all fronts. Despite the fact that many of the country's aristocrats and most influential men were Southerners, the agricultural South was ill-prepared for the War. As it dragged on for years, they felt the privations more acutely than did those in the more industrialized North. The War Between the States, as the conflict is still known in the South, was the United States' coming of age, and it was a bloody brutal transition.

Initially the enslaved were kept in ignorance of the politics of their day and duped by masters into believing that the Yankees were demons who would maim or otherwise harm them. However, as the war progressed, the truth of the situation was gradually accepted. It was a complex time of confusion, during which the enslaved in the South suffered along with their masters. Fear and uncertainty were daily fare, along with reduced rations. Indeed, most of the enslaved were unclear what the War was and how it would directly change their lives. Only as it progressed did the flickering hope dawn that the War might end their enslavement. Testimonies of the time from the former enslaved were rife with memories of the first glimpse of Yankee soldiers. Those who had been children remembered receiving candy or kind treatment from blue-coated soldiers marching through the South. The Union soldiers eventually arrived in Southern towns and hamlets, where the enslaved still went about their daily tasks. There were crops to plant and maintain and harvest, and as the fighting dragged on, the annual drudgery of the seasons repeated itself relentlessly, with mistresses taking over for the menfolk away at battle. The slave communication network that had so baffled and terrified owners throughout the period of enslavement, though, was at work. And then one day it came.

It began as a whisper that old Abe Lincoln, up in that place in the North known as Washington, where the white men sat in government, had made the decision to free the slaves. At first it seemed like just another of the rumors that made their way across the Southern states, giving hope to the overburdened and bringing the glimmer of possibility to those for whom each day was a fight against what others had imposed on them and called their destinies. It started on September 22, 1862, as a trickle, a corner of hope. Word slowly spread. Discussions were overheard by house servants in Virginia plying heavy silver ladles and proffering elegant fare on bone china platters, and this was passed along to unheated cabins where moss and rags plugged up the holes to keep out the winds of the upcoming winter. In North Carolina, it was silently signaled as folks picked bugs off tobacco leaves. In Georgia, it was whispered over bowed backs in cotton fields. In Louisiana, it was shared in the steaming heat of the boiling houses over vats of bubbling cane juice. President Lincoln had issued a proclamation that gave the seceding states one hundred days to abandon their pro-slavery positions. Could it be?

Then, on January 1, 1863, the day of the Jubilee finally arrived. President Lincoln signed the Emancipation Proclamation. As magnificent as the tidings were, news of the Proclamation didn't travel with the speed of today's modern information. Instead it made its way slowly across the American South. Many plantation owners felt it best to withhold the information until the crops had been gath-

ered. Some of the former enslaved, however, took it upon themselves to hasten the spread of the news and formed what was called
Lincoln's Legal Loyal League, or the 4-Ls; their mission was to bring
the news of Freedom. And, like a rising tide that enveloped the land
with the sureness of inevitability, the word passed through the tobacco fields of Virginia, through the rice-growing marshlands of the
Carolina and Georgia Lowcountry, through the cotton fields of Mississippi and Georgia, and out to the indigo plantations of the Sea
Islands. It sped along the cane breaks on Louisiana's sugar plantations, where some of the slave owners were black themselves, and
eventually arrived in the Texas outlands. Finally, all those who had
worked in slavery's fields could lay their burdens down.

Jubilee brought freedom and momentary rejoicing to the for-
merly enslaved, but while the War raged on, it offered little plan or
solution for the newly freed. Illiterate for the most part and raised
in a culture of dependency, they had no resources on which to de-
pend. Many, known as contrabands, sought out the Yankee army
and followed the soldiers, relying on them for food, clothing, and
shelter. Others set out on their own, looking for a new way of life.
Still others elected to remain with their masters and the security of
the only world that they'd ever known.

Confederate General Robert E. Lee's enslaved cook, William Mack
Lee, followed him for the entire four years of the War, cooking and
working as his butler. William Mack Lee recalled that the only time
he'd been chastised by his master during the entire course of the war
was when he'd killed a laying hen to provide a meal for a "crowd of
generals" that his master had invited to dine before the Battle of the
Wilderness. He dispatched General Lee's black hen, "picked her
good, and stuffed her with bread stuffing, mixed with butter"—
feeding the generals what he deemed an appropriate meal for men
of their rank. Like William Mack Lee, those who remained used the
resourcefulness acquired during enslavement to help their former
masters and mistresses survive the War and its aftermath.

In this manner, the Southern culinary symbiosis between black
and white continued throughout the War until its end. Then, in an
ironic coda, there was one final act of generosity. After Appomattox, the last rations distributed to the Louisiana regiment as they
marched in defeat to Burkeville Station to take the train for the last

journey home were several hundred ears of corn that they received from a freed black, who offered it saying, "They's the last I'll ever see." Each man was given two ears and a cup of sorghum: a grace note to the interwoven reliance of whites and blacks for sustenance during the entire period of enslavement.

General Lee's signing of the surrender at Appomattox did not signal the end of privations for the South's former enslaved. Rather, it heralded the beginning of new difficulties and challenges. With no master responsible for their care, the newly freed, who had deliberately been kept ignorant and illiterate, now found themselves without jobs, housing, and food. The shock of liberation combined with the lack of preparation for the momentous event killed many of the former enslaved. Others starved, and still others persevered, using the ingenuity and survival skills that they had learned in their long years of enslavement. Thomas Ruffin, a former North Carolina slave who was interviewed by the Works Progress Administration, remembered "We used to dig up dirt in the smokehouse and boil it dry and sift it to get the salt to season our food with. We used to go out and get old bones that had been throwed away and crack them open and get the marrow and use them to season the greens with." Ingenuity prevailed.

Following Emancipation and the War's end, separated and disconnected families attempted to find each other, and the black newspapers of the time were filled with advertisements looking for long-lost kin. Mothers and fathers were united with sons and daughters; husbands located wives; sisters discovered brothers who had been sold away. Others found no one. All went on facing the new dawn, working their way to a new future in freedom. They all relied on the skills that they had demonstrated so creatively during the period of enslavement: dressmaking, barbering, agricultural pursuits, metalwork, carpentry, and more. Large numbers of them would create new lives out of their knowledge of and abilities in the world of food.

CHAPTER 7

WESTWARD HO!

Migrations, Innovations, and a
Growing Culinary Divide

Dallas, Texas—

Everything seems bigger in Texas. Just driving along in a taxi on the road from the airport into town, I noticed the flags decorating the used-car dealerships appeared to be four times the size that they are elsewhere in the country. The weather is definitely twice as hot in June. Driving around the city with my new friend, a whippet-thin seventh-generation Texan, I was surprised at how Dallas seemed familiar. It fit into the pattern of many Southern cities that I knew. Shotgun houses huddled together, claiming their territory as if defying the troubled history of urban renewal that had also destroyed black neighborhoods, North and South. I could guess which of the old theaters had once housed thriving blues clubs.

I understood the class stratifications that were still evident in the proudly well-kept homes, differentiating between the substantial brick homes of the elite and the rickety clapboard ones of the less financially able. I could see the pentimento of a class divide that had always existed in the African American world but that became more firmly entrenched following Emancipation. There was a familiarity that came from living in a black neighborhood, albeit in the North, and from understanding that the migrations had transported blacks out of the South. We continued to drive, skirting the interstate that bisected the old 'hood like a snake eating away at its vitals. There was a stop at a barbecue place that, Texas style, included beef in its offerings and a trip to the black bookstore for black-related local books, and then it was time to move on. For I was in Dallas with a purpose: I'd been invited to speak at the African American Museum's Juneteenth celebrations.

Juneteenth is a Texas state holiday that celebrates the state's late acceptance of the Emancipation Proclamation. Black Texans observe their red-letter day with special fervor. At their inception, the Emancipation celebrations were times of reflection and featured prayer meetings and religious services giving thanks for deliverance from bondage. Gradually the heartfelt prayers of thanksgiving offered up by preachers in sonorous tones became secularized, and by the early twentieth century, Juneteenth was a time of cake-walks and parades with lots of high-stepping horses. Now celebrations are more likely to include beauty competitions and baseball games than the sermonizing of the past.

Throughout it all, though, the backbone of Juneteenth festivities has always been the table. In the early years, those who had toiled in sorrow's kitchen commemorated their liberty with some serious eating. Picnics and barbecues were the hallmarks of the early celebrations, and groaning boards covered with bright cloths offered specialties like barbecued ribs and fried chicken and myriad variations on summer produce like black-eyed peas, peaches, and watermelon.

Dallas's African American Museum is located on the state fairgrounds. There, despite a hazardous-air alert and temperatures of over ninety degrees, folks had come out to spend the day. Coolers were unpacked, lawn chairs pulled into convivial circles, and portable grills fired up. People gathered to listen to blues music, sample several types of homemade barbecue, slurp down gallons of super-sweet red soda, and enjoy a celebration of their freedom. Walking through the booths with the museum's director of education, I was struck by the longevity of African Americans in Texas. Later, as I ducked the torpid temperatures with periodic walks through the museum, I began to have a hint of our importance in Texas history. There were rooms devoted to the African antecedents of the cowboy culture and to those who had been enslaved in the northeastern part of the state. There was even a section devoted to Dallas's lost black neighborhoods, with cases filled with memorabilia from demolished homes and long-forgotten clubs: faded photographs in tarnished frames, cups and saucers from long-dismantled sets, fragments of programs from shuttered theaters.

As I strolled through the galleries, I realized that the vast open lands of the West seemed to naturally appeal to those who had lived in bondage in the Southeast. Although the first Africans arrived in the area that would become the American West in the sixteenth century as slaves of the Spanish, with the Emancipation and Jubilee that Juneteenth celebrated, African Americans' westward migrations began in earnest. The West offered space for adventurers and settlers, entrepreneurs and laborers—room so that the African American experience could expand in all its diversity.

◆ ◆ ◆ ◆ ◆

Pre-and post-Emancipation African Americans longed for a place where the past didn't hang over their heads like live oaks dripping Spanish moss. They wanted out of the South, and the new lands of the West beckoned. The country was moving westward and the region loomed large in the national consciousness as a place where adventurers of all races could find a stake and be evaluated on their merit and their hard work, not on their family lineage or the color of their skin. This look westward occurred at a time of increasing racism. The early decades of the nineteenth century were marked by the removal of Native peoples from the Southeast into the area of the country that would become known as "Indian Territory." They were an era of anti-black violence that lasted up until the Civil War and was characterized by race riots and repression. The West was a place where the past was eradicated and new beginnings could be made. Texas would become the gateway to the West in the final decades of the nineteenth century, but in fact, the migration from East and Southeast to West started earlier.

One unlikely starting point was the city of Philadelphia. In 1800, the City of Brotherly Love had the largest free black population in the country and was home to more than four thousand free blacks. In 1833, while Robert Bogle was catering to Philadelphia's upper crust, he and his fellow free African Americans in the city were searching for a way out of the problems of continuing racism in the United States. The third annual Convention for the Improvement of the Free People of Color proposed moving to western Africa, but after lengthy debate, it settled on immigration to Texas as a solution. Texas in 1833 remained a part of Mexico, a country with its own long history of enslavement of Africans. (Between 1521 and 1824, the date of the abolition of the foreign slave trade in Mexico, approximately two hundred thousand Africans were transported there.) Emancipation, though, had come early to Mexico, decreed in 1829 by mixed-blood president Vicente Guerrero. For free blacks at the Philadelphia convention, the neighboring country's abolition of slavery must have seemed attractive indeed, and hundreds migrated to the northern area of what is now Texas. But their expectations and hopes were dashed in 1836, when Texas became an independent slaveholding republic, a profile it kept through 1845, when it became a pro-slavery part of the United States. It remained slaveholding right up until Emancipation and was one of the last states to formally announce the Emancipation Proclamation, in 1865.

Another group of African Americans also arrived in the West in the early 1830s. They, though, traveled with the Native Americans and were blacks who had melded with members of the Five Civilized Tribes (Cherokee, Muskogee-Creek, Chickasaw, Choctaw, and Seminole) either as family members or as their slaves. They were a part of the forced marches to Indian Territory on the harrowing series of journeys known as the Trail of Tears. For these blacks, it began in 1831 with the first phase: the voluntary removal of the Choctaw Nation. It continued until 1838, when sixteen thousand Cherokees were forcibly taken from Tennessee, Alabama, North Carolina, and Georgia and resettled in what is today's Oklahoma. In 1832, George W. Harkins, a Choctaw, wrote in *A Farewell Letter to the American People*, "We as Choctaws rather chose to suffer and be free, than live under the degrading influence of laws, which our voice could not be heard in their formation." Surely his words resonated with the African Americans who traveled westward with the Indians and with all those enslaved in the South.

Two years after the 1848 Gold Strike in California that began the Gold Rush, the West continued to look best for yet another group of African Americans. California was admitted to the Union in 1850 as a free state. That year only one thousand blacks lived in the state of California, but by 1860, three thousand more had joined them, settling in the San Francisco and Sacramento areas. However, the compromise that admitted California to the Union as a free state resulted in harsher fugitive slave laws that contributed to greater repression of blacks enslaved and free in the North and the South. In the decades leading up to the 1860 secession of the Southern states and the Civil War, the country was increasingly polarized over the question of slavery, and the division was being played out in the western territories that were open for settlement.

California was free, as were Oregon Territory and Washington Territory; the issue was unresolved in the territories of New Mexico and Utah, and the question of enslavement in the Kansas and Nebraska territories was to be determined by popular sovereignty. Freedom was not guaranteed, as laws changed and territories filled with white settlers of varying political views.

Yet, blacks continued to trickle westward; they headed for Oregon Territory and journeyed to Colorado for the Pike's Peak Gold Rush of 1859. Following Emancipation, the trickle became a steady flow, including the cowboys, those who worked on the railroads that connected the again-reunited country, the homesteaders, and the Buffalo Soldiers who protected them. By the last decades of the nineteenth century, the westward migration had swollen to a wave. Relocating blacks found jobs and created employment in the areas of service where once they had toiled in bondage. They worked in fields, where their ingenuity and cultural flexibility allowed them freedom. They worked on the nascent railroads and in hotels and in boardinghouses. They catered to miners and homesteaders, settlers and outlaws, and opened restaurants and saloons in the small towns and cities that were springing up along the routes west. Along with their omnipresent desire for equality, the African Americans brought with them in their heads, their hands, and their hearts the African-inspired and American-inflected tastes of their former Southern homes.

Among the first to arrive in the western territories were the black cowboys who had worked in Texas and the Indian Territories before the Civil War. They had come as slaves, brought by their Anglo masters after 1845, when the independent republic was folded into the United States. A second wave of ranch hands, single, able-bodied men, came post-Emancipation. Both groups found work moving cows down the cattle trails, which emerged at the end of the Civil War, as routes of commerce expanded and central slaughterhouses were developed at burgeoning rail hubs that would take the meat to the rest of the country.

Interestingly, an archetype as quintessentially American as the Western cowboy may owe more than a little debt to the African continent. One of the many skills that arrived in the fetid holds of the slave ships was the knowledge of working with cattle. Nomadic

Fulani herdsmen lived in Western Africa, in an area that went from Senegambia to Nigeria and from Mali and the Niger River regions to the Sudan. They were accustomed to cow herding and had an understanding of animal husbandry. After their arrival in Virginia in the early days of the colonies, they began transforming the way that cattle were kept in the United States. Descriptions of herding in the Fulani-occupied regions of Western Africa closely resembled later ones in the South Carolina hinterlands and included patterns of seasonal north-south migration that are still used in Texas.

At the end of the Civil War, following this African-inspired system, cowboys black and white herded cattle off southern Texas ranches to the markets that lay to the north along routes that had developed over time. The most popular of the trails led from the Rio Grande to Abilene, Kansas. There, an entrepreneur named Joseph G. McCoy had established a hub where cattle could be penned and shipped to eastern markets on the Union Pacific Railroad. By 1867, the thrum of hoof beats could be heard seasonally along the route. That year, thirty-five thousand cattle were herded along the trail. By 1871, the number had swollen to seven hundred thousand, but by then the area was well settled and grazing lands were becoming scarce, so the loading of cattle was moved farther west.

Whether on the Abilene Trail or on any of the other routes that developed later, herding cattle was a lengthy, dusty, and arduous undertaking. For the entire journey, the only individuals that a cowboy saw were the other members of the crew. The average crew was made up of no fewer than eleven men—usually consisting of a trail boss, eight cowboys, a wrangler, and a cook. The trail boss was often the owner of the herd and had complete authority; the cowboys were in charge of keeping the cattle in line. The wrangler was usually the youngest member of the crew and the lowest in the pecking order. He was responsible for the cowboys' horses and for aiding the cook by collecting wood for the fire, loading and unloading the chuck wagon, and washing the dishes. The most important member of the crew, however, was the cook, who often became confidant and mediator for the entire crew, who depended on him for nourishment. The creation of meals to suit the varied tastes of the crew from dried ingredients, fresh-killed meat, and foraged greens demanded a skilled hand, and the job was often a thankless one. Yet because of the relative freedom offered by the task, there were a sizable number of black cowboy cooks.

On the early cattle drives, a cowboy carried his own food and prepared his own meals. By the time the trails were in place and the drives had become larger, each crew had its own cook, who had many duties and was responsible for enforcing discipline in camp and having meals prepared on time. His mobile kitchen, known as the chuck wagon, developed over time to suit the needs of a traveling commissary. The chuck wagon was a sturdy vehicle designed to carry water for two days and food supplies for the journey, including such staples as flour, beans, sugar, bacon, salt pork, coffee, molasses, and the omnipresent canned tomatoes, which flavored many of the meals. It also held minimal medical supplies and cooking utensils, including the indispensable Dutch ovens used to create the meals that ranged from delights to disasters. In the morning, the chuck wagon pulled out ahead of the herd, carrying the provisions and the bedrolls and on occasion even the legal papers showing ownership of the herd. Up before the rest of the crew, the cook built the fire and prepared breakfast before heading out to the next campsite, followed by the procession of cattle. At the end of the day he met the cowboys with a hot meal, their bedrolls and a glowing campfire that he had to keep going, along with a pot of the ever-present coffee brewing for the cowboys.

The cook was usually one of the oldest people on the trail, often a superannuated cowboy who could no longer take the rigors of the saddle. He was a man of trust, because in addition to the food and water supplies and the medicine kit, the cowboys' personal possessions often rode in the wagon. The cook, whether white or black, was the complete ruler of his domain. Not surprisingly, black cowboy cooks had to tread lightly in the mid-nineteenth-century minefield of racial mores. Yet, even black cowboy cooks retained a degree of autonomy. For them, as for any trail cook, transgression of their authority was not tolerated, and retribution could be swift and was always unpleasant, whether the crew member was white or black. A disrespectful cowhand might find that the cook had taken revenge in any number of ways, from cold coffee to a lost bedroll to a gristle-laden meal.

Although often a trail-hardened type, the cook served as doctor and dentist, father confessor and surrogate mother to the crew. The cook had to know how to forage for wild greens along the trail and also how to dress and roast the small game that might be hunted along the way. He also had to understand how to build a fire just so, ensuring that it would cook his meals evenly and wouldn't blow sparks back onto the wagon and set it ablaze. The cook, sometimes called *cosi* (short for the Spanish *cocinera*, meaning cook), had to be a master of outdoor cooking and judge where to place the sharply pointed irons that held the spits over the flames as well as man the Dutch ovens, skillets, and griddles. The cook's job was to tend to the crew, and a happy crew made a cook a treasure. There were trail roundup cooks who manned chuck wagons on the roundups as well as ranch cooks who manned the skillets in a more stationary environment.

Many of the cowboy cooks were like Sam, who remained without a last name, as remembered by John D. Young in J. Frank Dobie's *A Vaquero of the Brush Country*. Weighing in at over 220 pounds and at age thirty-five, Sam was a bit too heavy and a tad too old for life in the saddle. But, according to Young,

> he always had a cheerful word or cheerful song and seemed to have an affection for every one of us. When we camped in the vicinity of brush every cowboy before coming in would rope a chunk of wood and snake it up to the chuck wagon. That wood always made Sam grinning happy whether he wanted it or not.

Sam worked wonders on the fires he made from the wood the cowboys brought. Whenever the camp lingered long enough in one spot for the cowboys to hunt, Sam provided some of the most "luscious eating" known on the plains. When he had time to barbecue antelope ribs or roast buffalo steaks or wild turkey, the men had what Sam called a "wedding feast"—because it wed dinner and supper. Then the cowboys waited eagerly for Sam to sing out for them to wash their faces, comb their hair, and come and get it "while she's hot and juicy."

All black cooks were not as amiable or as talented as Sam. Zeno, a "French Negro" who cooked on the trail in 1872, was noted for keeping his baking soda and his calomel—a white tasteless powder used as a purgative and fungicide—in similar jars, with predictable results. With remarkable understatement, one cowboy recalled, "We were sick a lot, for despite the more than peculiar taste we ate Zeno's bread." Ate they did, truly awful grub like Zeno's calomel-laden biscuits, but also the tasty vittles like Sam's.

George, at the RL ranch in Montana, was remembered for his delicious pies and biscuits and his kindly way with the cowhands. Gordon Davis, a cook for legendary trail boss Abe Blocker, prefigured a scene from *Blazing Saddles* when he rode into town on his left wheel ox playing "Buffalo gals, won't you come out tonight" on his fiddle! Jim Simpson, a roundup cook and ranch cook in Wyoming, "really knew how to wrestle Dutch ovens and pots and pans." Others remain nameless, but in their reminiscences the cowboys remembered the black cooks and their skills, and their meals. They recalled sourdough biscuits so light that they seemed to float, beefsteaks served in rich brown gravy, bread pudding sweetened with molasses and dotted with raisins. All memories, though, were not fond. There were also recollections of tough steaks, tooth-cracking biscuits, and coffee that tasted like muddy water.

One dish that most recalled with relish was Son of a Gun Stew, also known as Son of a Bitch Stew. It, like the apple pies made from dried apples and dough rolled out with a beer bottle, was a staple of the cowboy cooks. The stew was prepared when a nursing calf was slaughtered en route and cooked up from pieces of the tenderloin with the addition of the fresh heart, liver, tongue, and brains of the animal well seasoned in a rich broth. The essential item that gave Son of a Gun Stew its distinctive taste was the young calf's "marrow gut" (a tube connecting the two stomachs of a calf that is filled with a marrowlike substance when a calf is on a milk diet). It added a flavor of rennin-curdled milk to the stew. For some, the use of a "skunk egg" (as onions were designated) was essential; for others, anathema. Some think that the dish was learned from the Comanche, but its use of innards and the fact that a sizable number of African Americans were chuck wagon cooks may indicate an African hand in the pot. What is certain is that from the molasses that seasoned the bread puddings, to the barbecuing of antelope ribs, to the ineffable spicing of the dishes, black cowboy cooks brought an African culinary hand to the pots of the West. They also subtly brought African American foods into the diets of Texas cowboys. As one food historian says, "Put together meat off the hoof, Mexican and Upper South foodways, the cooking tradition of the blacks, and you have West Texas eats."

The freedom of the wide open range beckoned the men who became cowboy cooks. But while the job of cowboy cook guaranteed freedom, the job did not generate great fortunes. The West, though, did offer ample opportunity for those with initiative and creativity to create sizable wealth. Following the 1848 discovery of gold at Sutter's Mill, a few blacks headed to California hoping to strike it rich, but the forty-niners were almost exclusively white males. Most of the blacks who traveled there sought their fortune by providing services to the newly minted millionaires. Some of them were women hoping to take advantage of the male-to-female ratio in post-Gold-Rush San Francisco, which was 158 to 100. Domestic services were much needed by the developing elite, and the highest wages in the early years of the gold rush went to female domestics. Black, Asian, and white women ran laundries and boardinghouses and worked as domestic servants and seamstresses. In this world, one African American woman transformed her culinary skills and domestic acumen into great personal wealth; her name was Mary Ellen Pleasant.

Although Mary Ellen Pleasant is known to history as "Mammy" Pleasant, in her lifetime she was known to have refused the title, on more than one occasion saying, "DON'T call me Mammy." Pleasant led a life that is the stuff of an eighteenth-century picaresque novel, crisscrossing the country in a series of adventures. Enough rumor and innuendo surround the shade of Pleasant to fuel a multipart miniseries. It almost seems as though the only hard information we have about her life is that she lived in San Francisco and made her fortune there.

Pleasant was given to embroidering the facts of her birth. It is thought that she was born sometime between 1814 and 1817. She turns up in Nantucket around 1827 working as an indentured servant for a storekeeper named Hussey. After she served out the terms of her bond, she remained with Hussey and through him became active in abolitionist causes. She continued to work with the Underground Railroad and ultimately made her way to Gold Rush California, arriving by 1852.

Mary Ellen Pleasant passed for white in California and used her first husband's name, Smith, among the whites. She found a job working for Case and Heiser, a company of commission merchants—the all-important middlemen who bought and sold goods for others and functioned as brokers in the growing economy. She oversaw the running of the boardinghouse for the merchants' employees. In a place with few women, this establishment and others like it were where the men who ran the city met to take meals. By the late 1850s, Pleasant was cooking for some of the most elite families and prominent bachelors of San Francisco. She used her opportunities well, capitalized on the information that was unwittingly revealed around the table, and began to make money with the aid of a young clerk she hired as her own broker, Thomas Bell. (Bell, who was also rumored to be her lover, did so well that he went on to become vice president of the Bank of California.) By 1875, they had amassed a considerable fortune at a time when the gold from California and the silver from the Comstock Lode flooded the city and created new millionaires daily. Pleasant eventually opened her own boardinghouse and became an adept manipulator of real estate and mining stock.

Pleasant was a complex character, and attempting to unravel the threads of her life has defeated more than one biographer. Certainly she was by far the most successful of the many African American women who made their fortunes by opening boardinghouses and restaurants to cater to the needs of the single men who made their way west. Like her male East Coast counterparts, Dorsey and Downing, Pleasant was a staunch Civil Rights activist; she gave money to finance John Brown's raid on Harpers Ferry and fought for the desegregation of streetcars in San Francisco. However, like Dorsey's and Downing's establishments in New York and Philadelphia earlier in the century, Pleasant's boardinghouses served the fledgling city's white elite; she employed, but did not cater to, people of color.

Although she owned at least three boardinghouses at different periods, her most famous boardinghouse was located at 920 Washington Street and featured, along with the best wines and elegant food served in its dining room, "lavishly furnished upstairs rooms which were set up as combined private dining rooms and bedrooms." In this opulent establishment, Pleasant engaged a staff of black workers and busily continued to make her fortune serving particularly potent drinks and using the nuggets of information that her guests dropped at her tables as the basis for her growing portfolio of investments. Pleasant has been reviled as a conniver who kept her boarders enthralled with strong liquor and fast women; some have even called her a madam. But she operated her boardinghouses in a world and at a period when in many places a warm body to share the bed was considered to be included in the cost of a room. Despite allegations and innuendo, Pleasant remains important to the story of African American cooking in the Untied States, for she was the most successful female African American culinary entrepreneur in the West. Using her taste, her business acumen, and her culinary abilities, she amassed a sizable fortune, became a force for equality in the growing city of San Francisco, and earned the sobriquet "Mother of Civil Rights in California."

Pleasant's recipes seem to have vanished along with the accurate account of her life. *The Mammy Pleasant Cookbook*, published in the 1970s, was purported to contain some of her recipes, although modified by the author, Helen Holdredge. According to the publisher, the author "tested the recipes and equated them to smaller amounts, in some cases adding ingredients unknown to cooks of that period." The 1970s recipes have certainly been adapted, but there may be glimmers of Pleasant's originals in ones like the Hoppin' John in the section titled "Missouri Plantation," notable for its use of black beans instead of the more traditional black-eyed peas; and a stuffed eggplant in the section "New Year's Supper" that would be at home on any New Orleans table. Certainly the recipes collected in the volume cover the scope of Pleasant's life and testify to the diversity of the cooking of African Americans at the time. They range from simple plantation fare such as sweet potato pone and chitterlings to traditional Western dishes like the Hangtown fry of oysters simmered in butter and served with eggs and cream. There are also truly sophisticated ones that may have been served to the San Francisco establishment, like Nasturtium Artifice, in which nasturtium flowers are stuffed with a mixture of cream cheese and cooked Oregon salmon seasoned with marjoram. The latter recipe is interesting, as, if reasonably authentic, it may indicate just how innovative Pleasant's cooking was. Cream cheese, although mentioned in an English dictionary in 1754 and known in France in the seventeenth century, only came into usage in the United States in the 1870s and would have been an expensive novelty in Pleasant's day. Until Pleasant's own recipes are located, we will never know precisely which ingredients and techniques are hers and which are Holdredge's. The range of recipes in the books is notable, as it reminds us of the culinary divide between the food of the slave cabins of the plantation South and the dishes of the Big House: those that blacks, free and enslaved, fixed for white patrons. As the country moved westward, blacks who had the culinary know-how to prepare and serve the types of elaborate meals desired by the white upper classes found that their fortune lay in catering to the newly affluent.

Barney Ford was just such an individual. The California Gold Rush was also the lure that attracted Ford to the West. Born in Virginia in 1822, he had grown up on a plantation in South Carolina. As a young man, he'd escaped his Southern bondage, most likely with the aid of the Underground Railroad, and made his way to Chicago, where he was taken in by abolitionists. There he married and learned the trade of barber. After the Gold Rush began, he and his wife headed out toward California in 1851. At that time, before the completion of the transcontinental railroad, there were three ways to head from east to west. The overland route was a journey of two thousand miles on trails subject to all manner of privations, including running out of fresh drinking water, and the fear of Indian raids. The length of the journey depended on seasonal weather conditions, and no traveler could estimate how long it would take. The sea route around Cape Horn was not much better, and the uncomfortable voyage could take as much as six months. A shorter sea route involved traversing the malaria-infested Central America rain forest in Panama to await ships to San Francisco on the Pacific coast. The Fords chose the latter route, but when their ship put in at the port of Greytown in Nicaragua, they disembarked and remained, deciding to open up a small hotel to serve others making the same journey. They were successful, and the United States Hotel, as it was called, was noted for its clean rooms and "home cooked American meals."

The Fords, though, did not remain in Nicaragua. The threat of war there and the discovery of gold in Colorado led them back stateside with a change in destination; they arrived in the area near Denver in 1859, and Barney attempted to make a claim. He was rebuffed because, as an African American, he was not allowed to stake one in his name. He attempted to use a white lawyer, but that too ended in disaster, when the lawyer had him thrown off the mountain he was trying to claim. His claim was then jumped, and all ended in ruin. The Fords began anew; this time, Barney fell back on the trade he'd learned in Chicago, set up a barbershop in downtown Denver, and began to build a clientele. But when the fire of 1863 burned much of Denver to the ground, including Ford's barbershop, it was back to the drawing board yet again. The fire led to Denver's 1863 "brick ordinance," in which all new buildings in the city had to be constructed with brick or stone. It was a challenge, but this time, with a nine-thousand-dollar grant from a local banker who had faith in his abilities, Ford opened his People's Restaurant on the corner of Sixteenth and Blake streets in downtown Denver a scant four months after the fire.

An advertisement for the newly opened People's Restaurant in the 1863 *Rocky Mountain News* reads:

FORD'S PEOPLE'S RESTAURANT,
Blake Street, Denver.

B.L. Ford would respectfully invite his old patrons and the
public generally to call and see him at his new and
commodious
Saloon, Restaurant and Barber Shop
On the site of his old stand. Gentlemen will find at
All HOURS his tables supplied with the
MOST CHOICE AND DELICATE LUXURIES OF
COLORADO AND THE EAST
Private Parties of Ladies and gents can be accomo-
dated with special meals, and Oyster suppers to order

> In his upstairs saloon
> His Bar Is stocked with
> The Very Finest Liquors and Cigars
> That gold or greenbacks can control of first hands in
> The eastern markets. Denver and Mountain Lager
> Received daily.
> Game of all kinds, Trout, &c. constantly on hand
> For regular and transient customers, and served up in
> Style second to no other restaurant in the west.

Customers flocked to the premises. The establishment included a restaurant, a saloon, and, in a nod to his former trade, a barbershop. Ford served Denver's elite and its newly rich, who were often rough-hewn miners. (This, after all, was the Denver of the "unsinkable" Molly Brown.) The menu that he proffered was far from the standard cornbread-based slave diet; it offered elaborate dishes prepared from the finest local, national, and international ingredients and designed to suit the taste of the city's sophisticates, which followed the tastes of those of Europe and New York.

The East Coast had begun to grow a restaurant culture among the rich in the early decades of the nineteenth century. Delmonico's restaurant opened in New York City in 1837 and became a must-visit stop in the city. The seven-page menu was printed in English and French and offered twenty veal dishes, fifteen seafood ones, eleven beef items, and a wide variety of appetizers, vegetables, pastries, and fruits. There was a range of alcoholic beverages, and the wine list even included *Premiers crus* Bordeaux. Delmonico's raised the national standard, and Barney Ford's clientele wanted equivalent fare. His trout, oysters, and game were served up in rich sauces prepared from the most expensive ingredients; they were paid for by Denver's growing upper class, who settled their checks not only with U.S. currency but also with the gold that they had mined. Ford was wildly successful and later expanded People's Restaurant into the Inter-Ocean Hotel. Known for serving "the squarest meal between two oceans," Ford recognized the commercial importance of the railroad lines that had begun to traverse the country and moved in to exploit their growth. By 1867, he had a second restaurant in Cheyenne, Wyoming, which developed into a second hotel, where he catered to those who arrived on the new train routes that were beginning to crisscross the West.

The first U.S.-built locomotive ushered in the age of rail in Charleston, South Carolina, in 1830. By 1862, the United States Congress had passed a bill that called for two railroad companies to construct a rail line that would join the Atlantic and Pacific coasts and promote western migration. The Central Pacific and Union Pacific companies were charged with the task. On May 10, 1869, the two lines were joined at Promontory, Utah, with the driving of a golden spike. The nation was joined. By 1895 four more lines were built that continued the growth of the country's rail routes. Finding a meal on train journeys was a haphazard affair. Travelers had to either provision themselves for the journey or dash from the train at stops to purchase food from local vendors like the black women waiter-carriers of Gordonsville, Virginia, who proffered fried chicken and coffee to travelers on the Chesapeake and Ohio line after the Civil War.

Then, in 1867, George Mortimore Pullman introduced his "hotel car," which immediately became the traveling rage. The idea was to provide the well-to-do with all the comforts of a hotel on the rolling stock that rackety-clacked itself across the continent. Pullman's hotel cars included a kitchen that measured three feet by six feet, a pantry, and even a wine cellar, in which the crew of four or five created an amazing variety of dishes, considering the cramped quarters. The cars were successful, but the elite felt that eating should be separated from sleeping, and the hotel cars were gradually phased out and replaced with new dining cars devoted exclusively to serving food. The first was named the Delmonico, in honor of the famous New York restaurant, which was the epitome of dining elegance. Pullman's original hotel cars arrived on the tracks shortly after Emancipation and offered employment for many newly emancipated house servants in the domestic roles that they had defined under enslavement. Writing in 1917's *The History of the Pullman Car*, Joseph Husband declared that "the Pullman Company is today the greatest single employer of colored labor in the world." He continued, in terms that speak eloquently of the prevailing views on African Americans, noting they are "trained as a race for by years of personal service in various capacities, and by nature adapted faithfully to perform their duties under circumstances which necessitate unfailing good nature, solicitude, and faithfulness."

The railroads, as they grew, provisioned their passengers and developed their own regional specialties. Long before "fresh" and "local" and "regional" became the bywords of a twenty-first-century culinary generation, the trains were creating menus that reflected their routes. Travelers could dine on ripe figs in California, Dungeness crab in Oregon, and fresh-caught trout in Idaho.

The railroads offered employment and another way for African Americans and their food to travel westward. By the end of the century, African Americans excelled in dining cars as cooks and as waiters, gaining secure jobs in difficult times and often receiving travel benefits for family members at reduced rates. In the later part of the nineteenth century, as train employees moved about the country and established themselves and their families at terminus spots like California's Oakland and Los Angeles and Washington's Seattle, they became the avant garde for the early-twentieth-century wave of black migration.

The success of Ford, like that of Mary Ellen Pleasant, was based on serving food to the white upper classes. Those who worked in the Pullman cars also catered to the elite; they were praised for their taste and flair, but most of the menus served had little to do with the recipes of Africa or the plantation foods of the antebellum South and were inspired by the prevailing taste and ideas of grand dining in Europe. They and others like them lived and made their fortunes in the West's burgeoning cities, rode in railroad cars, and supped in fancy eateries.

Most blacks who journeyed westward were too impoverished to pay the rail fares. They went instead by wagon and cart and all too often simply on foot. The region also offered them jobs at small settlements that boasted a saloon or a boardinghouse, a general store, and perhaps a stagecoach post. This was the West of the homesteaders: the everyday, ordinary folk on whose backs the region was built. The black homesteaders were largely made up of former slaves and those seeking new land and opportunities, and their fragile existence on the plains was subject to Indian raids and outlaws, dust storms and droughts. Africa's tastes came to the West in the cast iron skillets and Dutch ovens of these black homesteaders who emigrated post-Emancipation. These new Westerners found themselves in small towns and enclaves and remote settlements where they depended on the protection of their neighbors and of the army in the form of the Buffalo Soldiers.

The legendary Ninth and Tenth Regiments of the United States Cavalry were founded by General Grant in 1866, the former in the Division of the Gulf and the latter in the Division of Missouri. White officers willing to command black troops were difficult to find, and many—like George Custer of Little Big Horn infamy—refused to lead the regiments. Other officers were less prejudiced and signed on, and so did black recruits in droves. The newly emancipated blacks arrived despite lower pay and rampant discrimination and racism. They were, for the most part, raw and untrained, but less than a year later the Ninth and Tenth Cavalries were on the trail west to begin their more-than-two-decade history of unbroken service. The Ninth served in Texas, New Mexico, Kansas, Oklahoma, Nebraska, Utah, and Montana. The Tenth, based at Fort Leavenworth in Kansas, was responsible for Kansas, Oklahoma, New Mexico, and Arizona. The Buffalo Soldiers made up about 20 percent of the cavalry in the West and patrolled the Great Plains and in New Mexico and Arizona. Their duty in these outposts of the westward-moving country was to keep order, and that was a mighty task indeed, as they had to deal with Indian wars, border conflicts, and general lawlessness. The Native peoples counted them worthy adversaries and gave them the name Buffalo Soldiers for their tenacity and for the peltlike look of their curly hair.

Despite the soldiers' renown and exemplary record, discrimination from whites followed them constantly and even showed up in their company mess halls. The Buffalo Soldiers were the U.S. Army's stepchildren, and their commanders complained constantly about provisioning. Meals consisted of a monotonous pork diet and seldom deviated from the staples of coffee, bread, beans, molasses, cornbread, and sweet potatoes. In the larders of the Buffalo Soldiers there were none of the staples common at other Western army posts. There was no canned pears, crackers, sugar, cheese, molasses, or sauerkraut. Post surgeon at Fort Concho, Texas, William Buchanan complained constantly to his superiors about the food, arguing that it was inferior to that offered at other posts: The bread was sour and the meat of poor quality. The canned peas provided were so old that they had deteriorated and the contents were poisoned by tin and solder. Buchanan was so incensed that he filed a written complaint with the post adjutant. The only rations to greet the soldiers returning to camp from the various battles and skirmishes of the Red River War were the same monotonous foods that might have fed an antebellum Alabama field hand: hog, hominy, and molasses. On some expeditions, the soldiers were gifted with good weather and could hunt and forage to supplement their substandard rations. Then, there might be venison or antelope ribs or wild turkey to break the routine, but generally, poor meals and poor horses and straw bedsacks on bed irons in leaky barracks were the standard lot of the Buffalo Soldiers.

On occasions, though, when the commanders managed to obtain appropriate rations, there were festivities such as the one given by Commander Benjamin Grierson on Christmas 1876 for the entire garrison at Fort Concho. The regimental band played, and officers and men sat down to a meal of "sandwiches, turkey, buffalo tongue, olives, cheese, biscuits, sweet and sour pickles, candy, raisins, apples, and four kinds of cake—all washed down with gallons of coffee." The experience of the Buffalo Soldiers was another side of the tale of the movement west—one in which the racism of the country marched west, shadowing the footsteps of the migrants with their bundled quilts and flimsy carpetbags containing their meager belongings.

Kansas was a favored destination for those seeking to put down roots and establish themselves outside the South. The 1862 Homestead Act applied to other Western states and territories, but for blacks, Kansas was a known quantity; it had been a haven for fugitive slaves during the Civil War, and the name of the state continued to resonate in the minds and hearts of African Americans. The Homestead Act allowed any U.S. citizen regardless of race or gender who had never fought against the U.S. government to file an application and claim 160 acres of surveyed government land. The homesteader had to live on the land and develop it. After five years, the homesteader could file for his deed by submitting proof of residency and enhancements to a local land office. Following the Civil War, Union veterans could deduct their army time from the residency requirements. The local land office then forwarded the paperwork including a final certificate of eligibility to the General Land Office in Washington, D.C. There, claims deemed valid could also be acquired after living on it for six months, making minimal improvements, and paying the government $1.25 per acre.

By 1877, the year the last of the federal troops were withdrawn from the South, racism and repression had become so onerous for former slaves that a committee was formed by Civil Rights leaders with members from all sections of the South. The committee, at its own expense, sent investigators throughout the region to report on conditions. Their reports were devastating: lynchings, whippings by former masters, and a horrifying litany of abuses of the privileges newly earned. The committee appealed to Washington, but its entreaties went unheard. Land was requested in the West or an appropriation to ship people to Liberia, but this request remained unacknowledged. Finally, black delegates from fourteen states met again in Nashville under the aegis of black congressman John R. Lynch of Mississippi and resolved to support migration, declaring that "the colored people should emigrate to those States and Territories where they can enjoy all the rights which are guaranteed by the laws and Constitution of the United States." This declaration assisted what became known as the Exodus of 1879. Former slaves left in droves, with many of the newly formed African American churches sponsoring migrating groups. It is estimated that between twenty thousand and forty thousand African American men, women, and children made their way westward to Kansas in ten years. Their numbers were such that they swamped the facilities that had been readied for them and provoked a government investigation into the handling of the move and subsequent failure of the reception services. But move they did and endure they did. They called themselves Exodusters, building on the biblical imagery of an exodus to freedom that had pervaded many of the slave songs.

The Exodusters moved into a West of possibility. All-black towns, such as Nicodemus, Kansas, and Langston, Oklahoma, were being founded by the blacks who earlier had migrated to the area. Nicodemus's secretary, Reverend S. P. Roundtree, published a broadside on July 2, 1877, addressed "To the Colored Citizens of the United States." In it, he advised them,

> We, the Nicodemus Town Company of Graham County, Kan.,
> are now in possession of our lands and the Town Site of Nico-
> demus, which is beautifully located on the N.W. quarter of
> Section 1, Town 8, Range 21, in Graham Co., Kansas, in the
> Great Solomon Valley, 240 miles west of Topeka, and we are
> proud to say it is the finest country we ever saw . . . Now is
> your time to secure your home on Government Land in the
> Great Solomon Valley of Western Kansas.

The town was named for Nicodemus, a legendary slave who had
arrived in the United States on a slave ship and purchased his own
freedom. The living wasn't as easy as the optimistic Reverend
Roundtree predicted; the tidal wave of Exodusters had caused a
breakdown in services, and the newly arriving folks had to live in
dugout caves for the first year and contend with drought and crop
failure. But the town grew and prospered, until the Missouri-Pacific
railroad passed it by later in the century, after which it began to
languish. Zachary Fletcher, one of the town's original residents and
its postmaster, built its first hotel, the Saint Francis Hotel and Livery
Stable. By 1880 there were two hotels, a newspaper, a bank, a drug-
store, and three general stores. And by 1887, Nicodemus had an ice
cream parlor as well as a baseball team—poignant proof that the
African Americans leaving the South just wanted one thing: their
own piece of the American dream. In other parts of Kansas, the tidal
wave of Exodusters also overburdened the existing infrastructure.
Famine threatened, and aid was sought from as far away as England. Nicodemus survives until this day, but just barely—with a
population of about twenty souls in 2004 and a designation as a
National Historical Site.

Oklahoma was another favored destination, and by 1900, African
Americans in the state owned 1.5 million acres of land, worth eleven
million dollars. The state had more than two dozen all-black towns.
Soon Allensworth, California; Blackdom, New Mexico; Dearfield,
Colorado, and other towns like them were magnets to families leaving the South. Many were also stopping points for those who wanted
to journey farther west. They offered services to those who stopped
in the vicinity and, most important, the company of like people.

The black towns, however, were not the only places where African

Americans headed. Many settled in other small towns along the trails and served the cattlemen and cowboys. They lived in developing cities and in towns along the routes west, where many worked at livery stables and saloons and hotels, in jobs that they knew well from slavery. Still others clustered in cities, starting black neighborhoods in places like Denver, Colorado; Lincoln, Nebraska; Cheyenne, Wyoming; and St. Louis and Kansas City, Missouri. They moved near like folk who shared similar history and similar tastes. In most neighborhoods, Southern foodways were maintained with discreet signs posted in black-owned shop windows advertising an arrival of possum or pecans or other foodstuffs from the South.

During the western migrations, many blacks used the domestic arts and particularly their culinary skills to create advancement for themselves and their families, especially women. Black women were valiant in the West; they worked singly or alongside men and ran restaurants, hotels, and boardinghouses. Western Black women were five times more likely to be married than their white counterparts and, according to the 1890 census, were also better educated and more likely than whites to attend school for six months or more. Most of the black pioneer women are nameless, but they are not always faceless. Photographs of the era show stalwart women dressed in their Sunday best greeting the uncertain future with broad smiles or sitting proudly in front of sod houses and log cabins in places like Deerfield, Colorado; Reno, Nevada; and Tucson, Arizona. In one image, a family is gathered on the banks of the Mississippi River, staring into the distance as though waiting deliverance. A child sleeps on a pallet, a youngster sucks her thumb, and on the ground surrounding them are cast-iron pots, a Dutch oven, and an ironstone pitcher—silent witnesses to the food and foodways that were journeying West with them.

The post-Emancipation culinary history of African Americans solidified the development of two different tendencies of African American food. One presented the basic African-influenced pork and corn fare of the newly emancipated. The other celebrated the more European-oriented offerings of the former free people of color and the mulatto elite and included dishes like those created by blacks to serve to elite whites. Together the styles signaled the development of a multiplicity of dishes that make up the present-day African American culinary lexicon and speak to the diversity of the African American experience in the United States. In the twentieth century northward migration would fix the culinary class divide and bring this all out into the open.

WRITING IT ALL DOWN

Cookbooks are so prevalent in today's world that we take them for granted. We have only to reach up to our kitchen shelves or turn on the computer to have access to more recipes than we will ever be able to prepare. This, however, has not always been the case. The first American cookbook, *American Cookery*, was published in 1796 by Amelia Simmons, and the first Southern cookbook, *The Virginia House-wife*, by Mary Randolph, was published in 1824. These books, though, were only for the elite. Recipes were kept in family collections written down by generations of cooks or transmitted orally. And for most of the enslaved cooks, whether in the slave cabin or the Big House, oral transmission prevailed up until Emancipation and beyond. In most slaveholding sections of the country, it was illegal for enslaved blacks to be taught to read and write, and up to Emancipation and for decades thereafter, only the African American elite were fully literate. It is therefore remarkable that the first African American cookbook was published in the same decade that saw Emancipation.

Abby Fisher's 1881 *What Mrs. Fisher Knows About Old Southern Cooking, Soups, Pickles, Preserves, Etc.* was long thought to be the first African American cookbook. Then, in 2000, Michigan antiquarian book dealer Jan Longone acquired a slim volume that changed the trajectory of the study of African American food history. Longone found what seems to be the sole surviving copy of a book by Malinda Russell, a free woman of color. The book, *A Domestic Cook Book: Containing a Careful Selection of Useful Receipts for the Kitchen,* was published in 1866 in Paw Paw, Michigan.

Malinda Russell proclaims herself to be a free woman of color on the back cover of her cookbook, no doubt to set herself apart from the recently emancipated. However, the life that she details in her introduction lets readers know that while freedom was essential, in itself it was no guarantor of financial or physical comfort. Her life exemplified many of the hazards of westward migration. Born to a free woman who died while she was young, Russell tried to migrate to Liberia at the age of nineteen but was duped out of her savings and forced to make her way in the world. She turned to cooking to earn a living. She made her way through Virginia, North Carolina, and Kentucky, working at various jobs. She worked as a nurse, a laundress, owner of a boardinghouse, a cook, a baker, and a caterer. She was married and widowed and became the mother of a disabled child. A tireless worker, she managed to accumulate another nest egg, but it too was stolen from her. Russell left the South, "flying a flag of truce out of the Southern borders, being attacked several times by the enemy," and made her way to Paw Paw, Michigan, where she again tried to recoup her funds. The cookbook that has become known as the first African American cookbook was, at its inception, one western migrant's innovative way of trying to earn some cash.

Russell, in her introduction, pays homage to the African American tradition of Southern cookery and declares that she learned her trade from "Fanny Steward, a colored cook of Virginia." She equally states that she cooked "in the plan of the Virginia Housewife." Indeed, her 265 recipes mirror the brevity and style of Randolph's book and often are only a sentence in length. Not surprisingly, for one who had run a bakery, they include a preponderance of puddings and cakes. Although Russell spent considerable time in Virginia and claimed to have learned her culinary skills there, few recipes reflect the Southern palate. She offers fried oysters instead of fried chicken and charlotte russe and floating island instead of more traditionally Southern desserts. There is a sweet potato sliced pie and even one dish for okra, which she calls "ocher," but in general compass, her dishes reflect a cuisine more representative of the Middle American diet.

My grandmother would have said that Russell and Abby Fisher were as different as chalk and cheese. Fisher, the author of the work that had long been thought to be the first African American cookbook, was born into slavery around 1822. Little is known about Fisher other than that she married Alexander C. Fisher, from Mobile, Alabama, and that by 1880 they had migrated to San Francisco, where Mr. Fisher listed his occupation in the census as a pickle and preserve manufacturer. Abby Fisher's book was published the following year. In her one-paragraph "Preface and Apology" to the work, she indicates that she and her husband were "without the advantages of an education." In this she was like the millions of other enslaved who entered Emancipation without formal instruction. Some acquired the ability to read and write post-Emancipation, but thousands remained marginally literate at best.

The book's title, *What Mrs. Fisher Knows About Old Southern Cooking*, implies that people were interested in knowing just what Mrs. Fisher did know about old Southern cooking, and Fisher declares that she had been frequently asked by her lady friends and patrons—nine of whom are listed by name and address—to reveal some of her knowledge and experience of Southern cooking, pickles, and jelly making. She explains that she had more than thirty-five years' experience in the art of cooking "Soups, Gumbos, Terrapin Stews, Meat Stews, Baked and Roast Meats, Pastries, Pies, Biscuits, making Jellies, Pickles, Sauces, Ice-Creams, and Jams, preserving Fruits, etc." Her recipes are set out in careful detail "so that a child can understand it and learn the art of cooking." Most cookbooks of the era leave much unstated, assuming knowledge on the part of the cooks, but Fisher is meticulous and exacting in her instructions. She suggests that cooks not only sift but also brown the flour for her fruitcake recipe and that they beat whites and yolks separately. She advises readers that two pounds of sweet potatoes will make two pies. Her oyster gumbo recipe is thickened with filé (a sassafras powder) which she calls gumbo and in true Creole fashion (as one who spent time in Mobile would know) she reminds her readers to "have dry boiled rice to go to the table with gumbo in a separate dish. Serve one tablespoon of rice to a plate of gumbo."

Like Russell, Fisher celebrated the culinary legacy of Southern black cooks. But while Russell briefly acknowledges it in her introduction as the genesis of her culinary training, Fisher presents it on the plate, with detailed recipes for many traditional Southern and African American favorites as stuffed ham, corn fritters, and watermelon-rind pickles. Fisher and Russell, however, are more than simply the authors of the first African American cookbooks. In the pages of their works, they preserve the culinary cultures that created them and had enabled them and so many like them to survive and prosper during the western migrations. In this, each moved forward the African American quest for acceptance in American society and the growing culinary diversity of African American life.

CHAPTER 8

MOVIN' ON UP!

Resilience, Resistance, and
Entrepreneurs Large and Small

Chicago, Illinois—

I've always been more a Langston Hughes type than a Carl Sandburg person: one who is more at home in the urban enclaves of New York City than anywhere else. The hog butcher to the world ethic of the Second City was really not for me. Then, in the 1970s, when I was travel editor for *Essence* magazine, I made my first trip to the Windy City. The South Side of Chicago was still the South Side in those days, and friends made sure that I visited a series of clubs and joints, including Flukey's, a local club of some fame. Entering it was like opening a door into the past: The walls were hung with red flocked wallpaper, a long mahogany bar lined one wall. It looked like nothing so much as a nineteenth-century brothel. It was a time of wide-brimmed hats and swaggering men wearing platform shoes who flashed, made deals, and strutted like brightly colored peacocks. The barmaids called everyone "Baby" and "Sugar" and seemed to have been imported directly from some sweet home Down South. As the evening was softened more and more by bourbon and ginger ale, I began to realize that the crowd was made up of folks who shared common history, common roots. People circulated and exchanged news of the Mississippi hometowns that they shared. They asked about friends and families and passed around the copies of the local paper that the most recent traveler had brought back from down home. Now gone, Flukey's was an atavism, a bar like many others that must have existed in the days of the Great Migration, when folks who came from the same hamlets and small towns of the South clustered together. Flukey's gave me a real feel for the geography that led folks straight from Mississippi to Chicago. For them the Mississippi provided a way out of the Delta, due north: Natchez, Vicksburg, Memphis, St. Louis, and on into Illinois and Chicago.

I've been back to Chicago many times since then. On one memorable occasion my friend Marvin Jones, who is a chef, took me on a Chicago barbecue crawl. We made our way into corners where I'd have never dared to venture alone. I can still recall waiting in a line of folks in a narrow corridor, smelling the mix of smoke and char and the sweet pungency of the cooking meat in the air. We'd managed to get in line before the small joint ran out of barbecue and closed for the night. We feasted: sucking on the bone tips of the ribs and scarfing down the chopped pork barbecue off paper plates. The taste of the 'cue was sweet-tart with the red sauce that I'd had in some of my favorite Memphis spots. Memphis was a stop on the way north to Chicago, and some of the people simply settled there; others stayed only long enough to make more money and continue the journey north to Chicago. Connections between the two cities and the Mississippi Delta still run deep.

Chicago had long been a beacon for blacks leaving the South. Its big-shoulder ethos appealed to those who had little more than the strength of their backs and the acuity of their wit. Founded by black trading-post owner Jean-Baptiste Point du Sable, Chicago has always been a town of black entrepreneurs. None was more successful than John H. Johnson, who founded the Johnson Publishing Company there in 1942. Johnson migrated from Arkansas, and his success was the larger-than-life version of the smaller stories of entrepreneurial success that played out in the first half of the twentieth century. The tale of how he began publishing *Negro Digest* and then *Ebony* and founded his empire, which became the largest black-owned publishing firm in the world, is the stuff of legend. No trip to Chicago for me is complete without a visit to the offices of Johnson Publishing, where my friend Charlotte Lyons has been food editor of *Ebony* magazine for more than three decades, following in the steps of the first black food editor, Frieda DeKnight.

When first built, the headquarters of *Ebony* were not only the pride of the Johnson family who had founded the publishing giant but also a testimonial of accomplishment for African Americans all over the country. As recently as 2008, I was tickled to note some church ladies—hats firmly planted on heads and hands snugly in gloves—had made Johnson Publishing headquarters a stop on their Chicago tour and come just to visit the building and see where the magazine that had been so much a part of their lives was produced. The building is pure 1960s top of the line—exotic woods, art-hung corridors, executive offices with vast views of Grant Park across the street, its own archives and library. It reflects a pride in ownership that is part of the entrepreneurial feeling among African Americans, nowhere more so than in Chicago.

It is not without reason that the first black president of the United States was based in Chicago, for the city and the opportunity that it has traditionally offered African Americans embodies an ongoing African American quest for acceptance and equal success even in the twenty-first century. In the late years of the nineteenth century and the early decades of the twentieth, Chicago and other Northern cities must have glowed like beacons of possibility and opportunity for African Americans. Those, like John Johnson, who left the South to establish themselves in the North brought with them more than their dreams of a better life; they brought their willingness to work, their sense of family and community, and the resourcefulness and the resilience that would transform the food of their Southern homes into businesses large and small.

❖ ❖ ❖ ❖ ❖

Escaping slaves had followed the drinking gourd, located the north star, and made their way north to freedom for centuries. In the last quarter of the nineteenth century and for much of the first half of the twentieth, their emancipated descendants followed the same routes as their ancestors. Tattered clothing and knapsacks filled with meager belongings were replaced by scratchy new store-bought finery and flimsy cardboard suitcases, but the essential baggage that came in the hearts and heads of both enslaved and free was hope. Hope didn't change. It remained a constant—the hope for a new place to live free, the hope for a place with jobs that would allow a person to support a family, the hope for a place in a country where they could be themselves and be at peace.

They headed north out of a South that was increasingly hostile. Reconstruction ended in 1877 and the protections that the government attempted to put into place to protect the newly freed African Americans ceased. The promise of Reconstruction, with its more equitable tax system and attempts to integrate blacks into the American fabric of life, was over. The end of Reconstruction led to the imposition of a series of Jim Crow laws in the South that required the segregation of whites and black on public transportation and, later, in schools, public places, and restaurants. Slavery was gradually transformed into sharecropping. The white supremacist organizations that had been formed at the end of the Civil War grew. The Ku Klux Klan, which originated with Confederate veterans at the end of the Civil War, was rekindled, and a second Klan was founded in 1915. Violence escalated. Between 1889 and 1932, 3,700 lynchings of blacks were recorded in the United States. For many in the South, the rights won by the Civil War disappeared slowly into bleak lives of hardscrabble subsistence farming. The South held little for them; it was time to leave.

In 1910, seven eighths of African Americans in the country lived in the South below the so-called Cotton Curtain. By 1925, one tenth of the black population of the country had moved to the North. Between 1916 and 1918 alone, almost four hundred thousand African Americans—almost five hundred a day—stepped out onto dusty roads, pointed their faces toward the horizon, and headed north. They headed toward metropolises where there were jobs in the factories created by increasing industrialization. They arrived in cities like Chicago, Detroit, Pittsburgh, Cleveland, and New York and began to make their presence felt by creating neighborhoods and communities where they supported and sustained one another in their churches, their shops, their restaurants, and their gathering places.

Initially, Northern companies sent agents down to recruit labor, but as the trickle turned into a tidal wave, agents were no longer necessary. People did their own recruiting. Males who had journeyed northward to seek their fortunes found a toehold and sent for brothers and then families, and neighborhoods were established. The jobs were not the gold-paved streets of the blues or the easy money of the grapevine rumors, but segregated jobs that paid blacks less than whites and placed them in competition with the new waves of European immigrants. There were jobs in manufacturing and industry, and for those with specialized skills, there was the ability to make money in areas offering services not performed by whites for blacks even in the North. Doctors, dentists, and undertakers also came north, formed the nuclei of the new communities, and prospered.

The black press grew and fueled the northward migrations with its own columns and connections. Papers like the *New York Amsterdam News*, the *Pittsburgh Courier*, and the *Chicago Defender* were so much a part of the migration that some Southern cities banned them, feeling that they were luring away the blacks who had formed the basis of the Southern unskilled job pool. Yet still they came, following routes as worn as those of the Underground Railroad. Those from the Mississippi Delta headed due north to Chicago. Folks from Georgia, Alabama, and Upper Mississippi headed to Pittsburgh, Cleveland, and Detroit. Those from the Carolinas and Virginia made their way to Washington, Philadelphia, and New York. In the early years of migration, Chicago was a singular magnet. Between 1910 and 1920 Chicago's black population grew by 148 percent. The city's industrial expansion required strong backs and broad shoulders and people willing to get in and work, and Southern blacks responded. By the 1920s, however, the true mecca for many heading north from the sharecropping fields of the South was New York City, with its growing beacon for the black world: Harlem.

The Harlem they arrived in had not always been black. In the federal days and well into the nineteenth century, blacks in New York City had lived downtown and then in the area now known as Greenwich Village. As the city grew, they moved north. By the late nineteenth century, the majority of the black population had moved uptown to the upper Twenties and lower Thirties, to an area called the "Tenderloin." Following that, folks moved as far north as the San Juan Hill neighborhood, near West Fifty-third Street, where they had the opportunity to live in bigger and better-built apartments. Finally, around the turn of the twentieth century, the move uptown began. Harlem, originally spelled "Haarlem," was a suburb for the Dutch and German bourgeoisie that had been overbuilt. Landlords had difficulty finding tenants for their new buildings. The move of blacks into the neighborhood began slowly at first, centered on one or two buildings east of Lenox Avenue; then gradually the line moved west. It met with resistance and with reprisals and created bitter battles. When the tipping point was reached, white flight resulted and left Harlem wide open to new black tenants.

In Harlem, as in other northern communities around the country, the newly arrived had to survive on what African American writer Ralph Ellison called "shit, grit, and mother wit." They found their way and soon established their bailiwicks, as—like many of the developing black neighborhoods around the country—Harlem divided itself between the sacred and the profane: The Sunday saints were firmly on one side of the divide, and the Saturday-night sinners, with their bars and clubs, were equally firmly on the other.

Harlem soon offered a vibrant network of African American churches of myriad denominations that became the mainstay of the new communities, offering guidance in negotiating the complex byways to employment and serving as gathering places for the newly arrived by providing contact with others in like circumstances. Church functions became the social bedrock for those on the ecclesiastical side of the community divide. Births, weddings, funerals, and all of life's stages were accompanied by the resounding "Hallelujahs" and "Amens" of fellow brothers and sisters. Southern churches partnered with their Northern counterparts and pushed the move north as well by forming migration clubs—groups that monitored newspapers for jobs and cut through much of the red tape for those who were unskilled, often illiterate, and unable to negotiate the bureaucracy. Letters from the faithful in the North encouraged the journeys of those remaining in the South, and the umbilicus was maintained between Up North and the folks left back home.

The Saturday-night sinners also created their own Northern world: one where the juke joints and Saturday-night stomps of the South were transformed into blues clubs and jazz dens of the North. It was a time of progress but also a time of homesickness and uprootedness—when a pigfoot and a bottle of beer could bring relief from the travails of the Northern world that was not the promised nirvana. The Northern migrants found sustenance and like company in the small eateries that were being formed in newly nascent black neighborhoods. Often run by women who catered out of their rooming houses or apartments, these spots grew into small mom-and-pop restaurants known to those in the neighborhood for providing fried chicken and okra, hog maws and collard greens—in short, the comfort food the displaced Southerners craved.

Whatever side of the divide the migrants to New York occupied, all were subjected to higher rents than those living in other sections of the city. The Harlem apartments to which they were flocking had been hastily subdivided with flimsy walls and narrow hallways. Many were railroad flats with one room leading directly into the next and no privacy for those who lived there. Cold-water flats were the norm, and often the toilets were shared with others who lived down the dark hallways. Bathing facilities, if they existed beyond a galvanized tub, were in the kitchen, and often the bathtub might do double duty as a bed for an additional tenant to supplement the rent. Kitchens used coal stoves, with only the most modern landlords slowly changing over to piped-in gas in the 1920s and 1930s. Whatever refrigeration existed was provided by the ice man, who hauled blocks of ice up tenement steps for use in iceboxes, where it chilled food until it melted and had to be replaced again a few days later.

Blacks, though, were anxious to establish a foothold; they accepted the conditions and worked to make a good life amid the decay. Small entrepreneurs again turned to the skills they'd acquired doing domestic work and day labor in the South and used them to develop small businesses, which they grew into larger enterprises. In the creation of these small enterprises, they evidenced the same resourcefulness that had enabled generations to survive enslavement. Patsy Randolph used the castoffs of others to create pickles, pepper sauces, spices, and relishes, which she then sold. According to Frank Byrd, who cataloged some of Harlem's ways for the WPA:

> The biggest seller of this entire lot, incidentally, happens to be pickled watermelon rind. Her profits on this Southern delicacy amount to something well over ninety-five percent because the rinds cost her absolutely nothing. She has obtained the permission of store owners who sell individual five- and ten-cent slices at their street stands to collect all the rinds she wants from their baskets. At the height of the summer season, she takes these rinds home, prepares

and packs them in fruit jars, and sells them to a highly appreciative buying public that has long since been accustomed to this fine "down-home" dish that adds a tasty
flavor to meats, especially roast pork or the more widely
favored pork chops.

Others also improvised and took to the streets as vendors selling
Southern favorites like the individual described by author Ralph
Ellison in *Invisible Man*. Although his book is a work of fiction, Ellison, like Byrd, had conducted interviews for the WPA with Harlem denizens of the 1920s and 1930s and based the character on
reality. Echoing the thoughts of more than one Harlem migrant,
he wrote:

> Then far down at the corner I saw an old man warming his
> hands against the side of an odd-looking wagon, from which
> a stove pipe reeled off a thin spiral of smoke that drifted the
> odor of baking yams slowly to me, bringing a stab of swift
> nostalgia. I stopped as though struck by a shot, deeply inhal-
> ing, remembering, my mind surging back, back. At home
> we'd bake them in the hot coals of the fireplace, had carried
> them cold to school for lunch; munched them secretly,
> squeezing the sweet pulp from the soft peel as we hid from
> the teacher behind the largest book, the *World's Geography*.
> Yes, and we'd loved them candied, or baked in a cobbler,
> deep-fat fried in a pocket of dough, or roasted with pork and
> glazed with the well-browned fat; had chewed them raw—
> yams and years ago.

Ellison's evocation of the world—conjured up for the lonely
northern migrant by the aroma of roasting sweet potatoes—was
reenacted day in and day out on the streets of Harlem and other
Northern metropolises where traditional Southern foods were
offered to the newly arrived by a multiplicity of vendors selling
from stalls and carts along the main thoroughfares of the black
neighborhoods.

Life in crowded, less-than-welcoming apartments made Harlem
residents take to the streets and provided the uptown neighborhood

with a life and vibrancy that was commented on by most observers. Food vendors and street stands were a large part of the urban landscape. Indeed, it seemed to Frank Byrd and Terry Roth, who documented the Harlem street vendors of the period, that the cook-shack, pushcart, and horsecart vendors gave Harlem streets a "sprightlier" air than those in the downtown precincts. Vendors sold pigs' feet, fried chicken, and hot corn and other vegetables using syncopated rhythms and humorous rhymes. In this and in many other ways, they were direct descendents of the vegetable hawkers of Charleston and New Orleans and even of the black street-food sellers who had dotted the downtown New York streets in the colonial period and the early years of the nineteenth century.

Uptown, though, African Americans had a monopoly on street food and made their livings selling the foods they knew best: items that harked back to days of enslavement. Pig trotters were one part of the hog that lay unequivocally in the realm of African American food in the South. They were not elegant to eat and not meaty, but they offered an abundance of bones to be sucked of their skin, gristle, and small pieces of meat. They were also the trademark of one of the most successful Harlem food vendors. Harlem Renaissance writer James Weldon Johnson celebrated her entrepreneurial skills in an article in the March 1925 issue of *Survey Graphic*:

> "Pig Foot Mary" is a character in Harlem. Everybody knows "Mary" and her stand and has been tempted by the smell of her pigsfeet, fried chicken and hot corn, even if he is not a customer. "Mary," whose real name is Mary Dean, bought the five-story apartment house at the corner of Seventh Avenue and One Hundred and Thirty-seventh Street at a price of $42,000.

Johnson's story of Pig Foot Mary spoke to her entrepreneurial acumen and to her financial abilities. His is the abbreviated version. Lillian Harris Dean, Pig Foot Mary's *real* name, arrived in Harlem in 1901, a migrant from the Mississippi Delta area and became a local legend. As the story goes, she began working as a domestic. When she'd earned five dollars, she spent three on a baby carriage and a wash-boiler and the rest on pigs' feet. Then she set to work from the makeshift cart. Her hot pigs' feet were an immediate success, and she remained at her stand, located at the corner of 135th Street and Lenox Avenue (now Malcolm X Boulevard), for sixteen years. Her daily working uniform was a freshly starched gingham dress, once seemingly her only property, but soon she purchased a cook cart, married the owner of the adjacent newsstand, went into real estate, and eventually purchased not only the building mentioned by Johnson in his 1925 article but also others around Harlem. When she died in 1929, she had retired to California to live comfortably on the $375,000 that she had earned. Illiterate and initially alone, she had amassed a small fortune selling pigs' feet, chitterlings, and other black Southern classics like fried chicken, yams, and roast corn.

Fried chicken had traditionally been associated with African Americans, and it generated racial stereotypes that persisted well into the twentieth century of chicken-loving African Americans and their "Gospel" bird. The reality is perhaps a bit more banal. Fried chicken is a dish that could be consumed hot or cold and while on the go, and it was no doubt practical for those whose apartments provided scant cooking facilities. The sweet potatoes, mistakenly called yams, of which Ellison spoke so eloquently were another remembrance of things Southern. Other food vendors sold roast corn. Roasted ears had traditionally been offered on roadsides on the African continent and throughout the Caribbean and had been a street-food standby in New York City almost from the city's inception. Ellison's fictitious yam vendor, Pig Foot Mary, and others like them carved out careers and in some cases accumulated wealth. Often their fortunes were made by selling dishes that amply demonstrated the cultural resilience of some iconic black foods. Inadvertently, they also aided the northward movement of traditional African American foodways from the South.

While in Chicago and Detroit African Americans often lived next door to others from the same Southern region or adjacent Southern states, in New York the lure of jobs had reached beyond the borders of the United States. Migrants to the Big Apple met up with black immigrants from other parts of the globe who had also answered Harlem's siren song. They came from English-speaking Jamaica, Montserrat, Barbados, and Trinidad and Tobago and from French-speaking Martinique and Guadeloupe, and Papiamento and Dutch-speaking Aruba and Curaçao. They too followed the lure of available jobs, arrived in Harlem, and brought their foods to add to the mix. Alongside yam sellers and cobbled-together cook stands selling pigs' feet and fried chicken, Caribbean street vendors also hawked tropical fruits with their multilingual calls.

> Yo tengo guineas
> Yo tengo cocoas
> Yo tengo piñas también

They brought the rhythms of the islands to their cries as they roamed the streets selling the bananas, coconuts, and pineapples of their tropical climes. A 1928 article in the *New York Times* asked the question "What Tempts Harlem's Palate?" Author John Walker Harrington discovered that

> Harlem is the cosmopolis of colored culture, of gaiety, of art, and the capital of Negro cookery. Harlem's visitors come from the Southern United States, the West Indies, from South America and even from Africa. In what it eats, Harlem shows itself less a locality than an international rallying point. It is haven where food had the odd psychology, where viands solace the mind as well as feed the body.

Harlem markets were culinary melting pots of the foods of the African diaspora. The roots and tubers of the Caribbean, like *tania*, *eddoes*, and cassava, as well as the true yam from Africa, turned up in market stalls next to the sweet potatoes that had claimed their name in the American South. Harrington also noted "crystal fines, as Harlem calls them. They are like a combination of thin-necked squashes and puffy cucumbers, and are covered with fibers of soft whitish filaments . . . Duly shorn and cut into strips, these strange looking vegetables give body to soups and stews—particularly to gumbo." He was speaking of a form of the vegetable known as *chayote* in Mexico, *chocho* in Jamaica, *christophene* in the French-speaking world, and mirliton in New Orleans and which made its way into the soups and stews of Harlem's culinary melting pot.

The Southern foods of black Americans were the mainstays for many in the marketplace. Harrington also observed, "What broccoli is to Park Avenue, the select collards are to the colony of Upper Manhattan." The leafy greens had primacy of place in the uptown markets. Pork, he noted, is the "leading article of flesh diet," adding that "every part of the hog finds its way into the Harlem kitchen" and remarking on its use as a seasoning piece of meat in many of the dishes described. Braver than many, he sampled chitterlings, the small intestine of the pig, and said that "their savory odor is their chief lure to those who like them." Unclear to Harrington, the pungent odor of cooking chitterlings made them anathema in many an African American household, and the scrupulous processing their preparation entailed meant that they were only eaten in homes or restaurants where cleanliness reigned. Chitterlings and dishes like hog maw (the stomach of a pig) and Pig Foot Mary's pigs' feet defined African American food preferences harking back to the rural South. They were culinary throwbacks to the meals improvised by the enslaved from the less noble parts of the pig, which were their dietary standbys. In the markets and kitchens of Harlem of the 1920s, they met up with parallel dishes from the Caribbean featuring less noble parts of the pig and similar African-inspired tastes.

Throughout the period, street markets flourished alongside vendors of cooked foods, with small entrepreneurs hawking their wares and providing curbside service for housewives and those who wished to avail themselves of a Pan-African bounty.

Harrington wrote:

> On Saturday afternoons and nights the broad sidewalks of Lenox Avenue become groves and gardens and broad fields. Out of huge barrels loom red sugar cane, six or eight feet high, which later, cut in short lengths, is eaten as a stick candy by children. Plantains and bananas in all shades of green and yellow and dark red are ranged in inviting "hands." Pyramids of tanyans and eddoes loom: bushels of collards and stacks of gigantic yellow and reddish yams tempt the affluence of payday.

Ironically, this multicultural cornucopia was not the fare that most whites who journeyed to Harlem experienced. Harrington was writing in the heyday of whites "slumming" uptown in Harlem's clubs and nightspots, and his opening question—"What Tempts Harlem's Palate?"—reminded readers that the fare available in the markets was not to be found on the menus at the hot spots that made the Harlem of the era famous.

Blacks who arrived in Harlem in the 1920s arrived in a city in the throes of Prohibition. The January 16, 1920, enforcement of the Eighteenth Amendment slowly transformed uptown into a place of speakeasies and cabarets and created a vibrant nightlife that came to define the era. Connie's Inn, the Nest Club, Small's Paradise, and the legendary Cotton Club were among the most famous, but Harlem could boast something for virtually every taste, no matter how exotic. From 129th Street to 135th Street between Lenox Avenue and Eighth Avenue alone there were a dozen or so formal clubs and speakeasies offering elaborate floor shows with chorus girls and bands led by notables like Duke Ellington and Cab Calloway. There were also numerous smaller and often-illicit ones offering jazz, blues, transvestite drag shows, and all manner of entertainment. The most famous, like the Cotton Club, were strictly segregated establishments. Other than the performers, kitchen workers, and staff, no blacks were allowed in the clubs, whose atmosphere was bathed in a faux exoticism designed to evoke plantation days, with scantily clad bandanna-wearing light-skinned women as dancers or tropical fantasies complete with palm trees and jungle decor. Club owners were white, and kitchen staffs black. The menus they cooked were varied and created to appeal to a variety of downtown tastes. The black dishes that they served were invariably as falsely exotic as their decors. Cultural commentator Harrington queried:

> If the Negro is to win New York with the fare he likes, as he has won the rest of the world to his jazz and his spirituals, what shall we be eating one of these days? Not the menu of his night clubs and cabarets. Harlem's exhibition restaurants for white folks have mammies who fry chicken southern style and bake beaten biscuits. But such viands are like

Chinese chop suey—all for customers of other racial strains.

At the Cotton Club, the menu offered steak and lobster or shrimp cocktails, a selection of Chinese food like *moo goo gai pan*, Mexican food, and a smattering of Southern black dishes like the "mammy-fried" chicken decried by Harrington and barbecued spare ribs. Slumming "negropolitans," as upper-crust whites from downtown were known by tart-tongued black writer Zora Neale Hurston, dining in the famous clubs may have felt a frisson of delight and a kinship to black food as they sampled fried chicken and barbecued ribs alongside the lobster and the ersatz international foods purveyed by the white club owners. However, their ignorance of Harlem's true foods equaled their ignorance of Harlem's true life. The Harlem denizens they assumed to know had very different lives and daily diets more firmly rooted in the African American culinary culture of the Southern United States, with its emphasis on pork, chicken, and corn.

The Harlem residents relaxed from the drudgery of their jobs as laborers and domestics not at the notable local clubs, where Jim Crow policies meant that no blacks were allowed, but at rent parties. As with the entrepreneurial zeal that created yam sellers and street vendors, rent parties were born of resourcefulness and created by financial necessity. Given on Saturday or Thursday nights, the traditional days off for maids and other domestics, the fetes were designed to augment slim incomes while providing cheap entertainment for those who would not have been allowed to cross the thresholds of the famous clubs even if they could afford to. Rent gouging of newly arrived blacks meant that rents in Harlem averaged fifteen to thirty dollars a month higher than those in other areas of Manhattan. An individual who couldn't "make the rent" on an apartment would hold such a shindig, print up handbills, and set up shop. The handbills often featured rhyming couplets:

> *You don't get nothing for being an angel child,*
> *So you might as well get real busy and real wild.*

Or

If you can't do the Charleston or do the pigeon
  wing,
You sure can shake that thing.

As the parties became more prevalent, hosts and hostesses often advertised the Southern culinary specialties that would be sold.

Ribbon Maws and Trotters a Specialty
Fall in Line and Watch Your Step,
For there'll be a lot of browns with plenty of pep at
A Social Whist Party
Given by Lucille & Minnie
149 West 117 Street, N.Y. GR. Floor, W,
Saturday Evening, Nov. 2nd 1929

Furniture was cleaned out, chairs borrowed from a local funeral parlor, and voilà. The lights were turned down low, with a red or blue bulb added for atmosphere. A pickup band of out-of-work musicians was usually available, and a spread of Southern fare was set out. Items such as pigs' feet, Hoppin' John, ham hocks and cabbage, okra gumbo, sweet potato pone, and the tomato-infused rice that is called "mulatto rice" in Savannah might be served along with the ever-present fried chicken. Soon, someone was guaranteed to start singing, and a good time was had by all. A nominal fee was charged, and if the tenant was lucky, at evening's end there would be enough in the till to pay the rent for another month. Harlem Renaissance poet and writer Langston Hughes recalled:

The Saturday Night rent parties that I attended were often more amusing than any night club, in small apartments where God knows who lived—because the guests seldom did—but where the piano would often be augmented by a guitar, or an odd coronet, or somebody with a pair of drums walking in off the street. And where awful bootleg whiskey and good fried fish or steaming chitterlings were sold at very low prices. And the dancing and singing and impromptu entertaining went on until dawn came in at the windows.

The rent parties were another side of the entrepreneurial impulse. Some grew into regular events and even grew into mini clubs and clandestine temporary restaurants.

Harlem, like much of the African American world of the time, also had its class divide. While the mass of people worked daily at small jobs and menial tasks as domestics and laborers, there were also those exceptional people who had growing power, prestige, and wealth. The black political views of how the African American community little more than fifty years from enslavement would grow and prosper were divided between the ideas of two men: W. E. B. Du Bois and Booker T. Washington.

A seminal figure of the period, Du Bois was a Northerner who grew up in Massachusetts. He was educated at Fisk University, one of the historically black institutions of higher learning that had sprung up in the South post-Emancipation. Later, he became the first black man to be awarded a Harvard doctorate and also pursued graduate study in Germany. Du Bois argued that the "Talented Tenth," the educationally and socially advantaged 10 percent of the Community, would rise and "pull all that are worthy of saving up to their vantage ground" and held that a liberal arts education for that segment of the population was the key to African American success.

At the opposite cultural pole of the black world was Booker T. Washington, the other great black statesman of the period. His work provided contrast to that of Du Bois, as did his life. Washington had been born enslaved in Hale's Ford, Virginia, and received his freedom as a result of the Civil War. The differences in their birth defined the differences in their philosophical positions. Washington felt that agricultural and technical education would give blacks the tools with which to seek jobs in the workforce and that economic acceptance would lead to eventual social acceptance. In this, Washington espoused the growth of institutions such as Hampton Institute (founded in 1868 as Hampton Normal and Agricultural Institute) and Tuskegee Institute (founded in 1881 as Tuskegee Normal and Technical Institute) where students were taught trades. Washington was the president of Tuskegee Institute, the home school of the multitalented scientist George Washington Carver, whose research established myriad uses for several traditional African American foodstuffs, such as peanuts and sweet potatoes. Tuskegee did not offer the liberal arts curriculum espoused by Du Bois, but rather had courses of study leading to a bachelor of science degree in home economics, mechanical industries, physical education, agriculture, commercial dietetics, and education, as well as certificated courses in nurse training and special trade courses. As Washington put it, "we shall prosper in proportion as we learn to dignify and glorify labor and put brains and skill into the common occupations of life."

The debate between Du Bois and Washington defined the class divisions between the citizens of all the new black neighborhoods springing up across the country. At the top of the social spectrum sat Du Bois's Talented Tenth: educated, cultured, adept in European mores, and often disdainful of the uneducated masses who represented the other ninetieth percent of black society. They too entertained, but not at rent parties; they socialized at teas and debutante balls, soirées, literary talks, luncheons, and cocktail parties. Their foods, like their social style, emulated that of Europe, though they might enjoy fried chicken on occasion, as did Du Bois. They had no need of rent parties, and the pungent funk of boiling chitterlings or ribbon maws would never poison the air of their well-appointed abodes. Harlem Renaissance writer Dorothy West described the fare at one of the cocktail parties of the elite: "Cocktails, little sausages on toothpicks, black and green olives, cheeses with crisp little crackers, two-inch sandwiches, went in continuous file around the room."

There were few who crossed the great class divide. In Harlem, however, A'lelia Walker was neither patrician nor proletarian. In the community of artists and writers who created the Harlem Renaissance, she stood out. The daughter of Madame C. J. Walker, the first female black millionaire, who had made her fortune from hair products, A'lelia inherited her mother's sizable fortune and became the Harlem "hostess with the mostest." She entertained a Harlem high society that she virtually created, inviting blacks and whites, artists, gangsters, and businesspeople into her home. Her Harlem gatherings became legendary. She understood the culinary and cultural class divisions and the insidiousness of Harlem slumming. At one gathering, she is alleged to have fed her white guests pigs' feet, chitterlings, and bathtub gin and her black ones caviar, pheasant, and champagne.

Dubbed the "Mahogany Millionairess," Walker gloried in her

money and spent it lavishly. In a fit of entrepreneurial zeal, she had a floor of her Harlem brownstone designed as a club and a meeting place for artists and those who followed them. She named it the "Dark Tower," after the column in *Opportunity* magazine written by Countee Cullen, one of the Harlem Renaissance's leading lights. She ran the salon in the grand manner, but she began to charge her guests: fifteen cents to check a hat, a dime for a cup of coffee, and a quarter for lemonade. Sandwiches went for fifty cents. Those who had attended her grand soirées and dined lavishly at her expense were not willing to pay for her hospitality. She had misjudged her friends and the venture was not a success.

As the good times of the twenties faded into the dismal days of the Great Depression, Walker's fortune diminished, and she had to sell Villa Lewaro, her huge estate outside the city in Irvington, New York. However, she continued to dine well. Champagne was her signature drink, and she quaffed it until the end. In 1931, as the Harlem Renaissance waned, the woman that poet Langston Hughes had referred to as the "joy goddess of Harlem's 1920's" died at the age of forty-six following a dinner of lobster, chocolate cake, and champagne. Her death signaled the end of an era and the incipient end of the glory days of Harlem.

Prohibition lasted until 1933, but the gilded age of Harlem ended with the stock market crash of 1929. The Great Depression changed Harlem; the days of rent parties, cabarets, and clubs were gone, replaced by job losses and even harder economic struggles for the already strapped Harlem residents and for all those throughout the country. Blacks, who were in many cases only a generation or two from enslavement, knew that when the economy went bad in the United States, African Americans were the first to feel its tightening grip. By 1934, the jobless rate among black American men was at 40 percent in Chicago and 48 percent in Harlem. In the South it was worse, with 80 percent of black workers applying for public assistance. The tenuous footholds that had been gained in the boom years were rapidly eroded, and workers found themselves competing with newly unemployed whites for jobs previously considered "negro jobs." It was time for prayer and reorganization.

If the Harlem of the 1920s placed its emphasis on the Saturday-night rent parties and celebrations of the secular world, the Harlem of the 1930s turned to the church. Just as the churches north and south had been prime movers in the migration northward for so many, in the bad times of the deepening Depression they offered blacks north and south a way to band together. During these hard times, many former Saturday-night sinners joined the ranks of the Sunday saints. There were many denominations to choose from: African Methodist Episcopal, African Methodist Episcopal Zion, Christian Methodist Episcopal, National Baptist Convention Incorporated, National Baptist Convention of America Unincorporated, Progressive National Baptist Convention, and the Church of God in Christ, as well as smaller localized groups. One of the most important institutions of the 1930s, though, was outside the usual Christian denominations: Father Divine's Peace Mission movement. It was founded by a charismatic leader, used food and feasting as a focal point of worship, and insisted on self-help and entrepreneurship. It was a perfect faith for its era.

Father Major Jealous Divine was born somewhere in the South around 1876. His early life is unrecorded and shrouded in mystery and confusion; he traveled as an itinerant preacher in the South and the West. He began to come to national attention when he established himself in the Bedford Stuyvesant area of Brooklyn around 1914 with a few of his disciples and opened his apartments to the nonaffiliated for meetings and meals. These banquets were lavish and free. He also provided shelter to any who asked and respected his doctrines at low cost or for an extremely nominal fee. He preached a doctrine of sobriety and hard work, honesty, racial equality, and sexual abstinence. By 1919, Divine had moved to Sayville, Long Island, and recruited more members, some of them black servants of wealthy white families and some whites as well. Major Divine became Father Divine, self-proclaimed god. His flock grew, and people traveled to hear him speak and to hear his notions of racial equality. (His second wife, Sister Penny, was white.) Though they came by the hundreds to hear his speeches, in the depths of the Depression, many came to participate in the sharing of food at the banquets, which became one of the defining practices of the religion. Sara Harris, a former social worker who wrote about Father Divine in the 1950s, recalled attending one of the banquets in the 1970 re-issue of her work *Father Divine*:

> The food was brought in by a team of black, and white, waitresses in crisply starched uniforms practically before I'd been seated. What a fantastic feast it was: fricasseed chicken, roast duck, boiled beef, spareribs, fried sausage, lamb stew, liver and bacon, stewed tomatoes, spinach, brussels sprouts, string beans, asparagus tips, fruit salad, ice cream, and chocolate cake.
>
> Next to me a young black girl named Miss Love Dove, a high ranking secretary, told me that people paid what they wished for the sumptuous feast, and that those who couldn't afford to pay ate free.

The food at the banquets was passed down from the head table, where Divine sat, in such a way that the platter should not touch the table, lest the chain of blessings that flowed from Divine be broken. The food served ranged from traditional Southern fare to more-Europeanized items, like asparagus tips and brussels sprouts, in keeping with the mixed origins of the worshippers. While the faithful were eating, Divine spoke, preaching sermons that lasted for more than an hour and stressed positive visualization and the other virtues of his faith.

By 1931, his popularity had grown so much that some of his banquets drew as many as three thousand attendees. His doctrine of economic stewardship was a balm to the ears of blacks at the beginning of the Depression. The residents of Sayville did not approve of their neighbor, and he was brought up on charges of disturbing the peace and sentenced to a brief prison stay. The publicity, however, only increased Divine's popularity, and his Peace Mission movement grew. Upon his release from prison, Father Divine moved to Harlem, where he began to acquire property: real estate and housing projects, called "heavens," where members could live inexpensively and search for jobs, often within the cash-only businesses that Divine developed. The followers, called "angels," were given new names as well: Miss Beautiful Child, Miss Buncha Love, Miss Universal Vocabulary, Miss Moonbeam, Mr. Humility, John Devout, and the like.

Charismatic Father Divine was a holy entrepreneur, and the thousands of members of his international flock, both black and white, worked to create his financial empire. In return, Father Divine provided income and shelter for his disciples and his message of racial and economic equality helped many blacks (and whites) weather the days of the Depression. Among the many businesses that Divine acquired were hotels and restaurants, and all were run according to his principles—small bands of cooperatives came together to purchase and run businesses for the Peace Mission. As Harris states it:

> Divine restaurant owners want no return from the capital investments Father Divine has "blessed them to make." They don't want to earn from their restaurants any more than exactly what they absolutely need to live on . . . Divine restaurant owners are more than satisfied. Fifteen dollars provides them with board and lodging in approved hotels and kingdoms and with pocket money for approved outside expenses.

Father Divine's restaurants, like all of Father Divine's businesses, were housed in Father Divine–owned buildings and paid for in cash. Father Divine felt that "if you pay a million dollars for a hotel or ten cents for an item in F.W. Woolworth and Company, you must pay cash." There were additional savings, as the ingredients for the restaurants came from Father Divine's farms or stores operating for the good of the cause, and the waitstaff and kitchen help were Divine's followers with minimal needs and wants who could be paid minimal wages. It was a masterful plan wherein little was necessary that was not provided by Father Divine's organization.

It worked well. Father Divine's following, though, began to ebb with the restarting of the economy. When Divine died, in 1965, his holdings were estimated at ten million dollars. Food remained an integral part of his ministry, and his Peace Mission was known up until the time of his death as a place where one could obtain a home-style meal featuring many traditional African American dishes for little money or for the simple utterance of the phrase "Peace, it's truly wonderful!" that became Divine's hallmark. Divine's second wife continued the mission into the twenty-first century.

The Depression slowly lifted its veil of misery as the nation pulled out of its slump and prepared to again go to war. The "War to End All Wars" had not done its job. Europe was again sinking into disunity and dissension, and soon the United States was drawn into another global conflict. This time, African Americans, further from enslavement than they had been on the eve of World War I, were determined to play their part in the country's war effort and determined to do so with full equality. The armed forces thought otherwise; they were still segregated. African Americans who enlisted in great numbers were once again relegated to menial tasks in the services. They provided backup to the fighting troops and generally worked in cleanup and in food service. Low-level jobs were typical, but there were incidents of great valor even from those who were not allowed to take full part in the war effort.

One individual who displayed such valor was Dorrie Miller, who worked in the mess hall on the USS *Arizona* when the bomb was dropped at Pearl Harbor. Despite never having been given any instruction in the use of antiaircraft guns, he manned one and brought down two enemy planes before being wounded. His reward from the U.S. government was a medal. He was then returned to his job in the ship's mess without a promotion. There were few other places for him to work in the white man's army. The Tuskegee Airmen were notable exceptions, but even they usually accompanied bombing missions; they did not fly them! The return from the war was, for many former fighting men, the last straw. They who had witnessed the relatively biasless life in Europe were determined that their efforts for equality be acknowledged. As the voice of the period, Langston Hughes, put it,

> the Negro soldier had been to many lands, seen many peoples, and been treated with a dignity and sensibility, even by his foes, that was alien to him in his own country. The die cast, he could never return in spirit to racial complacency in America, and certainly not to the old days of Uncle Tom . . . In fact, Uncle Tom was probably slain in Normandy, at Anzio or Iwo Jima, never to be resurrected again by the army of brave young black men returning to America with a new sense of freedom and purpose.

If Uncle Tom died at Anzio, Aunt Jemima was killed off in the home front war plants. As one woman put it, "it took Hitler to get me out of Miss Anne's kitchen." Black women also participated in the war effort as nurses and ambulance drivers. On the home front, they raised "victory gardens," went without nylon stockings for the war effort, saved tinfoil, and became gold-star mothers when their offspring were killed in the conflict. Most important, they who had a long history of working outside the home went to work in the factories in unprecedented numbers. At war's end, they too did not want to return to the subservient domestic roles that they had previously played in the life of the nation; they joined the returning veterans in a push for greater Civil Rights and access to the American dream in full.

As World War I had paved the way for the northern migrations and the growth of black wealth in the North, World War II paved the way for the final push for Civil Rights legislation. The period in between had been a proving ground in which migrating African Americans amply demonstrated both resourcefulness and resilience and an ability to survive. For patrician and pauper, the period showed how, with entrepreneurial strength and hard work, African Americans' culinary abilities continued to provide a springboard to financial success and community growth. It was a paradigm that worked for the educated as well as the unschooled migrant. This culinary entrepreneurship came at a time of increasing internationalism on the tables of the African American community, as people from the Caribbean and Latin America mingled with those up from the South on the streets and in markets and restaurants. Returning veterans male and female had been seated at the restaurants and cafes of Europe and knew that it was time for them to sit down at the country's tables and lunch counters as equals at home. They became the force behind the tidal wave of change that fueled the Civil Rights movement of the 1950s.

❖❖❖❖❖❖

GETTING THE WORD OUT:
LENA RICHARD AND
FREDA DEKNIGHT

Food was becoming a science in the country during the period of the Great Migration. Francis Merritt Farmer published the *Boston Cooking School Cookbook* in 1896, standardizing measurements and transforming the way America cooked. Home economics became a growing field of endeavor. Historically black schools that had placed the emphasis on the agricultural and the technical, like Hampton University, Tuskegee University, and Bethune-Cookman University (founded in 1905 as the Daytona Educational and Industrial Training School for Negro Girls), offered curricula centered on the practical. Those in the food-related courses of study learned cooking and proper service—courses designed to train them for jobs as domestics and in service jobs on the railroads and in hotels and restaurants.

Between 1936 and the end of the 1940s, Tuskegee even published a journal devoted to African Americans in the food and hospitality trades titled *Service*. The cover of the first issue, published in August

1936, features a triptych of photographs of blacks working as waiters, porters, and cooks with an inset photograph of Booker T. Washington, the president of Tuskegee and the thinker who espoused a doctrine of teaching technical skills as a way of empowerment. Articles include "The Importance of Salads" and extol the "Virtues of Efficiency," while sections titled "Table Talks," "Cock of the Walk," "Front!" and "All Aboard!" feature items of special interest to waiters, cooks, bellmen, and porters, respectively. Issues of *Service* detail the varied and wide-ranging universe that the world of African American food had become. They include recipes for banana doughnuts and Brazil nut sundaes and offer a glimpse of a larger world through articles on travel to Argentina and the Bahamas. But interspersed among the glowing mentions of progress and success are topical pieces like the one detailing the foods for the war effort grown by "Negro farmers" and a 1942 piece titled "The Klan Rides." *Service* was focused at blacks in the hotel, restaurant, and cafeteria businesses, and the journal got the word out: Its circulation reached all of the South as well as the District of Columbia and beyond, to New Jersey, New York, Illinois, Michigan, Ohio, Pennsylvania, Connecticut, and Massachusetts, where the Great Migration had taken African Americans.

The title of Tuskegee's journal coupled with its wide circulation remind that, as they had in the past, large numbers of black men and women turned to food and food service as a way of paying the bills. The articles within equally remind that, outside the world of black institutions or work in the service industries (railroads, food-processing plants, hotel and waitstaff work), there were few job opportunities other than working in domestic service for white families. Increasingly, though, a growing number of black domestic scientists and home economists began to expand the horizons and get the word about African American cooking to the black public and the world at large. Two women who were pioneers in this were Lena Richard and Freda DeKnight.

Lena Richard of New Orleans, like so many others of her time, began work as a domestic. Born Lena Paul in New Roads, Louisiana, in 1892, she moved to New Orleans at an early age. By fourteen she was being paid to help her mother and her aunt do domestic work and cook in an Esplanade Avenue mansion in that city. By the time she'd finished school she was hired by the Vairin family, who so valued her culinary talents that they sent her to perfect her skills at a local cooking school and then at the Fannie Farmer Cooking School in Boston. She graduated in 1918, but discovered that her culinary gifts were unique. She recalled "I found out in a hurry they can't teach me more than I know . . . When it comes to cooking meats, stews, soups, sauces, and such dishes we Southern cooks have Northern cooks beat by a mile." Richard gradually used her expertise and by 1920 was catering from her home. By 1937, she had opened a cooking school, small gumbo shops, and a catering business. She privately published a cookbook in 1938 and promoted it around the city. In 1939, she was enough of a celebrity to publish *Lena Richard's Cook Book* locally in New Orleans. Mentions in the press by such notables as Clementine Paddleford of the *New York Herald Tribune* and James Beard created a large audience for the work and it was published internationally in 1940 as *The New Orleans Cook Book*, the first work on the cuisine of the Crescent City to be published by an African American. Richard was also an innovative marketer and sold her book wherever she cooked as well as at New Orleans department stores. She also sold her book through an agreement with Father Divine who, after meeting Mrs. Richard, promoted it to his followers, making it available to them for two dollars, or one third of the list price.

As a caterer, Richard cooked mainly for whites; indeed, the first edition of her work is dedicated to Alice Baldwin Vairin, the woman for whom she initially worked as a domestic. However, along with dishes like ground artichoke mousse and lobster salad, Richard also included dishes from a more traditional African American culinary lexicon: banana fritters, fried chicken (albeit creole style), and cornbread, as well as a significant number of dishes that are uniquely Louisiana creole such as *daube glacé*, pralines, and baked mirlitons. Mrs. Richard's culinary renown grew and she was invited to cook outside of New Orleans, at the Bird and Bottle Inn in Garrison, New York, and in Colonial Williamsburg, Virginia. The expeditions proved successful, but she always returned to her home city.

There, in 1947, she became the first African American woman to have her own television show. She did this in the segregated South at a time when a television set was still not common currency in the homes of most whites. Almost twenty years before Julia Child used television to transform the way Americans thought about food, Richard in New Orleans was using the new medium of television to get the word out about herself and about African American food.

If Richard was an African American culinary entrepreneur with a growing national presence, Freda DeKnight became the national, if not international, face of African American food when John Johnson appointed her as the first food editor of *Ebony* magazine in 1946, shortly after the magazine's establishment. Johnson recognized that knowledge of proper nutrition was a necessary part of the growing world of possibility for African Americans, and DeKnight fit the bill.

Unlike many in the first half of the twentieth century, DeKnight did not come to matters culinary from domestic work. She was born in Topeka, Kansas, and had a peripatetic childhood, attending convent school in South Dakota and high school in St. Paul, Minnesota. She was trained in home economics, had a twenty-year career as a caterer in New York City, and for a time jointly operated a Harlem restaurant known as the Chicken Coop with African American actor Canada Lee.

As *Ebony*'s first food editor, the Kansas native became the magazine's culinary ambassador, speaking to the public both black and white and doing cooking demonstrations around the country. At *Ebony*, DeKnight was also instrumental in setting up what was the first Home Services Department at any African American publication. She described this in an early memo:

> We have an efficient Test Kitchen in our Home Office where recipes and products are tested and new ideas are originated for advertisers, a service we are very proud of . . .
>
> We also publish "Food Hints," which is a monthly release reaching over 75,000 women all over the country and as far away as South Africa. It consists of helpful menus, tips on plentiful foods and household equipment, and had proven to be one of the most popular features of the Home Services Department.

Advertisers sought DeKnight's endorsements for products; her columns, recipes, and photograph appeared in the magazine; she spoke at colleges and high schools both black and white, and did hundreds of cooking demonstrations around the country. She authored numerous pamphlets of cooking hints and recipes for such diverse *Ebony* clients as Carnation Evaporated Milk and the Golden State Insurance Company. Perhaps her most lasting legacy is her cookbook *A Date with a Dish*, published in 1948, which showcases some of the recipes that she had collected and created for *Ebony*. It is still in print in an updated version, *The Ebony Cookbook*, fixing the cooking of the mid-twentieth century for generations yet to come.

The careers of both Lena Richard and Freda DeKnight heralded a new age of African Americans in food, one in which blacks professionally trained in food preparation and the domestic sciences used developing media outlets like *Ebony* magazine and new technology like television to create national and international reputations and teach the world about the growing scope and diversity of African American food.

CHAPTER 9

WE SHALL NOT
BE MOVED

Sit-ins, Soul Food, and Increasing
Culinary Diversity

Atlanta, Georgia—

The capital of the New South had held little attraction for me. My first trip there was a humiliating quest for an errant boyfriend that ended with tears, a breakup, and a two-day hangover; it was my first trip to the South. The only good thing about that trip more than thirty-five years ago is that it allowed me to see "Sweet" Auburn Avenue before it became "gentrified." Somehow, I knew enough to take time out from my fruitless mission to sample some of the legendary fried chicken at the old Paschal's restaurant. Paschal's is one of the restaurants where Martin Luther King and his disciples planned some of their Civil Rights strategy. Even in that bad time for me, as I sat in the restaurant, I wondered which booth Dr. King had occupied and what his favorite dishes had been. I was told that the fried chicken figured largely on the menu at those meetings.

It seems that every Southern city has a similar restaurant in the former black part of town. During the Civil Rights Movement, it was the place that became the hub where people from the movement met and planned their strategy. Birmingham has one, as do Memphis, Mobile, and Montgomery. New Orleans has Dooky Chase, and Atlanta has Paschal's and also had Deacon's, although it, like many others, did not survive. Back in the day, they all had similar finished-basement-type decor, with red vinyl booths and knotty-pine paneling on the walls. They also had homey waitresses who cajoled diners into eating more than was good for them and wore nylon uniforms that fitted tightly across ample bosoms, often with a highly starched handkerchief perched like a corsage on one side. The menus all harked back to the comfort food of the South: Pig was the preeminent meat, and the pungent aroma of chitterlings often perfumed the kitchen. Pigs' feet were also offered, and great delight was taken in sucking the hot-sauce-dotted meat off the bones. Pork chops were cooked to a solid well-done and smothered with thick brown gravy. Side dishes included tender candied yams (yes, they were sweet potatoes), dripping with sugar and cinnamon in every bite. There were always greens—be they collards, turnips, or mustards or a mix of all three—handpicked over and freshly cooked. They were served with smoked pig or, in later years, a smoked turkey wing. Okra figured significantly on most menus, turning up in gumbo or served as stewed okra in a mix of tomato and onion or as Southern succotash with corn and tomatoes. For dessert, there was an array of the teeth-achingly sweet confections that had become hallmarks of African American food: bubbling cobblers filled with seasonal fruit, bread puddings, rice puddings with and without raisins, fluffy coconut cakes, densely rich pound cakes, yellow cakes with chocolate frosting, and more (though red velvet cake had not become ubiquitous at this point). Then there were the pies—flaky crusts made with lard topped by or under-pinned with freshly made fillings: sweet potato pie, syrupy pecan pie, and nutmeg-scented apple pie. There was always rice in the kitchen to put under the rich cream gravy that accompanied the fried chicken, and the bread basket boasted fluffy squares of hot corn-bread and often hot biscuits. These places were also open for break-fast, and those fortunate enough to greet the day in them ate biscuits and syrup: karo, cane, or sorghum, and only occasionally maple. There were eggs aplenty done to order, sausage patties (not links), and South or North there were grits.

Some restaurants, like Atlanta's Deacon's and New York's Cope-land's, did not survive the late-twentieth-century changes in Afri-can American dietary and dining habits and the gentrification of their neighborhoods that later years would bring. Others, like Chi-cago's Army and Lou's, seem preserved in the amber of their times. Paschal's, though, had, like Atlanta, grown and prospered since my first visit. A recent trip to the city that I have come to understand and enjoy led me to stay in the hotel-restaurant complex that Pas-chal's has become. The rooms were motel minimalist, but the res-taurant was trendy, popular, and the poster child for the New Atlanta: it displayed all the possibilities that exist there for those with gumption and nerve.

Paschal's and other places like it, South and North, were pivot points of history: places where black entrepreneurship met up with the growing national movement for Civil Rights for African Ameri-cans. They were hubs in vibrant African American communities.

In the North, they were refuges for homesick expatriate black Southerners, places where those who had ridden the trains and walked the roads northward in search of better opportunities could gather and indulge their physical and psychic need for the food of their remembered Southern pasts. In the South, the restaurants were places where African Americans knew that they would be welcomed in the days when welcome was most assuredly not offered by white establishments. In the 1950s and 1960s they became gathering places for dissent—places where the next chapter in the African American quest for full equality would be strategized and plotted, organized and launched. It is somehow fitting that so much of the organization of the Civil Rights Movement took place around tables in home kitchens and restaurants like Paschal's and others. After all, during the 350-year-plus history of African Americans in this country, we were relegated to the kitchen and kept in actual or metaphorical servitude. The food that flourished in these restaurants during the 1960s and 1970s came to be known as soul food because it fed the spirit as much as the body on the long march to institutionalized equality.

◆ ◆ ◆ ◆ ◆

The die was cast when President Truman desegregated the U.S. Armed Forces in 1948, shortly after the end of World War II. The postwar era in the United States was one of unprecedented optimism and growth for the middle classes. Returning soldiers could take advantage of the G.I. Bill and get a subsidized education. Homes were being built in new suburbs and people were moving out from the cities. Affluence was all around. Supermarkets sprouted across the country; the aisles were filled with new products to go into the shiny refrigerators and freezers that many now acquired. Men got out their Hawaiian shirts and their aprons and headed to their newly acquired backyards to light up barbecue grills and indulge in another national fad. "Quick" and "convenient" were the watchwords of the day for the myriad American women who had gone into the job market to help the war effort and who did not return to their former role as tenders of home and hearth at its end. Products like Minute Rice, fish sticks, Lipton onion soup mix, and Betty Crocker and Pillsbury cake mixes proliferated on the shelves. Those who had seen the war in Japan and Italy, France and the South Pacific, had also experienced different foods, and the national taste profile expanded. Hope seemed to be a glowing beacon on the horizon for many Americans, but not for African Americans.

For African American soldiers returning from the war, life was different. Some certainly were able to take advantage of the benefits the war had brought, but there was also a renewed sense of the urgent need for full equality. After all, they'd bandaged the wounded, fed the forces, helped on the home front in the armament factories and the naval yards; they'd done all the dirty work. The glorious Tuskegee Airmen had even guided American bombers to their destinations, never losing a plane. It was time for the country that had ignored or neglected them for generations to step up and finally make things equal. Returning black soldiers arrived home with a different attitude toward the second-class citizenship that had been their lot. Different racial attitudes in Europe had also confirmed that the American way of life was not the only way. There was a better way to be, and it was time for the United States to understand that. African American soldiers were not coming home from the fronts to be shut out of the American dream once again.

Returning African American soldiers came back to a South that was rigidly segregated: education, housing, public accommodations, and dining were strictly delineated according to color. Jim Crow laws still affected Southern voters, making the disenfranchisement complete. In the North, an increasingly affluent white middle-class population moved to the newly constructed suburbs. They left the Northern blacks—who had moved to the urban centers in search of jobs that were declining in a postwar economy—relegated to living in inner-city neighborhoods that were slumping into deterioration. Then, in 1954, the Supreme Court decision in the case of *Brown v. the Board of Education of Topeka* began a series of legal decisions that eradicated the Jim Crow laws and brought the possibility of full equality closer to reality. It declared, "We conclude that in the field of public education the doctrine of 'separate but equal' has no place. Separate educational facilities are inherently unequal." The decision, followed in 1955 by another referred to as *Brown II,* mandated that the dismantling of the unequal school systems should begin with "all deliberate speed." Change was about to come to America.

After an initial brief period of calm, during which it looked as though the process might be attained through legislative means, the decisions were met with massive resistance on the part of white Southern hard-liners, who were more than willing to fight to maintain the "Southern way of life." The lynching of Emmett Till in 1955 defined in the minds of many African Americans north and south just what the "Southern way of life" had been for blacks for more than 350 years. The press for equality escalated. The Montgomery bus boycott brought Rosa Parks immortality and Martin Luther King Jr. fame and set the stage for and defined future protests. The increasing protests depended on highly organized black communities with capable and committed leaders. They were well orchestrated to not only attain small goals but also focus national attention on the South and on the need for racial equality in the country. Activists used a network of black churches. They also met at local black restaurants, like Atlanta's Paschal's and New Orleans's Dooky Chase, and in private homes, where they gathered around kitchen tables to strategize over platters of the traditional foods of the African American South—like fried chicken, collard greens, and macaroni and cheese—as they planned their campaigns.

The Southern Christian Leadership Conference (SCLC), a loose confederation of churches, community organizations, and civil rights groups, was formed, and it started to gain prominence and the support of liberal whites north and south. Soon it began to challenge the power of the National Association for the Advancement of Colored People (NAACP), the traditional black leadership organization, which had been instrumental in the passing of the historic *Brown* decisions in 1954. SCLC advanced the movement, but most important, SCLC began to train student activists on black college campuses in the South who provided the next wave of protest. This wave did not start at the kitchen tables or the black restaurants where King and his followers had planned the Montgomery bus boycott. Rather, it started at the lunch counter of a five-and-dime store, where the menu ran to hamburgers and grilled cheese or chicken salad sandwiches.

This phase of the fight for equality began in Greensboro, North

Carolina, on February 1, 1960, when Ezell Blair Jr., Franklin McCain, Joseph McNeil, and David Richmond, freshmen from North Carolina's Agricultural and Technical College (A&T), sat down at a Woolworth's lunch counter at four thirty in the afternoon, requested service, and launched the sit-in movement that would become the tocsin tolling the death knell of the segregated South. The rules of social behavior in the segregated South were complex. Blacks were able to shop in the store and indeed had worked behind the lunch counter serving food; however, they were not able to sit down to eat at the establishment. That was about to change that afternoon when the four young men took their places and simply waited for service while doing their schoolwork. They were not served, although they waited until the shop's closing. The next day, others joined them: students from Bennett College, a black all-girls' school in Greensboro, as well as some whites from the University of North Carolina's Women's College. Although the four had begun their campaign without a mandate from any of the larger Civil Rights or community organizations, their protest quickly galvanized the area, and by the fifth day, there were hundreds of students crowded into the downtown shops, peacefully demanding their rights. The sit-ins galvanized the country, demonstrations were staged in more than one hundred cities in the South and the North, and the lunch counter rapidly became a national symbol of the South's inequalities.

The images of the well-dressed college students quietly sitting and the humiliations that they suffered as they remained impassive and dignified transformed the country, and the campaign soon spread nationwide. Blacks and whites in the North and West picketed large chains that had segregated facilities in the South, while in the South sit-ins spread rapidly to Nashville and Atlanta, where the campaign was broadened to include the desegregation of all public facilities as well as equal access to education and employment. The Greensboro protests ultimately resulted in the desegregation of that city's lunch counters. In Nashville, major restaurants desegregated by May 1960, and the Atlanta protests resulted in the capitulation of the local business and political community in September 1961.

Although many of the leaders of the developing protest movement had been trained in passive resistance by traditional organizations like the NAACP and the SCLC, some younger activists feared that the momentum of the movement would fade. They called for continued nonviolent action but also acknowledged that more militancy might be required. A conference was called from April 15 to 17, 1960, to keep the protests moving forward. Addressing delegates who came from thirteen states and more than fifty different high schools and colleges, Ella Baker, a Shaw University student and an SCLC organizer, reminded them that it was about "more than a Hamburger"—an aptly culinary image for a movement that began with four young college students deciding to sit in for their lunch and their rights. The culture-changing protest was not about the mainstream food that was served at the lunch counters: the sixty-five-cent roast turkey, fifty-cent ham and cheese sandwich, or even about America's totemic apple pie, offered for fifteen cents. It was simply about equality. The sit-ins drew the curtain back from the country's dirty little secret and showed the inequality of American life to the world. Anyone alive during that era can vividly remember the images of the clean-cut young students, the unbridled furor of those who opposed them, and the victory the students won. Food became metaphor for society.

The Civil Rights organizations brought the movement to the daily consciousness of a nation, and gains were won. But it took the Freedom Riders; more boycotts; the murder of Medgar Evers in Jackson, Mississippi; a march on Washington, D.C.; the bombing of four little girls in a Birmingham church; the assassination of President John F. Kennedy; and countless other acts of violence before the Civil Rights Act of 1964 was passed. The act banned discrimination in places of public accommodation, including restaurants, hotels, gas stations, and entertainment facilities, as well as schools, parks, playgrounds, libraries, and swimming pools. The 1964 act, unlike some that had preceded it, had potential for enforcement, since it mandated that government funds could be withheld from any program that did not comply. It created the Equal Employment Opportunity Commission to ensure that there was no longer discrimination in the country based on race, or on color, gender, religion, or country of national origin. The yoke had been lifted, but the battle for full equality was not over by any means.

The Civil Rights Movement in the United States in the 1960s was a crucial turning point in the history of African Americans and food: It not only emphasized the importance that food had held within the African American context but also placed the important role that African Americans played in the food of the country front and center. In a memorable photograph of the second day of the Greensboro sit-in, the four young men, Blair, McCain, McNeil, and Richmond, sit at the counter. On the other side of the counter is a server, an African American who seems more than abashed to be placed in such a position. The menu offerings posted on the walls are the simple fast food of a prior generation: sandwiches, plate lunches, and sweet desserts, culinarily nothing worth fighting for. The story is a complex one, unlocking a history of racial interaction in the country. While many Southern whites were content with being served by African Americans who held the job of restaurant cook, home domestic, or lunch counterman, they were not prepared to share their space at the counter or the table with those from whose hands they were served daily. The inherent absurdity of the racial contradiction that for centuries was emblematic of the South resonates in that photo capturing the era's transforming moment.

While the sit-ins were being held in the South, planning activities for civil disobedience around the country took African Americans and their food to a wider audience. Kitchen tables and black restaurants had become, along with churches of all denominations, traditional planning places for the movement. At them, white liberals from the North, who'd traveled to the South for sit-ins and later for Freedom Rides and voter registration and protest marches, got what for many was their first taste of the savory, well-seasoned traditional African American menu. When they returned home, they ventured into black neighborhoods in search of restaurants serving the same dishes and contributed to the mainstream awareness of the traditional black diet. The popularizing of African American traditional foods went hand in hand with a growing pride in race and in self in the African American community.

For the younger generation, the Civil Rights Movement morphed into the Black Power movement, and there was a growing pride in things black and in the culture that had survived enslavement. It went hand in hand with a hunger to learn more about the black experience and a national feeling of solidarity among blacks. In the early 1960s this pride manifested itself in what could be termed a "soul" movement. Much ink has flowed on the origins of the word "soul" as it applies to the African American experience in the United States, and more will almost certainly flow, but the 1960s created a place where for the first time in many lives there was a palpable pride in the uniqueness of the African American experience in the United States. The word "soul" was at first used among blacks to establish a cultural community, as in "soul brother" and "soul sister." It was initially used to denote kinship in the struggle, in much the same way as the terms "brother" and "sister" had been honorifics in the black church for generations. However, as with many other African American cultural innovations, the term was rapidly coopted by the mainstream, and soon there were soul combs on the market along with soul T-shirts, soul hairdos, soul handshakes, and certainly soul music. The term "soul food" harks back to this era, when everything that was black and of the moment had soul, and the word's use signaled a change in attitude toward the food of the African American South.

Soul food has been defined as the traditional African American food of the South as it has been served in black homes and restaurants around the country, but there is wide-ranging disagreement on exactly what that food was. Was it solely the food of the plantation South that was fed to the enslaved: a diet of hog and hominy supplemented with whatever could be hunted or foraged or stolen to relieve its monotony? Was it the traditionally less-noble parts of the pig that were fed to the enslaved, like the chitterlings and hog maws and pigs' feet, the taste for which had been carried to the North by those who left the South in search of jobs? Was it the foods that nourished those who danced at rent parties in Harlem and who went to work in the armament factories during World War II? Was it the fried chicken that was served by the waiter-carriers who hawked their wares at train stations in Virginia or the chicken that was packed in boxes and nourished those who migrated to Kansas and other parts of the West? Was it the smothered pork chop that turned up in the African American restaurants covered in rich brown gravy or the fluffy cornbread that accompanied it?

Soul food, it would seem, depends on an ineffable quality. It is a combination of nostalgia for and pride in the food of those who came before. In the manner of the Negro spiritual "How I Got Over," soul food looks back at the past and celebrates a genuine taste palate while offering more than a nod to the history of disenfranchisement of blacks in the United States. In the 1960s, as the history of African Americans began to be rewritten with pride instead of with the shame that had previously accompanied the experience of disenfranchisement and enslavement, soul food was as much an affirmation as a diet. Eating neckbones and chitterlings, turnip greens and fried chicken, became a political statement for many, and African American restaurants that had existed since the early part of the century were increasingly being patronized not only by blacks but also by those in sympathy with the movement. In the North, those who patronized soul food restaurants also included homesick white Southerners as well as the occasional white liberal who wanted a taste of some of the foods from below the Mason-Dixon Line.

As had often been the case in African American society, there was a culinary class divide that must be acknowledged. At one pole were those whose social aspirations led them to eat dishes that emulated the dietary habits of mainstream America and Europe. At the other were those who consumed what was a more traditional African American diet: one that harked back to the slave foods of the South. In the 1960s, soul food based on the slave diet of hog and hominy became a political statement and was embraced by many middle-class blacks who had previously publicly eschewed it as a relic of a slave past. It became popular and even celebrated.

A look at the cookbooks of the period confirms the enormous impact that the term had on the minds and indeed the palates of many. Most African American cookbooks published prior to the 1960s and in the early part of the decade referenced the plantation South or the historic aspect of the recipes with titles like *Plantation Recipes*, *The Melrose Plantation Cookbook* (to which folk artist Clementine Hunter made numerous contributions), and the National Council of Negro Women's *Historical Cookbook of the American Negro*. Others invoked the name of a well-known local cook or caterer, like *Bess Grant's Cook Book*, published in Culver City, California, and Lena Richard's eponymous cookbook, published in New Orleans, Louisiana. The trend continued through the early 1960s, with such works as *His Finest Party Recipes Based on a Lifetime of Successful Catering*, by Frank Bellamy of Roswell, Georgia, and *A Good Heart and a Light Hand: Ruth L. Gaskins' Collection of Traditional Negro Recipes*, published in Annandale, Virginia.

By the late 1960s and early 1970s, soul food had gained a powerful allure, and a tidal wave of cookbooks with "soul food" in the title was unleashed, including Bob Jeffries's *Soul Food Cookbook*, Hattie Rinehart Griffin's *Soul-Food Cookbook*, and Jim Harwood and Ed Callahan's *Soul Food Cookbook*—all published in 1969. The same year also saw the publication of *Princess Pamela's Soul Food Cookbook*, by the owner of an East Village restaurant in New York City that had become a mecca for whites who wanted a taste of "authentic" African American cooking.

If the period of the Civil Rights movement began with traditional African American cookbooks extolling the virtues of greens, macaroni and cheese, neckbones, chitterlings, and fried chicken, it ended with a transformation of the diet of many African Americans. By the end of the decade and throughout the 1970s, brown rice, smoked turkey wings, tahini, and tofu also appeared on urban African American tables as signs of gastronomic protest against the traditional diet and its perceived limitations to health and well-being, both real or imagined. One of the reasons was the resurgence of the Nation of Islam.

The Nation of Islam (NOI) originated in the early part of the twentieth century but came to national prominence in the 1960s under the leadership of Elijah Muhammad, who preached that peaceful confrontation was not the only way. In Chicago, Detroit, and other large urban areas, the Nation of Islam offered an alternative to the Civil Rights Movement's civil disobedience, which many felt was unnecessarily docile. It preached an Afro-centric variation of traditional Islam and provided a family-centered culture in which gender roles were clearly defined. Food always played an important role in the work of the Nation. As early as 1945, the NOI had recognized the need for land ownership and also for economic independence and had purchased 145 acres in Michigan. Two years later, it opened a grocery store, a restaurant, and a bakery in Chicago. One of the major tenets of the religion was the eschewing of the behaviors that had been imposed by whites, who were regarded as "blue-eyed devils." Followers abjured their "slave name," frequently taking an X in its place and adopted a strictly regimented way of life that included giving up eating the traditional foods that were fed to the enslaved in the South.

NOI leader Elijah Muhammad was extremely concerned about the dietary habits of African Americans and in 1967 published a dietary manual for his followers titled *How to Eat to Live*; in 1972 he published another, *How to Eat to Live, Book 2*. As with much about the Nation of Islam, there is considerable contention about Muhammad's ideas and precepts, which are a combination of traditional Islamic proscriptions with an idiosyncratic admixture of prohibitions that seem personally biased. He vehemently opposed the traditional African American diet, or "slave diet," as he called it. Alcohol and tobacco were forbidden to Nation of Islam members and pork, in particular, was anathema. Elijah Muhammad enjoined his followers:

> Do not eat the swine—do not even touch it. Just stop eating the swine flesh and your life will be expanded. Stay off that grandmother's old fashioned corn bread and black-eyed peas, and those quick 15 minute biscuits made with baking powder. Put yeast in your bread and let it sour and rise and then bake it. Eat and drink to live not to die.

Pork is *haram*, or forbidden, to traditional Muslims. Pork, especially the less-noble parts, was also the primary meat fed to enslaved African Americans. Pork in any form was anathema to NOI members, as were collard greens or black-eyed peas seasoned with swine. The refusal of the traditional African American diet of pig and corn was an indictment of its deleterious effects on African American health, but also a backhanded acknowledgment of the cultural resonance that it held for most blacks, albeit one rooted in slavery. Pork had become so emblematic of African American food that the forbidding of it by the Nation of Islam was radical, and the refusal to eat swine immediately differentiated members of the group from many other African Americans as much as the sober dress and bow ties of the men and the hijab-like attire of the women. Forbidding pork made a powerful political statement, but the real culinary hallmark of the Nation was the bean pie—a sweet pie, prepared from the small navy beans that Elijah Muhammad decreed digestible. It was hawked by the dark-suited, bow-tie-wearing followers of the religion along with copies of the Nation's newspaper, *Muhammad Speaks*, spreading the Nation's gospel in both an intellectual and a gustatory manner.

Under Elijah Muhammad's leadership and that of his ministers Malcolm X and Louis Farrakhan, the Nation of Islam grew into a formidable force in the 1960s and 1970s, gaining numerous members around the country.

The mid-1960s were a time of turbulence and trouble on the national and international fronts. The 1963 assassination of President Kennedy opened a Pandora's box. In 1965, Malcolm X was assassinated and the Watts riots occurred. In 1967, Bobby Kennedy was assassinated. In 1968, Martin Luther King was assassinated and riots broke out all over the country. The country's racial transformation occurred in an unprecedented clashing of blacks and whites, as blacks increasingly refused to accept what had for centuries been the status quo. A growing awareness of the history of African Americans and the race pride that was the result of the Civil Rights Movement resulted in a quest for more information about the African American experience and of blacks' links around the world with other communities in struggle.

As a result of the gains of the Civil Rights Movement, there were a small but growing number of black students enrolled at predominantly white institutions around the country. Their increasing numbers, which rose 100 percent between 1950 and 1969, led to the call for black studies, and in 1968, San Francisco State College became the first institution of higher learning in the country to establish a black studies department. The institutionalized study of the history of African Americans went hand in hand with the growth of a cultural nationalism movement that celebrated African American culture in all realms and contributed to an increasing awareness of an African world, as a greater number of African Americans began to have an international approach.

This international approach gained increasing importance as the 1954 *Brown vs. Board of Education* decision not only galvanized those in the United States but also served as a rallying cry to others around the world in countries where people of color were living under colonialism and imperialism. The battles won and the methods used in the United States provided a road map to independence for many. Indeed, many of those who became leaders in the independence movements in the Caribbean and on the African continent had been students in the United States. If the 1960 photograph of four young men sitting at a lunch counter sums up the early part of the Civil Rights Movement, a 1957 photograph of the duchess of Kent dancing with a kente-cloth-clad Kwame Nkrumah at the independence celebrations for Ghana visually codified the opening of the African movement toward independence.

Fights for basic civil rights in the United States paralleled those in the Caribbean and on the African continent, where the battle for autonomy and the ability to govern their own countries continued through the 1960s. The dates of independence for African and Caribbean nations resonate alongside the dates of gains in the march toward full equality for African Americans. The litany of independence days began with the 1957 independence for Ghana, the former British colony along the Gold Coast, and the turbulent 1958 independence of Guinea from France. The year 1960 marked a raft of independences for former French colonies, as Senegal, Ivory Coast, Chad, Gabon, Mali, Madagascar, Niger, Togo, Benin, and Upper Volta hauled down the tricolor and proudly hoisted their own flags. The same year, Nigeria gained independence from Britain. The map was gradually transformed from British imperial pink and French imperial turquoise into a raft of new nations. Africans, Caribbean peoples, and African Americans looked at one another across political divides and cultural contradictions and recognized that an international community was being born.

One of the ways that they all connected across cultural divide was food. As a growing number of cultural nationalists began to travel and visit other countries where people of African descent lived, they brought back recipes for dishes that were added to menus and to festivities. While the Harlem of the 1920s saw street vendors selling plantains and the root vegetables that are traditional in the foods of Africa and the Caribbean, in the intervening years they had largely disappeared from African American markets. By the 1960s, true yams, *eddoes, tania,* and dasheen had been relegated to neighborhoods around the country with predominantly West Indian and African populations—neighborhoods that existed because the 1965 Immigration Act had relaxed quotas, opened the American borders to a wider number of immigrants, and allowed for greater immigration from far-reaching areas of the African world.

The mid-1960s were a time of increasing internationalism and growing awareness of self in the African American community. The creation of the holiday Kwanzaa by cultural nationalist and black studies advocate Ron "Maulana" Karenga in 1966 marked another turning point. Using a traditional East African harvest festival as inspiration, Karenga created a nonreligious seven-day celebration rich in ritual that's designed to uplift and unify African Americans. The year-end holiday is rooted in the *nguzu saba,* or seven principles, Karenga created to extol the virtues of unity, self-determination, collective work and responsibility, cooperative economics, purpose, creativity, and faith. In keeping with its Pan-African inspiration, Kwanzaa uses Swahili (the language of African unity) as its official language. There are no culinary expectations for the holiday, like the Thanksgiving turkey or the Christmas goose, but Kwanzaa's seven nights of ritual make symbolic use of food throughout: ears of Native American corn are placed on Kwanzaa tables to represent the children in each household, and a basket of fruit symbolizing abundance is an integral part of the traditional centerpiece.

The final day of Kwanzaa, which falls on New Year's Day, is given over to the Karamu festival and designed to celebrate African American communities past and present by honoring African American elders and community leaders as well as African and African American ancestors. The day is traditionally capped by a communal meal with people bringing dishes created from family recipes or foods from around the African Diaspora. Karenga's writings do not offer recipes, but dishes such as Kawaida rice, a

vegetable-rich brown rice, became traditional to those who celebrated with him in the holiday's early years. Kwanzaa celebrations
around the country include dishes from the African continent, the
Caribbean region, and even South America, as well as sweet potato
pie, fried chicken, greens, and other traditional specialties of the
African American South.

Increasing numbers of African Americans chose to celebrate
Kwanzaa in the late 1960s and early 1970s as a part of a growing
awareness of their own African roots. The Peace Corps and continuing missionary work by churches black and white sent African
Americans to the African continent, resulting in more widespread
knowledge of the African Diaspora and expanded gastronomic
horizons, and contributed to a growing sense of shared culinary
underpinning. In larger cities and college towns, dishes of West
African *jollof* rice and Ghanaian groundnut stew began to be found
on dinner tables alongside more traditional favorites.

Then, in 1977, the publication of the autobiography of writer
Alex Haley, *Roots*, and the subsequent television miniseries based
on it transformed the way many African Americans thought of
themselves and of Africa. Blacks were galvanized by *Roots*, and
large numbers made pilgrimages to the African continent with
hopes of discovering their own ancestral origins. (Coinciding with
the release of the television miniseries, a travel organization began
to offer trips to Dakar, Senegal, for $299, a price that was afford-
able for many who might otherwise never have traveled to the
continent.) They boarded the planes by the hundreds and on the
other side of the Atlantic found myriad connections between African American culture and that of the motherland. One major connection they discovered was West Africa's food. They visited
markets and recognized items that had for centuries been associated with African American life: okra, watermelon, and black-eyed
peas. They tasted foods that had familiar savors and learned new
ways to prepare staples of the African American diet like peanuts,
hot chilies, and leafy greens. In Senegal, they tasted the onion-
and-lemon-flavored chicken *yassa* and the national rice-and-fish
dish, *thieboudiennse*; in Ghana, they sampled spicy peanut stews;
in Nigeria, they savored a black-eyed pea fritter called an *akara*.
African Americans began to taste the culinary connections between

foods they knew and those of the western section of the African continent.

This new knowledge found its way to a larger public, as the avant garde of African American cookbook authors took a more international approach and reflected a sense of the African Diaspora in their work. *Vibration Cooking: Or, The Travel Notes of a Geechee Girl*, by Verta Mae Smart Grosvenor, and *The African Heritage Cookbook*, by Helen Mendes, look at the traditional foods not just of the American South but also of an international African culinary diaspora and contain recipes for dishes from the African continent and the Caribbean as well as traditional Southern ones.

Africa, its diaspora, and their foods, though, were only a part of the expanding African American culinary paradigm; cookbooks of the period also evidence wider-ranging African American attitudes about what to eat and how to eat, like 1974's *Dick Gregory's Natural Diet for Folks Who Eat: Cookin' with Mother Nature*, by the eponymous comedian, and 1976's *Soul to Soul: A Soul Food Vegetarian Cookbook*, by Mary Keyes Burgess of Santa Barbara, California. The traditional foods of the South were still being written about in works like *Spoonbread and Strawberry Wine: Recipes and Reminiscences of a Family*, by Norma Jean and Carole Darden. Using genealogical research that had been popularized by *Roots* as well as recipe and memoir, the Darden sisters crafted a 1978 cookbook that tells the story of their family through food. It also tells of the diversity of African American food.

Up until the 1970s, the food of African Americans could be loosely categorized by class. The upper classes ate a more European-inspired diet, while the underclass consumed a diet evolved from the slave foods of the plantation South. Regional differences played a lesser role. The South always took primacy of place at the table, but those living in the North and West also had their own dietary habits, like a predilection for potatoes instead of rice or an affinity for beef instead of the more traditional pork.

The 1970s, however, exploded all hypotheses. Certainly many African Americans still clung to the traditional foods of the South. However, after the decades of Civil Rights gains and with the growing awareness of the African continent and its diaspora, increasing numbers of blacks of all classes throughout the nation began eating a diet that was widely varied and reflected a newly discovered pride in African roots and international connections. The African American diet of this era was one that continued to celebrate the traditional foods; it also encompassed the vegetarianism espoused by Dick Gregory, allowed for the dietary concerns of Elijah Muhammad and the Nation of Islam, reflected the international diversity of the African Diaspora, and even acknowledged the culinary trends of the time. In short, in the 1970s, the food of African Americans began to evolve into a cuisine that honored hog maws and collard greens and yet allowed for West African foufou, Caribbean callaloo, brown rice, and even tahini. Just as Rosa Parks's sitting down on a Montgomery bus changed the face of public America, civil rights workers at kitchen tables, black restaurants in urban enclaves, and four students at a North Carolina lunch counter transformed the African American foodscape and brought it out of isolation. Black food in its increasing diversity was no longer segregated on the blacks-only side of the menu, but squarely placed on the American table.

◆◆◆◆◆◆◆

YOU WERE WHAT YOU ATE:
FOOD AS POLITICS

The 1970s were a time of political consciousness on all fronts. How one dressed—dashiki or three-piece suit or shirt jacket—subtly advertised a point of view. For women, long skirts or short, afro or straightened hair all took on great significance. How one ate was equally fraught with political subtext, and a meal with friends of differing political stripes could be transformed into a minefield of culinary dos and don'ts.

Members of the Nation of Islam were identified by their bow ties and their well-pressed suits. They were also recognized by their diet, which was without any hint of swine. It was a highly codified regimen with foods that, although they were considered healthier than the newly named "soul food," retained some aspects of the traditional African American taste profile—sugary desserts and well-cooked vegetables. There was no alcohol to be seen, and dessert was more often than not a bean pie—one of the religion's hallmarks.

Dashiki-clad cultural nationalists ate a diet that was multicultural and infused with international flavor. The calabashes and carved wooden bowls that appeared on their batik tablecloths were likely to be filled with dishes like the spicy *jollof* rice from western Africa, or the seafood-rich stew of leafy greens known as *callaloo* from the Caribbean, or a Louisiana filé gumbo, or one of the newly created health-food-inspired dishes with a real or ersatz African name. Anything might turn up on their tables.

The upwardly mobile bourgeoisie continued to dine on Eurocentric foods and to emulate the culinary styles that James Beard, Julia Child, and Graham Kerr, the Galloping Gourmet, were bringing to the television sets weekly. Beef bourguignonne, beef Wellington, and cheese fondue were party standbys. In the privacy of their homes or those of their friends, they might indulge in some chitterlings or a slice of watermelon, but unless done to evidence culinary solidarity with others, it was not their public position.

The classic foods of the African American South—stewed okra and butter beans, pork chops and fried chicken—maintained their place at the table as well. These were the foods of rural Southerners and those Northerners and activists who wished to signal their solidarity with the more traditional arm of the Civil Rights Movement. For some, they remained the daily dietary mainstays; but for most, they evolved into the celebration food of family reunions and Sunday dinners.

Those with no special allegiance to any one faction ate what they wished or whatever was placed in front of them. Their tables might groan under a meal of Southern fried chicken and Caribbean rice and peas or be set with the finest family china upon which would be placed chitterlings and a mess of greens. The gastronomically flexible developed a chameleonlike ability to change with the prevailing culinary trend and political view.

By the end of the 1970s, food, like all aspects of African American life, had become a battleground for identity. The period's multiplicity of gastronomic and political positions and their dietary restrictions were difficult to navigate and confounded more than one diner. The political table wars were fierce, and ostracism, often accompanied by indigestion, awaited anyone who unwittingly crossed the dietary dividing lines. However, the new foods and the myriad cooking styles they brought into the African American culinary lexicon expanded African American taste, globalized the foodways of the African American world, and paved the way for the African American culinary omnivore of the last decades of the twentieth century and the twenty-first century.

CHAPTER 10

WE ARE THE WORLD

Making It in an Expanding
Black World and Joining
an Unbroken African
Culinary Circle

Bedford Stuyvesant, Brooklyn, New York—

I have lived in this neighborhood for more than twenty years. Labeled one of the country's African American ghettos in the turbulent 1960s, Bedford Stuyvesant benefited from an infusion of money and interest generated by Bobby Kennedy's championing of the Bedford Stuyvesant Restoration Corporation, which boosted African American home ownership and encouraged black enterprise in the community. I arrived a decade or so too late for the first wave of subsidized housing and the community spirit that it engendered; I was lured from my Greenwich Village apartment and my "That Girl" urban life by a brick row house. With a unique open floor plan and ample room for entertaining, the house struck me as a quirky place with loads of room for my thousands of cookbooks and my ever-growing collections. The neighborhood was in transition, but I hoped that with my "protective coloration" I'd be able to navigate the changes from Manhattan living without too much difficulty.

Little did I realize that I was spoiled. By the time I made my transition to Brooklyn life, I had written two cookbooks and was a food lover of the first order. I, like many other foodies—as we would later be called—had my culinary epiphany in France, where I'd lived for two years. In the Village, I was used to the abundant fresh produce at Balducci's, around the corner from my apartment, and the meat counter at Jefferson Market, which was a bit beyond that, as well as the atmospheric French butcher shop on my corner that sold tiny lamb chops and beautiful packages of freshly made pâté and seemed transported from the Left Bank.

In my new neighborhood supermarket, I was confronted by less-than-pristine vegetables, and mainly the basics—greens, turnips, carrots, broccoli, cauliflower, potatoes, and onions. There were no mushrooms, no fancy lettuces, no haricots verts. Salad meant iceberg lettuce, and for fruit I had a choice among apples, bananas, oranges, and the occasional pitiful-looking pear. Gone were seasonal treats like fresh raspberries in the summer and asparagus in the spring. (I knew better than to even think I'd spot a fiddlehead fern or a Jerusalem artichoke.) The meat counter was equally disappointing: There mostly were pork and chicken products and steaks that always seemed to be too thinly sliced. There was no lamb in sight, but customers were offered instead an assortment of nitrite-filled prepackaged luncheon meats. There were aisles and aisles of canned vegetables, packaged foods, sugary cereals, and fruit drinks containing little fruit juice. The real surprise was that the food cost as much or more than it did in the finest shops in Manhattan! The restaurant options were equally limited. Yes, the fish market offered delicious fried-fish sandwiches and there was a West Indian deli, but aside from Chinese takeout, there were three possibilities: McDonald's, Burger King, or Kentucky Fried Chicken. It was my first real acquaintance with America's culinary apartheid. Long before the term "food justice" became common currency, I rapidly learned that African Americans and indeed all who shop in ghettoized areas out of the mainstream were being offered second-rate comestibles sold at first-class prices and fast-food joints. We were getting stuck with overprocessed foods, low-quality meats, and second- or third-rate produce. It was a lesson I will not forget.

However, it was not all grim; there were advantages to Bed Stuy as well. I was heartened by the families who lived next door and the villagelike atmosphere on Fulton Street, two blocks away. I liked the fact that on summer weekends a gentleman would park his car across from my house, open the trunk, and sell watermelons; and I loved his sign, which read WATERMELON SWEET LIKE YOUR WOMAN. It was a place that reminded me of the 1950s, when I'd grown up, more than the 1980s.

When I lived in the Village, I had to journey uptown to Harlem whenever I felt like some collard greens or when I wanted black-eyed peas for the Hoppin' John deemed necessary to start the New Year off right, not only by me but also by most of Harlem, black Americans everywhere, and many white Southerners. In Brooklyn, there was no such difficulty; my local supermarket sold these African American staples year-round, and the greengrocer offered African American Southern seasonal specialties like raw peanuts. What the greengrocers lacked could be found on the back of trucks parked on Atlantic Avenue, where enterprising men hauled sausages, greens, sweet potatoes, and more up from North Carolina and did thriving business selling to those who still craved the foods of their Southern homes. The neighborhood was also home to a large West Indian population, so alongside the basic American produce, the local greengrocer also had dasheen, plantains, mangoes (in season), and a wide variety of root vegetables—*eddoes*, yams, cassava—as well as shelves of Trinidadian curry powder, Barbadian brown sugar, and vats of salted codfish and pickled pigs' tails. There were small containers at the checkout counter filled with the fresh thyme sprigs and the Scotch bonnet chilies that are essential to much of the food of the Caribbean world. What was exotic in other parts of the city became everyday for me.

In the twenty-plus years I've lived in my neighborhood, I have watched as the place and my supermarket changed. In the first decade of the twenty-first century, my neighborhood has gentrified but not so much that it's not still an African American neighborhood— at least for the next few years. The foodscape, however, is evolving rapidly. I can now get Chinese, Indian, and Japanese food delivered. A burgeoning Senegalese neighborhood has grown up around a mosque and is home to several small restaurants selling *thieboudienne* and chicken yassa to taxi drivers and adventurous locals. Folks even proudly boast of the Applebee's restaurant that opened a few years back. My supermarket as well has taken on a new look. The abundance of pork and chicken products is still there, as are the thin steaks, but the new dietary habits of African Americans and the upward mobility of the neighborhood are reflected in the goods sold. The produce counter now offers an abundance of fresh salads: arugula, mesclun, baby spinach, and spring mixes alongside the collards, dasheen, and kale. I can even find sun-dried tomatoes and haricots verts. A bakery purveys freshly baked croissants and pound cakes as well as bagels. I can find flour tortillas and wraps for spring rolls as well as wheatgrass health potions and tahini. The shelves still have their sugary cereals and canned foods, but they also display Greek yogurt, soy milk, and even tofu.

The changes in my neighborhood supermarket reflect, more than anything, the transformation of the African American diet in the final years of the twentieth century and the opening ones of the twenty-first. The traditional Southern diet of pig and corn is still consumed, but increasingly it has become celebration food for many families, eaten only on Sundays, on holidays, and at family reunions. The black middle class continues to increase, and upwardly mobile African Americans eat more widely ranging foods. The culinary explorations of the 1960s have added dishes from the African continent and the Caribbean to the menu.

There has also been an expansion of the black world. The designation "black American" no longer means up from the South. It can also encompass folks from the Caribbean, Central and South America, and the African continent itself. All brought recipes from their homelands to enrich the mix. These dishes supplemented the traditional Southern specialties and the recipes that blacks and the rest of the country received weekly from television shows with stars like Julia Child and Graham Kerr. At an African American party today it is possible to find the fried bean fritters from Brazil known as *acarajé* served along with Jamaican meat patties or the Trinidadian roasted chickpeas called *channa* that originated in India or, yes, fried chicken and a mess of greens. Beverages might include Senegalese *bissap rouge*, Southern mint julep featuring top-shelf bourbon, Guyanese rum and ginger ale, or a mellow California merlot. The choices and the range of food are limited only by the imagination. At the dinner table in the twenty-first century, African Americans, like the rest the country, are culinary omnivores, and we can truly say that, on the table, we eat the world.

❖ ❖ ❖ ❖ ❖

By the end of the 1970s it seemed as though the major battles engaged for centuries were winding down, if not completely won, and that the seeds of full equality long planted had finally sprouted. Black people had moved forward, but there were still hurdles to surmount and gains to be made. Despite their conservative agendas, President Ronald Reagan and his successor, George H. W. Bush, placed blacks in their administration's in high positions. Blacks continued to make political gains on the local and state levels as well. In 1964, there were only 103 black elected officials nationwide; by 1994, there were nearly 8,500, and blacks were mayors of four hundred U.S. cities, including New York and Washington, D.C. Political activist

Jesse Jackson ran for president in 1984 on a platform that united the concerns of blacks with those of poor whites and other minorities. His Rainbow Coalition was built on grassroots strategies he learned working with Dr. King in the Civil Rights Movement. He lost in 1984, but made a decent showing, and when he ran for president a second time, in 1987, he garnered one third of all the votes cast in the Democratic presidential primaries.

Black gains were not just on the political front. African Americans made strides in business, in sports, and in many other fields of endeavor. Black magazines like *Essence* and *Black Enterprise* followed the trail blazed by John Johnson and counterpointed the other publications' headlines about unemployment and familial dysfunction by presenting successful blacks from all walks of life to readers both black and white. They offered articles on the new entrepreneurship, book reviews, social commentary, in-depth interviews of black writers, artists, and businesspeople, as well as sections on travel and on wine and food. The latter were obligatory, for the country had changed as well. In the 1960s it underwent a culinary revolution with television chefs like James Beard and Julia Child. By the late 1970s and the early 1980s, food had become one of the country's central cultural forces.

Ironically, the food that was increasingly on the country's mind was for the most part neither fresh nor always nourishing; it was readily available and cheap. As women joined the workplace in record numbers in this period, food became a matter of convenience. Breakfast could be purchased at McDonald's, lunch at Burger King, and dinner brought home from Kentucky Fried Chicken. Family life also changed in the 1980s, and increasingly Americans lived in single-family households that survived on processed or fast foods. Even in households where the nuclear family still held sway, family dinnertime was becoming a thing of the past. Differing household schedules meant that individuals grabbed whatever they could and ate on their own timetable while watching television or chatting on the telephone or engaged in other pursuits. Often what they grabbed was fast food; in 1993 alone, Americans ate twenty-nine billion hamburgers! Fast-food chains expanded, as did the waistlines of average Americans. Obesity, not surprisingly, became a growing concern of the supersized country, and reports from the American

Medical Association regarding cholesterol levels and the health hazards of eating junk food raised alarm. The poor and the working classes, like those in my Brooklyn neighborhood, were growing fat and unhealthy on genetically engineered foods, processed foods, and fast-food meals.

On the other side of the culinary divide, the country's elite celebrated with lavish meals in over-the-top restaurants, which proliferated. Wealthy diners around the country savored a new American cuisine inspired by regional dishes. America became one of the world's dining destinations, with San Francisco and New York City developing into much-visited dining meccas. New American cuisine became the watchword, and American chefs like Larry Forgione in New York, Jasper White in Boston, Mark Miller in Santa Fe, and Alice Waters in Berkeley, California, championed the flavors of the country's regional cuisines. They served them up to the top tier of the public in a nation that spent almost one third of its food dollars on restaurant meals, whether upscale or down. Those who only watched the lifestyles of the rich and famous on their television sets attempted to duplicate the same meals in increasingly elaborate home kitchens using one of the thousand cookbooks that were published every year. Others simply sat down in front of their television sets, tuned into one of the rapidly multiplying cooking shows, and munched away on their hamburgers or Kentucky Fried while dreaming of other fare.

Americans on all ends of the social spectrum became enthralled by a cadre of celebrity chefs: cooks who made fortunes from food. However, African Americans who had toiled in homes and restaurants since the origins of the country were once again on the fringes of the new bonanza. One who almost made it was an earnest twenty-five-year-old black chef who created nouvelle cuisine dishes at a downtown Manhattan bistro known as Odeon. Patrick Clark came to popular attention in the 1980s. He was fiercely dedicated to his profession and wildly enthusiastic; with the zeal and wonder of the youngster he was, he could and did talk about his culinary ideas for hours.

Clark was a second-generation chef whose father had cooked for the Restaurant Associates group in an era when blacks worked hard but garnered little fame. At home, he'd grown up on traditional Southern specialties like smothered pork chops and fried chicken, but he also had been introduced to more-omnivorous fare through his father's profession. He trained at New York City Technical College and apprenticed at Eugénie-les-Bains, France, under Michel Guérard, one of the originators of *cuisine minceur* (the diet branch of nouvelle cuisine). As a classically trained black chef with an exceptional culinary pedigree, he was poised to enjoy the benefits of fame and fortune.

Clark arrived on the New York restaurant scene when fine dining was the social pastime of the well-to do and the city abounded with pricey restaurants purveying all manner of food. In Odeon's first review he was awarded two stars by the *New York Times*. He soon became one of the city's most revered chefs and expanded his culinary repertoire subtly, adding some of the Southern tastes of his African American world to the regional cuisines of America that were being rediscovered by chefs around the country. Clark's culinary realm grew, and by the mid-1980s he was appointed chef at Café Luxembourg, a second restaurant opened by Odeon owner Keith McNally.

Although lauded by his peers and praised in the media, Clark wanted the single sign of success that other chefs enjoyed: his own establishment. By 1988, he had found backers and was able to open his own restaurant, Metro, a lavish endeavor. Unfortunately, it opened right after the stock market crash of 1987. Metro was created for the high-flying 1980s, with stratospheric prices and equally elevated overhead. In the new economy, it was doomed; Clark closed it in 1990. He then moved to Los Angeles and became executive chef at Bice, an Italian restaurant. But the celebrity culture of the city and its finicky dining ethos did not suit Clark's temperament, and after a two-year sojourn he returned to the East Coast, this time to Washington, D.C. There he became chef at the Hay-Adams Hotel, where the Clintons were frequent diners. By the spring of 1994, upon the retirement of White House chef Pierre Chambrin, Clark's name was on the short list to become the Clintons' White House chef. Clark, who would have been the first official African American White House chef, demurred. Activists and civil rights leaders, aware of the honor that went with the request, were saddened by his refusal of the post, but Clark stood firm, citing loyalty to the Hay-Adams and wariness about the loss of personal identity and creative flexibility that came with the job, despite its prestige. In 1995, though, Clark left the Hay-Adams and returned to New York, where he became the chef at Tavern on the Green. Clark's promise was never fully attained. He died in 1998 from congestive heart failure at forty-two.

It was a shock from which the black culinary world is still recovering, because although blacks had been cooking for the white elite for centuries, Clark was the first black who seemed poised to enter the high-flying realm of twentieth-century superstar chefs. Although aware of the honor, Clark did not want to be categorized by race. "I consider myself a chef. The press has considered me a prominent black chef," he boldly stated. He remained, however, keenly aware of his roots and his past. At Tavern on the Green, he installed the first barbecue grill and added items to the menu inspired by the classic African American Southern tastes he'd learned at his family's table. More important, Clark also spent much of his free time mentoring young black culinary students and working with different organizations to raise funds for scholarships for them. The brevity of his life, cut short in the prime of his career, deprived him of several of the accolades received subsequently by his peers. Patrick Clark's true renown came from the respect in which he was held by fellow chefs, from the delight of diners who ate at the various restaurants where he cooked, and from the ongoing admiration of a new generation of young black chefs for whom he became the "north star."

Clark was a superstar chef yet spent most of his career working at establishments owned by others. The harsh reality was that even in the high-flying 1990s, restaurant ownership was difficult: Costs were prohibitive; backers were difficult to find; and banks were usually leery of loaning to African American chefs, who were still thought to know only how to prepare food from the classic Southern black repertoire. It required more than the creative entrepreneurship of Thomas Downing or Barney Ford to open a restaurant in the 1990s. It seemed that the days when blacks gained fame and fortune through food had ended just at the point when the culinary realm became a profession of honor and not a service job.

Then, in 1994, *New York* magazine restaurant critic Gael Greene wrote an article titled "Soul Food Now," which signaled the next step for the diverse traditions of African American food. Ironically, the three seminal voices of African American food of the period were women who had started their culinary journeys decades earlier: Edna Lewis in New York, South Carolina, and Georgia; Sylvia Woods in New York; and Leah Chase in New Orleans.

Edna Lewis was a quiet woman from Virginia whose regal bearing and uncompromising insistence on fresh ingredients and optimum taste made her the doyenne of fin de siècle African American food. It might seem odd that a superstar of the 1990s was born in 1916, in Freetown, Virginia, and was the granddaughter of an emancipated slave. But although Lewis's culinary career began much earlier, she reached the heights of her profession in the 1990s. As a child in Freetown, she was entranced by the flavors of the foods that she and her relatives had grown and harvested, and her taste memories of those meals informed her cooking decades later. Lewis said: "As a child, I thought all food tasted delicious. After growing up I didn't think food tasted the same, so it has been my lifelong effort to try to recapture those good flavors of the past." Lewis moved to New York at age sixteen and held a variety of jobs until she found her calling in 1949, when she became the cook at a small clublike restaurant in Manhattan called Café Nicholson. The restaurant, opened by antiques dealer John Nicholson, became a gathering spot for the bohemians of the day and soon "Miss Edna" was cooking her fresh-tasting honest country food for Tennessee Williams, Diana Vreeland, Marlon Brando, Truman Capote, and other members of the literati of the period.

As had many others before her, Lewis made her fame preparing food for whites in a setting where few if any blacks ventured. But while she might serve deceptively simple roast chicken, lemony-dressed salads of Boston lettuce, Gallic mussels with herbed rice, or cheese soufflés, the food that she cooked was always inspired by the country tastes of her Virginia home, demanded fresh ingredients, and used time-honed culinary skills. Lewis left Café Nicholson in the 1950s and cooked professionally at a number of other places. She gradually slipped from the growing culinary mainstream. Instead, she wrote, worked at the Museum of Natural History, and became a fixture at Manhattan's annual Ninth Avenue

Street Festival, an early celebration of the diversity of the city's food. Food, though, was always a driving passion, and by the 1970s Lewis could add cookbook author to her résumé; her *Edna Lewis Cookbook* was published in 1972, followed by *A Taste of Country Cooking* in 1976 and *The Pursuit of Flavor* in 1988. Each extolled the virtues of the fresh, seasonal ingredients that she had always championed.

Lewis, although long known to the culinary cognoscenti, joined the ranks of the gastronomic superstars in the 1990s, when she was lured out of retirement and named chef at Gage and Tollner, a venerable Brooklyn eatery. There, in the gaslit restaurant, which dated to the last decades of the nineteenth century, Lewis again wowed New Yorkers with her delicate hand with cornbread and biscuits and her deft way with the pickles and condiments that are such a part of the Southern table.

By the mid-1990s Lewis left New York, but she continued to cook, first in Chapel Hill, North Carolina, and then at Middleton Place Plantation in the South Carolina Lowcountry. At each spot, her insistence on fresh ingredients simply prepared remained primary. Throughout the 1990s and virtually until her death, in 2006, Lewis became a culinary fixture, always speaking with quiet authority. With her African-fabric dresses and her regal bearing, she garnered accolades and awards and became one of the most visible African American chefs. For years, she journeyed only by train, preferring the pace of the era of her birth to that in which she was widely acclaimed. In her later years, Lewis found an apprentice and soul mate in Scott Peacock, a young Southern white chef, and controversially, they lived together, cooked together, and collaborated on her last book, *The Gift of Southern Cooking*, a work that attempts to bridge the divide between the differing styles of black cooking and white cooking in the South. Lewis's food represented one facet of the African American culinary repertoire—one that emphasizes the freshest-available local ingredients and the studied preparation of simple foods. A soul food resurgence brought the traditional diet back to tables, and later the neo-soul movement would join both tendencies.

For much of the twentieth century, virtually every city in the United States large enough to have an inner city had its "soul food" restaurant. These black-owned restaurants still occupied pride of place in black neighborhoods, where they flourished and became thriving businesses, bringing their owners fame and increased fortune in the mid- to late 1990s. Many of them were survivors of the initial wave of black-owned restaurants that prospered and became icons in their communities during the period of the Great Migration and during the Civil Rights Movement. They all offered a taste of traditional foods: cornbread on the table in the bread basket, hot biscuits with breakfast, and a tall thin bottle of hot sauce among the table condiments.

Sylvia's in Harlem was one of these restaurants. Known to Harlemites for decades—along with other soul food places that have now disappeared, like Wells and Copeland's—it came to new fame in the 1990s and today is arguably the best-known soul food restaurant in the world. Like Edna Lewis, Sylvia Woods is an atavism—a survivor of another generation whose career has found new vigor in the twenty-first century. Sylvia Woods, the self-proclaimed "Queen of Soul Food," opened Sylvia's Restaurant in Harlem in the turbulent decades of the Civil Rights Movement. In a classic tale of black entrepreneurial success that mirrored those of black culinary entrepreneurs of earlier times, Sylvia worked her way from waitress to luncheonette owner to restaurateur to tycoon. It all began in 1954, when she was informed of a job at a local eatery. Sylvia's willingness to work hard, her eight years' tenure in the job, and a bad investment by the luncheonette's owner resulted in her being offered ownership of the spot, which originally consisted of a counter and a few booths.

In 1962, Sylvia's opened, serving the traditional pork and greens, cornbread, and fried catfish of the American South. It flourished and became a Harlem landmark. After a mention by *New York* magazine restaurant critic Gael Greene, it became the African American restaurant best known by tourists and visitors from as far afield as Brazil and Japan. Even today, tour buses disgorge groups by the hundreds to sample her African American meals. Especially lively are Sundays when a gospel brunch combines African American breakfast foods like grits and sausages with the rousing music of the black church; the place is packed not only with camera be-draped tourists looking for a taste of African American culture but also with Harlem natives, who remain loyal. All are served a menu featuring greens and pork chops, fried chicken and cornbread, all the totems of African American food.

Leveraging the fame conferred by Greene and other journalists, the diminutive Woods became the symbol of soul food to much of America, yet no one was more surprised at her success than she. But successful she is. Her face, topped with a chef's toque, now appears on a line of Sylvia's products, like canned black-eyed peas and collard greens, that is available at supermarkets around the country. Today, the booming enterprise includes not only the Harlem restaurant and the nationwide line of Sylvia's Food Products, but also a full-service catering hall and several cookbooks.

If Sylvia Woods is the "Queen of Soul Food" in New York City, Leah Chase is New Orleans's "Empress of Creole Cuisine." Like Woods, Chase is a country girl and a survivor of another era. She too journeyed to the big city and found a job working in food service. But there their stories diverge, for Chase met and married musician Edgar "Dooky" Chase II, whose parents owned an eatery that catered to local patrons in the black Tremé neighborhood of New Orleans. Chase envisioned a larger, more formal place like the white establishment in which she had worked in the French Quarter. She initially transformed the menu, expanding it from offering only sandwiches to serving hot meals at lunchtime to black men who were beginning to work in offices as the city was gradually being desegregated. She started out as a hostess, but soon she was redecorating the restaurant and eventually began working as chef. Five decades later, white-haired and feisty, she is still in the kitchen, and Dooky Chase restaurant (still a family-run endeavor) has grown into a New Orleans landmark. Chase has served Republican and Democratic presidents and has seen the notable and the notorious come to her art-filled establishment in Tremé to sample *mamère*'s crab soup and other dishes. Although gifted with great culinary curiosity and also an innovative cook, Chase is also a traditionalist. On Mondays there will always be red beans and rice; there will be fish on Fridays. Once a year, on Holy Thursday, there will be a crowd for the bowl of gumbo-z'herbes, a creole Lenten creation made from an odd number (nine, eleven, or thirteen) of greens— some store-bought, like collards and kale; some foraged, like sourgrass—that are prepared with sausage and ham. Dooky Chase celebrates Creole cooking, and the menu reveals some of the sophistication and culinary diversity of African American culture. It offers not only fried catfish and peach cobbler but also such uniquely creole New Orleans dishes as grits and grillades, seafood and okra gumbo, and jambalaya.

Sylvia's and Dooky Chase's continue to be successful, but by the last decades of the twentieth century, many of the other classic soul food eateries were forced to shut their doors. Health concerns about the high-fat, high-calorie traditional African American diet, rising rents brought about by gentrification, and an ignorance of the true tastes of traditional African American foods among a generation raised on fast food signaled their death knell. Then, in 1997 *Cooking Light* magazine named soul food one of the culinary trends to watch, and the neo-soul movement that had been percolating quietly got fully underway. Soon upscale dining spots serving improvisations on traditional African American fare—like Los Angeles's Georgia and Hartford, Connecticut's Savannah—flourished. *Satisfy Your Soul*, a guide to African American, African, and Caribbean restaurants published the same year listed more than 250 around the country. New York was the culinary epicenter and featured numerous upscale black restaurants outside Harlem, many of them owned by famous blacks, like Sean "Puff Daddy" Combs' Justin's and singers Nick Ashford and Valerie Simpson's Sugar Bar. There was a range of others—like the Motown Café, Soul Café, Mekka, and the Shark Bar—where newly affluent "buppies" (black upwardly mobile professionals) met after work to drink and mix. The neo-soul restaurants traded on African American nostalgia for the traditional foods of the past, but each added a nod to changing culinary conventions and the health concerns of the day. They showcased African American culinary innovations and were an incubator for a new wave of culinary entrepreneurs.

One of the precursors of the trend was owned by former model B. Smith, who opened her eponymous restaurant on the edge of New York's theater district in 1986. It was a gamble, but the place rapidly became a hangout for black professionals; it was one of the few places downtown where they could congregate among like folks. The restaurant thrived, driven by the bar scene, and eventually moved to larger digs a few blocks away. The menu revivified old Southern favorites like fried green tomatoes, crab cakes, macaroni and cheese, and mashed sweet potatoes, and it also gave a nod to Caribbean influences, with pigeon peas and rice and fried plantains. They were served alongside dishes like curried coconut oysters with a coconut wasabi dip and "Swamp Thang," a sauté of shrimps, scallops, and crayfish napped with a Dijon mustard sauce and presented over a bed of greens. Smith grew from success to success. With her model bearing and polish, she was the perfect crossover culinary icon for the period. Eventually she moved out of the metaphoric "kitchen" and became a brand, following in the footsteps of Martha Stewart, perhaps the most successful of all the culinary entrepreneurs. Mediagenic Smith has been so successful with her endeavors that she has penned cooking and lifestyle books, had her own radio show, and was the host of her own television series. Her B. Smith with Style Home Collection is sold at Bed Bath and Beyond stores around the country, she became the spokesperson for a range of products, and she now owns three eponymous restaurants.

B. Smith's had been open for several years when Café Beulah opened downtown in the early 1990s. Café Beulah, however, was a new kind of African American culinary endeavor: one that combined African American food with a setting full of black and white celebrities and bold-face names. Also located downtown, outside of Harlem, it offered a menu of foods described as "Southern revival" by Alexander Smalls, the *force majeure* behind the place. The bistro-like décor—tile floors, cream and white walls, and a burnished wood bar near the entrance of the small eighty-seat spot—offered no hint to its ethnicity. That was subtly done by the photographs decorating the walls showing blacks at play, including one of blacks in a car in Paris with the Arc de Triomphe in the background! The menu was like no other: chicken liver paté wrapped in collard greens, macaroni and cheese terrine, and free-range fried *poussin* with wild rice cake and Lowcountry succotash. Here was an African American place that dared to "signify," or slyly comment on, American attitudes toward soul food and expectations of black restaurants. While the menu was sassy, many of the dishes, like the seafood and crab gumbo and the hush puppies, offered Carolina Lowcountry food in almost classic presentation.

Part of the lure of Café Beulah was the people-watching. A former opera singer, Smalls treated Café Beulah as his own personal salon, and the place attracted a crowd of black notables, from opera singer Kathleen Battle to writer Toni Morrison, giving the spot a frothy feel appropriate to the fin de siècle. Café Beulah closed before the century did, in 1998, but Smalls went on to open two other restaurants: Sweet Ophelia's and the Shoebox Café, an eat-in/take-out place in Grand Central Station. However neither matched the excitement and verve of Café Beulah, and the restaurant-phobic aftermath of 9/11 regrettably put a temporary end to Smalls's restaurant empire.

Uptown, in Harlem, another former model, Norma Jean Darden, staked her claim. Two decades prior, in 1978, she had penned one of the first black cookbooks of the post-Civil Rights era, *Spoonbread and Strawberry Wine*, with her sister, Carole. The book, an intriguing mixture of memoir, anecdotes, and recipes, tells the multigenerational tale of their family through the foods they loved to cook and eat. Illustrated with family photographs and telling a compelling family story in the *Roots*-dominated period, it quickly became an African American classic. Based on the book's success, Darden was also empire building by the 1980s. In 1983, she established Spoonbread Catering and became one of Harlem's best-known caterers, providing food on the set of *The Cosby Show* and keeping uptown's partygoers well fed. Her catering success resulted in the establishment of the restaurant Miss Mamie's Spoonbread Too in 1998. Located on the West Side of Manhattan, with easy access from Harlem and from downtown, Miss Mamie's was successful and in 2001 spawned a second restaurant, Miss Maude's Spoonbread Too.

Darden's endeavors, like those of Smith and Smalls, played on both sides of the African American culinary divide. Her restaurant menus remained rooted in the traditional Southern fare—grits, candied yams, banana-bread pudding, collard greens, macaroni and cheese, smothered pork chops, North Carolina barbecue, and what was dubbed the best fried chicken in the city by the *New York Post*. Her catering menu offered African American classics but also foods more international in scope, including such items as foie gras mousse on chickpea chips with blackberry chutney, miniature biscuits with ham or turkey and honey mustard, miso-seared scallops, lamb tagine, and cornbread-stuffed chicken with rosemary gravy. However, the South rose again in desserts like miniature peach cobblers served with whipped cream and mint, sweet potato tartlettes, sweet potato soufflé, and red velvet cake. The combination suited New Yorkers who still wanted their soul food spots, even if they did include other items on the menu.

The multiplicity of African American cooking styles and their intersection with those from other parts of the African Diaspora and from around the world that were served in the neo-soul restaurants became the hallmarks of African American food in the last decade of the twentieth century and the opening one of the twenty-first. Cookbooks celebrated them and continued to proliferate, as African American cooks and chefs re-created their favorite dishes in print for home cooks, food journalists and dietitians culled their best recipes, and food historians documented and traced some of the roots and variations of the food of the African Diaspora. Cookbooks also recorded the cooking of African American churches and detailed heritage recipes from historically black colleges and black fraternal organizations. The regional aspects of the foods of the African American South came under scrutiny, as did those of the African continent and throughout the diaspora. The University of Alabama library now boasts an African American cookbook collection that has thousands of volumes—a testimonial to the prolific output of the black culinary authors of the period.

A few black chefs and a small but growing number of black foodies attended not only mainstream food events but also created their own, like Joe Randall's A Taste of Heritage, where they cross-pollinated and shared recipes and inspirations; and Taste of Ebony, held for three successive years in the mid-2000s, which lavishly celebrated black chefs for an invited public that tasted wine from South Africa and black-owned California vineyards and sampled the offerings of black caterers and chefs from around the country and across the globe. Other events, like Harlem's Men Who Cook, gave the general public a feel for what was going on in the country's African American home kitchens. Growing numbers of African Americans began to attend culinary schools and try to make their way to the summit of the culinary world.

The future, though, was not always rosy. Despite increasing opportunities and a growing appreciation of African American foods, there were still proportionately few African Americans who had risen to the ranks of superstar chef. The question of why so few African American chefs was much debated. Many recognized that the role of chef offered little inducement to those who had been enslaved for centuries, then traditionally relegated to lower-level service roles receiving low pay and no glory. Those who could afford the often-expensive tuitions at culinary schools discovered upon graduation that despite their abilities, they were often ghettoized, and the soul food debate still raged. "Part of the problem with African-American chefs is that people don't think of us as cooking anything other than ribs or barbecue," argued black chef Joe Randall, a forty-three-year veteran of the hospitality and food service industry. Even one who had attained the coveted status, Patrick Clark, while stating that he felt no prejudice directed toward him personally, recognized the difficulty for young black chefs. It seemed that despite a long history of culinary attainment, black chefs might again be thwarted from grabbing the brass ring of full culinary equality as signaled by financial success. But the final chapter remains unfinished.

In the post-millennium era, the food world has continued to grow and has become more complex. Food justice has become a major topic, addressing the systematic gastronomic disenfranchisement that is suffered by people in poor countries around the world as well as in the nation's poorer neighborhoods. The cry for fresh, seasonal, and local ingredients has brought people black and white to farmer's markets searching for fresh foods produced by individuals not agribusinesses. Urban gardening has gripped the imaginations of many, and blacks who are generations from Southern dirt now find themselves harvesting crops of tomatoes grown on a fire escape or taking snippets of rosemary from a window box. African Americans, like all in the country, continue to be culinary omnivores, eating not only the traditional foods of the African American South but also foods from the far-flung African Diaspora and the rest of the world as well.

New waves of immigrants have arrived from the African motherland, set up restaurants, and reacquainted us with tastes of our long-departed homeland. Morou Ouattara cooks recipes learned from his Ivoirian grandmother in the Washington, D.C., area and Pierre Thiam reinvents Senegalese classics in Brooklyn, New York. Bryant Terry creates vegan soul food in Oakland, California. Around the country, African American chefs are stepping up to stoves and creating foods that are expressions of the sum total of the black cultural experience: African, Southern, Caribbean, and more. And it seems that we are finally on our way to having our media superstars. The four currently most likely to succeed all represent different aspects of black diversity and are unlikely standard-bearers for the centuries-old traditions of African American cooking: a couple and a former hotel chef from Atlanta and an Ethiopian raised in Sweden.

Pat and Gina Neely are the more traditional of these chefs. They began their journey to fame in 1988, when the four Neely brothers opened a barbecue restaurant in downtown Memphis, a city known for its mastery of the genre. The Neelys' place prospered, and soon the family businesses numbered three. A segment with weatherman cum food critic Al Roker of the *Today Show* took news of the brothers' way with barbecue national. In 2008 Pat and Gina were given their own television show on the Food Network—the cable media juggernaut that created such culinary superstars as Mario Batali, Emeril Lagasse, and Paula Deen.

Down Home with the Neelys cemented their national prominence, and thanks to the power of television, they have become arguably the best-known African American cooks in the country. However, their renown did not come without controversy. As one of the very few African American cooking shows with national distribution, *Down Home with the Neelys* came under close scrutiny, especially from blacks. The virulence of the critics amply demonstrated how complex the world of black food had become. The format of the show, the dishes prepared, and the patter Pat and Gina Neely engage in while cooking have all been analyzed on culinary Web sites. At the show's inception, most viewers were outraged by everything from the dishes prepared on the air to the dialogue. A strawberry cake prepared with cake mix, Jell-O, strawberries, and whipped cream came under particular fire, as did the family's "loud and boisterous" manner. The level of sexual innuendo in the couple's banter and the personal style of Gina Neely were other points of dismay. African American viewers were particularly concerned that the show not be a throwback to behavior considered stereotypical and not a representation of the diversity and sophistication of African American lifestyle and cooking. Changes were made, and today *Down Home with the Neelys* remains one of the Food Network's most popular shows and indeed one of the few shows by black chefs that is available to a national television audience.

While the Neelys' food riffs on the classic Southern tastes of the African American past, G. Garvin's food and presence are designed for the black audience that watches TV One—the black television station that was begun in 2004 as an alternative to BET. Garvin trained in the kitchen, working his way up the ranks from dishwasher to line cook to sous chef and beyond. After a two-year stint in European kitchens, he returned stateside to work in hotel kitchens and private restaurants in Atlanta and on the West Coast. Mediagenic and as smooth as chocolate crème brûlée, Garvin has become a media presence complete with appearances on late-night talk shows, sponsorship deals with food brands, and a foundation that helps young men by teaching them discipline through cooking. Garvin's success, though, seems restricted and has not yet reached the national culinary cognoscenti.

For most Americans, black or white, mention "black superstar chef" and one name will come up—and one name only—Marcus Samuelsson. If the Neelys exemplify the populist level of African American food, and G. Garvin is representative of an increasing sophistication of black viewers and eaters, Marcus Samuelsson is the harbinger of a different African American future.

At the close of first decade of the twentieth-first century, African Americans are more diverse than ever before in history. An African American president sits in the White House. Like the president, Marcus Samuelsson is representative of the new and increasing diversity of those labeled "African Americans." They represent newer and recently arrived immigrants and their descendants, all of whom have no personal link to the history of African American enslavement in the country or the diet it spawned. Samuelsson was born in Ethiopia, adopted by a Swedish family, and taken to Göteborg,

Sweden, where he and his sister were raised. The tastes of hog and hominy that were traditionally ascribed to the enslaved and their descendants are tastes he learned as a chef after his coming to America. Samuelsson's culinary training is classic; early on he began to cook under the instruction of his Swedish grandmother, a professional cook, and he later trained at the Culinary Institute in Göteborg and completed apprenticeships in Switzerland and Austria.

Like Patrick Clark before him, Samuelsson attained fame at an early age. He arrived in New York City in 1991 to apprentice in the kitchen of Aquavit, serving the crisp, clean tastes of Scandinavia to New Yorkers in a décor that seemed transported from the lands of the midnight sun. Three years later, he became the restaurant's executive chef and shortly thereafter became the youngest chef ever to receive a three-star review from the *New York Times*. Other accolades followed, and in 2003 he was named best chef in New York City by the James Beard Foundation. Coming from a Swedish restaurant, Samuelsson has been unfettered by the racial assumptions of the dining public and therefore has been able to cast a wide culinary net. His restaurants have offered not only the food of his native Sweden but also served Japanese-American fusion food and the food of the African continent.

Young, ambitious, and multitalented Samuelsson also authored cookbooks in English and Swedish. The first *Aquavit and the New Scandinavian Cuisine* celebrated the food of his adopted homeland. *En Smakresa* (A Journey of Tastes), published in Sweden, detailed Samuelsson's personal journey of tastes, and *Street Food* speaks about the snacks that are a part of the daily lives of the world. Samuelsson's culinary journey further evolved when, at the behest of *Gourmet* magazine, he journeyed back to Ethiopia for the first time. The trip proved revelatory and revolutionary. Reacquainted with the continent of his birth, Samuelsson began an odyssey that culminated in another book, *The Soul of a New Cuisine: A Discovery of the Foods and Flavors of Africa*. A television miniseries for the Public Broadcasting Service, numerous appearances on television cooking competitions and at food media events, a coffee deal with Starbucks, a new cookbook on American food, *New American Table*, and a series of videos for AOL are only some of the long list of projects that have made Samuelsson the best-known African American in food at the end of the first decade of the twenty-first century. Samuelsson has now taken his African American culinary journey full circle and in December 2010 opened a place on 125th Street in Harlem that focuses on fresh, local, and seasonal American foods—the Red Rooster. The location is totemic for African Americans, and the name is that of a legendary Harlem bar. In a tip of the toque to not only the location but also the culinary history of the African Americans who made Harlem famous, the menu highlights some traditional Southern black foods, including fried chicken, macaroni and cheese with bacon, and bread pudding. The culinary circle is unbroken.

The traditional foods of the African American South, the pig and the corn that allowed so many to survive enslavement and its aftermath in this country—continue to be celebrated in restaurants with white tablecloths and pitted Formica. They appear in classic soul food establishments and provide the ongoing themes upon which multiple improvisations are wrought by chefs, black and white. In private homes they're served as grandma's recipes at Sunday suppers and family reunions. The tastes of the African motherland and its diaspora have also come full circle with Ghanaian groundnut stew and Caribbean peas and rice becoming new culinary classics. African American food has grown to encompass a world of possibility and of taste. The United States' increasing cultural diversity, along with the omnivorous curiosity of all Americans, means that we're all tasting and sampling one another's foods daily. A menu is as likely to include Brazilian-style collard greens served alongside Southern fried chicken with a salad of garden fresh heirloom tomatoes dressed with soy and sesame, a side of Cuban *yuca con mojo*, and a classic Grand Marnier soufflé for dessert.

Finally, we seem to be nearing the goal. Sure there's room for improvement. Certainly there should be a greater television presence of African Americans that showcases our gastronomic diversity. Restaurant ownership remains a problem, especially during these harsh economic times. Certainly the scope of the black culinary repertoire should not be limited but rather should be acknowledged. Catering should be valued and recognized as a historic path to success, especially for women, and let's finally get beyond the "soul food" label. We've journeyed far, and the rest is attainable in the bountiful world of American food. It is a simple request to be acknowledged for the integral part that we have played in the formation of the American culinary ethos, to sit down at the table of success with the members of the food community, and to begin to truly eat and live high on the hog. I, for one, am looking forward to it. My mouth is watering and I can hardly wait.

CODA: A FINAL DEFINITION

African Americans have a long love affair with food, one perhaps unequaled in the history of the country. For centuries we've brought the piquant tastes of Africa to the New World. With particular relish we eat (*nyam*) "grease" and "grit," whether it's a bologna sandwich and a peanut pattie tucked into the bib of overalls for a workman's snack or a late-night supper of chitlins and champagne eaten off fine bone china. Some of us delight in a sip of white lightning from a mason jar in a juke joint, while others delicately lift little fingers and savor minted ice tea or a cool drink while fanning and watching the neighbors on the front porch. Good times or bad, food provides a time for communion and relaxation.

It's so much a part of our lives that it seems at times as though a Supreme Being created us from a favorite recipe. There was a heaping cupful of cornmeal to signal our links with the Native Americans, a rounded tablespoon of biscuit dough for Southern gentility, a mess of greens and a dozen okra pods for our African roots, and a good measure of molasses to recall the tribulations of slavery. A seasoning piece of fatback signals our lasting love for the almighty pig, and a smoked turkey wing foretells our healthier future. A handful of hot chilies gives the mixture attitude and sass, while a hearty dose of bourbon mellows it out and a splash of corn liquor gives it kick. There are regional additions such as a bit of benne from South Carolina, a hint of praline from New Orleans, and a drop of at least twelve types of barbecue sauce. A fried porgy, a splash of homemade scuppernong wine, and a heaping portion of the secret ingredient called love fill the bowl to overflowing. When well mixed, it can be either baked, broiled, roasted, fried, sautéed, or barbecued. The result has yielded us in all hues of the rainbow from lightly toasted to deep well done.

We are now a new people. All the world comes together in us and on our plates: Africa, the Americas, Asia, and beyond. We eat hog maws or pickled meat, potatoes or plantain, sweet potatoes or yams or both. Our greens are collards or callaloo or bok choy, and we serve them with everything from a ham hock to a smoked turkey wing to tofu. We savor fine aged *rhum agricole* and still know how to knock back a good Mason jar of corn liquor or a glass of cachaça.

With a start like that, it's not surprising, then, that we have our own way with food. We've called it our way for centuries and incorporated our wondrous way with food and eating into our daily lives. We have rocked generations of babies to sleep while crooning "Shortenin' Bread," laughed to the comedy of "Pigmeat" Markham and "Butterbeans and Susie," danced the cakewalk, tapped our feet to the music of "Jelly Roll" Morton, shimmied with wild abandon to gutbucket music in juke joints, gotten all hot and sweaty over salsa or sat down with friends and "chewed the fat." We've had the blues over the "Kitchen Man," searched for our "Sugar Pie Honey Bunch," called our "Sugar Honey," and longed to be loved like "Lilac Wine." When we found the one, we celebrated with a "Pigfoot and a Bottle of Beer" or just kicked back and hollered, "Pass the Courvoisier."

In short, we've created our own culinary universe: one where an ample grandmother presides over a kitchen where the pungent aroma of greens mixes with the molasses perfume of pralines, and the bubbling from a big iron gumbo pot punctuates her soft humming. This is a universe where Aunt Jemima takes off her kerchief and sits down at the table, where Uncle Ben bows his head and blesses the food, the Luzianne coffee woman passes the plates, and Rastus, the Cream of Wheat man, tells tall tales over a taste of whiskey to the Banania Man. It's the warmth of the kitchen tempered by the formality of the dining room and the love of family that extends over generations and across bloodlines. With the improvisational genius that gave the world jazz and salsa, as well as rumba, rap, and reggae, we have cooked our way into the hearts, minds, and stomachs of a country.

RECIPES

Sauce Gombo

This simple vegetarian version of a classic West African sauce comes from Benin, a nation that sent many to the United States in the hold of slave ships. In Benin, it might be eaten over pounded yam or another traditional starch. Here, it can be served over rice.

Serves 4

   1 cup water
   1 pound fresh okra
   2 medium ripe tomatoes, peeled, seeded, and
      coarsely chopped
   1 habanero chili, pricked with a fork
   Salt and freshly ground black pepper to taste

Wash and top and tail the okra, then cut it into rounds, discarding any blemished or hard pods. Place the okra, tomatoes, chili, and the water in a heavy saucepan and bring to a boil. Lower the heat to medium and simmer, covered, for about 10 minutes, or until the okra is fork-tender. Remove the chili when the dish is hot enough for your taste. Season with salt and pepper and serve hot over rice.
        —*The Africa Cookbook: Tastes of a Continent*

Yassa au Poulet

This is the first dish that I tasted on the African continent, and it launched me on my culinary journey of connections.

Serves 8

> ⅓ cup freshly squeezed lemon juice
> 4 large onions, sliced
> Salt and freshly ground black pepper to taste
> 5 tablespoons peanut oil
> 1 habanero chili, pricked with a fork
> 1 2½- to 4½-pound frying chicken, cut into
>   serving parts
> ½ cup water

The night before, prepare a marinade by mixing the lemon juice, onions, salt and pepper, 4 tablespoons of the peanut oil, and the chili in a deep bowl. When the marinade has reached the desired heat, remove the chili. Place the chicken pieces in the marinade, cover the bowl with plastic wrap, and refrigerate it overnight.

When ready to cook, preheat the broiler. Remove the chicken pieces from the marinade, reserving the marinade. Place the pieces on the broiler rack and grill them briefly, until they are just lightly browned on both sides. Set them aside. Remove the onions from the marinade with a slotted spoon. Heat the remaining tablespoon of oil in a deep skillet, add the onions, and sauté them over medium heat until they are tender and translucent. Add the remaining marinade to the skillet and cook until the liquid is heated through. Add the chicken pieces and the water and stir to mix well. Lower the heat and simmer, covered, for 30 minutes, or until the chicken pieces are cooked through. Serve hot over white rice.

—*The Africa Cookbook: Tastes of a Continent*

Rice Gruel

This is simply rice that is boiled until it breaks down into a porridge, much like the rice porridges that were served aboard slave ships. This one is made considerably tastier by the addition of sugar and cinnamon. In some parts of the world, rice gruel is served as a meal for the ill or as a breakfast food with additions that make it either sweet or savory.

Serves 2 to 4

> 3 cups water
> 1 cup rice
> 2 teaspoons brown sugar or to taste

In a large saucepan, bring the water to a boil. Add the rice and cook it, covered, for 30 to 45 minutes, or until the rice has become soupy. You may need to add more water. Serve in a bowl topped with the brown sugar.

Grits

Grits are one of the Southern uses of corn that settlers adopted from the Native peoples.

Serves 4

> 4 cups water
> 2 tablespoons butter
> Salt to taste
> 1 cup whole-grain grits

Place the water, butter, and salt in a pot and bring it to a boil. Gradually add the grits, return it to a boil, then reduce it to a simmer. Cook the grits, stirring occasionally so they don't stick or form a skin, until they are creamy and done to your liking. It takes about 25 minutes, but many people like to cook them much longer. If you do, you may have to add more water.

Summer Southern Succotash

*Various types of succotash were eaten by tribes on the east-
ern seaboard. They were later adopted and adapted by African Americans to include such ingredients as okra, tomatoes,
and even black-eyed peas. This summertime succotash uses
okra, corn, and tomatoes.*

Serves 6 to 8

    6 large, ripe tomatoes, peeled, seeded, and
        coarsely chopped
    2 cups fresh corn kernels
    1 pound fresh okra, topped and tailed, and cut
        into ½-inch rounds
    1 habanero chili, pricked (optional)
    1½ cups water

Place all the ingredients in a medium saucepan and add 1½ cups of
water. Bring to a boil, then lower the heat, cover, and cook for 15
minutes, until the ingredients are well mixed and cooked through.
Remove the chili when the dish has the desired spiciness. Serve hot.

Snow Eggs

*There are few extant recipes from early African Americans.
This one is attributed to James, cook at Monticello, and
thought to be by James Hemings.*

Separate 5 eggs and beat the whites until you can turn the vessel bottom upward without their leaving it. Gradually add 1 table-spoon of powdered sugar and ½ teaspoon of any desired flavoring. (Jefferson used orange flower or rose water.)

Put 2 cups of milk into a saucepan, add 3 tablespoonfuls of sugar, flavoring and bring slowly to a boil. Drop the first mixture into the milk and poach until well set. Lay them on a wire drainer to drain.

Beat the yolk of 1 egg until thick, stir gradually into the milk. Add a pinch of salt. As soon as the custard thickens pour through a sieve. Put your whites in a serving dish and pour the custard over them. A little wine stirred in is a great improvement.

—*Thomas Jefferson's Cook Book*

Gumbs—A West India Dish

Okra entered the diet of the general population early on, as indicated by this recipe for stewed okra (here spelled "ocra") from the 1824 edition of a popular cookbook.

Gather young pods of ocra, wash them clean, and put them in a pan with a little water, salt and pepper, stew them till tender, and serve them with melted butter. They are very nutricious [sic] and easy of digestion.

—*Virginia House-wife*

Gumbo

Peel two quarts of ripe tomatoes, mix them with two quarts of young pods of ochre, and chop them small; put them in a stew pan, without any water; add four ounces of butter, and salt and pepper to your taste, and boil them gently and steadily for one hour; then pass it through a sieve into a tureen, and send to table with it, crackers, toasts, or light bread.

—The Kentucky Housewife

Fried Porgies

During the period of enslavement, blacks used what little free time they had to hunt and fish in order to supplement often scant rations. Porgy, was one of the fish that turned up in the pots. It remains an African American favorite at fish fries and Friday dinners.

Serves 6 to 8

12 medium porgies, cleaned, with heads and fins
    removed
¼ cup freshly squeezed lemon juice
Oil for frying
1 tablespoon seafood boil
¼ cup yellow cornmeal
¼ cup flour
Salt and freshly ground black pepper to taste
½ cup mayonnaise

Place the fish in a large bowl and sprinkle them with the lemon juice. Cover and let sit while you heat 2 inches of oil for frying to 250 degrees in a heavy cast iron skillet.

While the oil is heating, pulverize the seafood boil in a spice grinder and mix it together with the remaining ingredients in a brown paper bag. When ready to cook slather the fish on both sides with mayonnaise, then place a few fish at a time in the mixture and shake the bag to ensure that they are well covered.

Place the fish in the hot oil a few at a time and fry them for 2 to 3 minutes on each side, or until they are golden brown. Drain the fish on paper towels then place them on a warm platter. Repeat the process with the remaining fish until all are done. Serve at once.

—The Welcome Table

Possum with Sweet Potatoes

Skin a possum, and remove the head and feet. Wash carefully and salt heavily inside and out. Place the possum in a deep covered pan with a few cups of water and stew it for at least 1 hour. Then boil eight sweet potatoes in salted water, adding 2 tablespoons of butter and 1 tablespoon of sugar. Place the potatoes in the pot with the possum, lay $1/2$ dozen strips of bacon over the possum, sprinkle the top with thyme and marjoram, and place uncovered in an oven to brown at 400 degrees, basting frequently.

—A Taste for War

Calas

Calas are rice fritters that hark back to the Grain Coast of West Africa. The Vai people of the rice-growing regions of Sierra Leone and Liberia were represented in the Southern slave census. To them, the word for uncooked rice is kala. The word means "a stalk of cereal" to the Bambara people of West Africa and for the Gullah people of the South Carolina and Georgia Lowcountry, kala means rice. The fritters were one of the items hawked on the streets of New Orleans by women of color.

Serves 6

2¼ cups cold water
¾ cup raw long-grain rice
1½ packages dry yeast
½ cup lukewarm water
4 eggs, well beaten
¾ cup granulated sugar
¾ teaspoon salt
3 cups flour
Vegetable oil for frying
Confectioners' sugar for dusting

Place the cold water and rice in a saucepan and bring to a boil over high heat. Lower the heat and cook the rice for 25 to 30 minutes, or until it is soft and tender. Drain the rice, place it in a bowl, mash it with the back of a spoon, and set it aside to cool. In a separate bowl, dissolve the yeast in the lukewarm water, and then add it to the cooled rice. Beat the mixture for 2 minutes to aerate it, then cover the bowl with a slightly moistened towel and set it aside in a warm place to rise for 3 to 4 hours.

When ready to prepare the fritters, add the eggs, granulated sugar, salt, and flour to the rice mixture. Beat it thoroughly, cover it, and set it aside for 30 minutes. Heat 4 inches of oil in a heavy pan to 375 degrees. Drop the batter by the tablespoonful into the hot oil, frying a few at a time until golden brown. Drain on paper towels, then dust with confectioners' sugar and serve hot.

—The Welcome Table

Roasted Corn

Roasted ears of corn on the cob were a traditional treat during the period of enslavement, when they were roasted in the dying embers of a fire. Today they can be done on a barbecue grill.

> 4 ears of corn, husked
> Salt, cayenne pepper, and butter to taste

Heat the coals in the grill until red hot and then allow them to cool. Grease the rack and then place the ears of corn on it. Cook the ears for 5 to 7 minutes, turning them so that they are slightly charred but not burned on all sides. Serve immediately.

Son of a Gun Stew

Son of a Gun Stew was a cowboy favorite that used the less-noble parts of the animal. It was a treat for range riders, as it was served only after an animal was freshly slaughtered.

Serves 8

> 1 pound beef neck meat, cut in small pieces
> 1 beef heart, chopped
> 1 set beef brains
> ¾ pound marrow gut, cut in small pieces
> ⅓ pound calves liver, chopped
> 1 teaspoon salt
> 3 cloves garlic, minced
> 5 jalapeños, stemmed, seeded, and chopped
> Water
> 4 tablespoons tomato paste
> 6 cups beef broth
> Salt and pepper to taste

Cover the first eight ingredients with water in a large stockpot. Simmer for 6 to 7 hours, until meat is done. Check the stew occasionally and add water if necessary.

Stir the tomato paste into the beef broth and add to pot. Bring to a simmer for 10 minutes. Check seasonings and add salt and pepper if desired.

—Adapted from Texas Cooking Online,
     http://www/texascooking.com/recipes/sonofagun_stew.htm

Watermelon-Rind Pickles

This classic Southern condiment reminds of the ingenuity of those who made something from nothing. This recipe makes pickles similar to those served by my grandmother from Virginia, Grandma Jones.

Makes approximately 4 pints

    9 cups watermelon rind, cut into 1-inch cubes
    ½ cup salt
    2 quarts plus 2 cups water
    1¾ cups cider vinegar
    ½ cup balsamic vinegar
    2 cups dark brown sugar
    1 lemon, sliced thin
    2 sticks cinnamon, crushed
    1 teaspoon whole cloves
    2 teaspoons cracked allspice

Prepare the watermelon rind by removing the green skin and all but a small amount of the red meat. Place the prepared rind in a large bowl and soak it overnight in a brine prepared from the salt and 2 quarts of water.

When ready to make the pickles, drain the watermelon, wash it with fresh water, and drain it again. Place the rind in a large non-reactive saucepan, cover it with water, and simmer it for 15 minutes, or until it is fork-tender. Place the remaining ingredients, including the 2 cups of water, into a second nonreactive saucepan and bring them to a boil. Then lower the heat and simmer for 15 minutes, or until you have a thin syrup.

Drain the watermelon rind, add it to the syrup, and continue to simmer until the rind becomes translucent. Place the rind pieces in hot sterilized jars, cover them with the unstrained syrup, and seal them according to proper canning procedures. The pickles will keep for several months, if they last that long.

—The Martha's Vineyard Table

Pigs' Feet

Pigs' feet don't have much meat, just bone and gristle, but sucking the bits of meat off the bones and savoring the chewy skin is a treat for those who enjoy this traditional African American delicacy.

Serves 4 to 6

6 to 8 whole pigs' feet, split
2 bay leaves
6 peppercorns, cracked
½ cup cider vinegar
Hot sauce to taste

With a sharp knife, scrape the pigs' feet to remove all hair. (Recalcitrant hairs should be removed by singeing or by cutting off the piece of skin.) Place the pigs' feet in a large stockpot, cover with water, and bring to a boil. Allow the feet to boil for 3 to 5 minutes, then pour off the water and the scum that has accumulated. Rinse the feet and the pot. Replace the feet in the pot and cover them with water again. Add the bay leaves, peppercorns, and cider vinegar. Bring the liquid to a boil, then lower the heat and cook the feet for 2½ to 3 hours, or until the meat begins to fall off the bone. Remove the pigs' feet, drain them, place them on a platter, and serve hot, accompanied by the hot sauce of your choice.

—*The Welcome Table*

Fried Chicken

This is my mother's version of the classic Southern dish.

Serves 4 to 6

2½- to 3-pound frying chicken, cut into pieces
Vegetable oil for frying
½ cup flour
¼ cup white cornmeal
1½ tablespoons Bell's seasoning
Salt and freshly ground black pepper to taste

Wash the chicken pieces thoroughly and pat them dry with paper towels. Place the remaining ingredients in a brown paper bag and shake the bag to mix them well. Then add the chicken pieces to the bag a few at a time and shake it to ensure that each piece is well coated with the mix. Heat the oil to 350 degrees in a heavy cast iron skillet. Place the chicken pieces in the skillet and fry, uncovered, for 15 to 20 minutes, turning the chicken as it browns. Check for doneness by pricking the chicken with a fork; the juices should run clear with no trace of blood. Remove the chicken and drain the pieces on paper towels. Serve hot, warm, or at room temperature.

Note: The chicken is traditionally drained on pieces of brown paper bag, not on paper towels, but the latter will do just fine.

—*The Welcome Table*

Macaroni and Cheese

This dish is an African American classic. It has deeper roots in the culinary repertoire than is usually assumed and even turns up in other locales in the African diaspora like Barbados, where it is known as macaroni pie.

Cook macaroni broken up into short length in boiling salted water. Boil uncovered for twenty or thirty minutes, then drain. Fill a buttered pudding dish with alternate layers of macaroni and grated cheese, sprinkling pepper, salt, and melted butter over each layer. Have top layer of cheese, moisten with rich milk, bake in moderate oven until a rich brown.

—*Rufus Estes' Good Things to Eat*

Bean Pie

This is a variation of the bean pie that represented the Nation of Islam to many. It was sold on the streets and in restaurants run by mosques around the country. This version was given to me by my friend Charlotte Lyons, who is the food editor of Ebony magazine.

Makes one 9-inch pie

1 9-inch pie shell, baked for 10 minutes and
   cooled
2 (15-ounce) cans great northern beans, drained
3 eggs, slightly beaten
1¼ cups sugar
¼ cup unsalted butter
1 teaspoon vanilla extract
1 teaspoon ground cinnamon
1 teaspoon freshly grated nutmeg
½ teaspoon freshly ground allspice
1 teaspoon baking powder
⅓ cup evaporated milk

Preheat the oven to 350 degrees. Place the drained beans in a bowl and beat them with an electric mixer until they are smooth. Add the eggs, sugar, butter, vanilla, and spices. In a separate bowl, add the baking powder to the evaporated milk and pour it into the bean mixture. Beat the mixture well and then pour it into the partially baked pie shell. Bake the pie for 50 minutes, or until it is firm. Allow the pie to cool before serving.

—*The Welcome Table*

Smothered Pork Chops

It's all about the gravy in these traditional pork chops. In this recipe, the gravy is almost stewlike and flavored with clove, cinnamon, and allspice.

Serves 4 to 6

6 (1-inch thick) center-cut pork chops
3 tablespoons bacon drippings
1 lemon, thinly sliced
2 medium onions, thinly sliced
1 small green bell pepper, cored and sliced into
    rings
1 small red bell pepper, cored and sliced into
    rings
4 large ripe tomatoes, peeled, seeded, and
    coarsely chopped
1 cup water
2 tablespoons distilled white vinegar
Pinch of ground clove
Pinch of ground cinnamon
Pinch of ground allspice
Pinch of celery seed
Pinch of cayenne pepper
2 tablespoons sugar
Salt and freshly ground black pepper to taste

In a heavy skillet, brown the pork chops in the bacon drippings. Add the lemon, the onion, and the bell pepper slices and continue to sauté. In a small bowl, mix the tomatoes, water, vinegar, spices, sugar, and salt and pepper until they become a thick sauce and pour it over the pork chops. Cover the skillet and simmer the chops over medium heat for 45 minutes, or until they are tender and the tomato mixture has turned into a thick gravylike sauce.

—*The Welcome Table*

Brazilian Greens

In the twenty-first century, we have learned that not all greens are cooked with bacon drippings and a ham hock. This is the way that they accompany feijoada, the national dish of Brazil. The greens may be kale or collards or a mix, but I prefer to use collards.

Serves 4 to 6

2 pounds fresh young collard greens
3 tablespoons olive oil
8 cloves garlic, or to taste, minced
1 to 2 tablespoons water
Hot sauce to taste

Wash the collard greens thoroughly and bunch the leaves together. Take the bunch, roll it tightly, and cut it crosswise into thin strips. (This is a method that the French call *en chiffonade*.) Heat the oil in a large, heavy skillet over medium heat, then cook the garlic, stirring it until it's only slightly browned. Add the collard strips and cook them, stirring constantly for 5 minutes, so that the greens are soft but retain their bright color. Add a tablespoon or two of water, cover, lower the heat, and continue to cook for 2 minutes. Serve hot with the hot sauce of your choice.

—*Tasting Brazil*

Grandma Harris's Greens

My Grandma Harris didn't just use one green in this recipe. Instead, she prepared a mixture of bitey mustard greens and turnip greens along with the more classic collards. They were fantastic.

Serves 6

4 pounds mixed collard, mustard, and turnip
  greens
8 strips bacon
6 cups water
Salt and freshly ground black pepper to taste

For serving:
Hot sauce
Chopped onions
Balsamic vinegar

Wash the greens well, picking them over to remove any brown spots or blemishes, then drain them well, cut out the thick central stems, and tear the greens into bite-size pieces. Place the bacon strips in a large, heavy saucepan and cook them over medium heat until they are translucent and the bottom of the pan is covered with the rendered bacon fat. Add the greens and the water and bring to a boil over medium heat. Reduce the heat to low and continue to cook, covered, until the greens are tender—about 2 hours. Add salt and pepper to taste.

Serve the greens hot, accompanied by hot sauce, chopped onions, and vinegar.

Note: In some parts of the South, cooks add a pinch of sugar to their greens. My grandmother did not.

Garlic-, Rosemary-, and Lavender-Scented
Leg of Lamb with Spicy Mint Sauce

*This is a leg of lamb that might currently turn up on my table
for a party or a Sunday dinner.*

Serves 6 to 8

4- to 5-pound shank-end-half leg of lamb
6 large garlic cloves
1½ teaspoon dry lavender
1 tablespoon stripped fresh thyme
2 tablespoons sea salt
2 tablespoons mixed peppercorns
1 tablespoon thyme
1 tablespoon herbes de provence

Preheat the oven to 450 degrees. Trim all the excess fat and fell
from the leg of lamb, then pierce the lamb skin with 15 or so small
incisions. Place the garlic, lavender, and thyme in a small food pro-
cessor and pulse until you have a thick paste. Place a bit of the paste
into each of the incisions in the lamb. Lace the remaining dry ingredients together in a spice mill and pulse until you have a coarse
mix. Rub the mix all over the lamb, covering it entirely. Place the
lamb on a grill rack in a roasting pan and place it in the oven. Cook
at 450 degrees for 15 minutes, then lower the heat to 350 degrees
and continue to cook for 1 hour, or until the internal temperature
registers 140 degrees for rare, 150 degrees for medium rare, or 160
degrees for well done on a meat thermometer. (Cooking times will
vary according to the shape of the lamb and the heat of your oven.)
When it's done, allow the meat to rest for 15 minutes, then carve it
parallel to the bone in long thin slices and serve warm with Mint
Sauce (see below).

Mint Sauce

> 1 jar mint jelly
> 1 small jalapeno chili, or to taste, minced
> 2 tablespoons dark rum

Place the mint jelly in a small saucepan with the jalapeno chili and rum and cook over medium heat, stirring occasionally, until the sauce is warmed through. Serve warm in a sauceboat to accompany the lamb.

—The Martha's Vineyard Table

ACKNOWLEDGMENTS

High on the Hog is a work that has been in my head for decades, so it is impossible to acknowledge all who contributed to it personally and by name. You know who you are and please know that I am grateful for the conversations held, the meals shared, the sustaining phone calls, and more. I must also acknowledge all those who came before me in the area of food history and especially the trailblazers in the area of African American food history; I am only a link in the chain.

Some, though, must be thanked by name, and so I want to express my deep gratitude to those who helped me with research: Jan Bradford, Patricia Hopkins, Daniel Hammer, Georgia Chadwick, John T. Edge, Novelette Brown, Nishani Frasier, Shirley Sands, Susan Tucker, Karen Leatham, and librarians and research assistants, bookstore owners, postcard vendors, antique dealers, colleagues, and others. To all my editors past and present who have made me a better writer: Judith Kern, Pam Hoenig, Sydny Miner, Bill LeBlond, Robert Christgau, David Johnson, Audrey Peterson, and Corie Brown and the folks at Zesterdaily.com.

Thanks are also due my multi-continental extended "family," who nourished me both physically and mentally during the writing of this book, including in New York, Jane Daniels Lear and Sam Lear, Elaine Greenstein and Jose Medina, Jacqueline and Bill Reeves, Vanessa Abukusumo and family, William Freeman, Cheikh Oumar Thiam and family, Makale Faber Cullen and Rico Cullen, Yvette Burgess Polcyn and family, Martha Mae Jones, Thomas Jayne and Rick Ellis, Tom Gibson, Linda Cohen, Shikha Dalal and family, Vasu Varadan, and my friend, counselor, and quiet mentor Maya Angelou. A tip of the hat to Eddie Garcia, mailman extraordinaire, and my neighbors the Payne Hall family, especially "Miss" Julia, who is my cats' new godmother. Friends and colleagues at Queens College and Dillard University have been especially helpful, particularly their respective presidents, Jim Muyskens and Marvalene Hughes, and Nancy Comley, Frank Franklin, Michael Cogswell, Ricky Riccardi, Danille Taylor, Tony King, David V. Taylor, Bettye Parker Smith, Jerry Ward, Gail Bowman, Zena Ezeb, and Corthel Clark. In New Orleans, the Costa family, Gail McDonough, Leah Chase and family, Lolis Eric Elie and family, Ron and Nancy Harrell, Michèle and Ulrick Jean Pierre, Ann and Matt Konigsmark and family, Liz Williams, Daphne Derven, John Batty, Poppy Tooker, Ken Smith, Simon and Shelly Gunning, Michael Sartisky, Nadine and Simon Blake, Priscilla and John Lawrence and the team at HNOC, Kerry Moody, Patrick Dunne, and the Lucullus ladies—Roberta, Rebecca, and Michelle—all aided, abetted, and suffered through my madness. The Charleston Crew, including Mitchell and Randall, Kit and Mary, Nichole Greene, Lou Hammond, and Elizabeth and Paul Kitchen, keep me smiling always. The Martha's Vineyard contingent, Olive Tomlinson, Keren Tonnensen, Mitzi and Flip, Gretchen Tucker Underwood, Madelon Stent Gibell and Ron Gibell, "Aunt" Vivian Douglass, Charlayne Hunter-Gault and Ron Gault, Holly Nadler, Doug Best, Rhonda Conley, David Amaral, Anne Patrick, Daryl Alexander, Ron and Paula, Ron and Anne, and the Blitzer family, haul me around and drag me away from my computer when I get too serious.

Thanks are also due those who started me on my journey by giving me my first tastes of the food of the continent of my ancestors: In Benin, the Komaclo, Houemavo, and Grimaud clans, especially Theodora, Theophile Linda, Alain, Yves, Serge, Aimée, Albert, Christo, Alexi, and Bobby. In Senegal, Anna Kamara and Nichole Ndongo Cool—long-lost sisters recently returned to the fold. My spiritual family at Casa Branca do Engenho Velho continues to sustain me, especially Mae Tatá, Sinha, Gersoney, and Belo. Friends far and near like Peter Patout, Patricia Wilson, Patricia Lawrence and Noel, John Martin Taylor, Maricel Presilla, Judith Carney, Dr. Debbie, Fritz Blank, William Woys Weaver, and Martha Rose Schulman became involved with this project, and I thank them as well. There is always someone whom I inadvertently forgot; if it is you, please know that it is not through lack of gratitude. I could have not done this without the daily support of "my" universe.

Finally, abundant thanks are due Susan Ginsburg, my agent, who worked tirelessly to make this pig kosher, and her assistant, Bethany, who on paper and on the phone always recognized my voice, and newly arrived Carrie, who reminds me "no worries." To all of the team at Bloomsbury—publisher George Gibson, who paired me with Kathy Belden; Mike O'Connor, who understood; Sabrina Farber, who holds the piggy's purse strings; Peter Miller and Jonathan Kroberger, who got the word out about the pig; Laura Phillips, who kept the pig moving; my appreciative copyeditor, Maureen Klier; and especially Kathy Belden, editor become friend, who believed in me and in this project even when I doubted myself. She encouraged me daily, corrected and counseled me almost as often, and in the end got this little piggy to market!

It seemed at times during the three-year period that I spent writing this book that I'd dropped out of my own life—

To those who missed me—I'm back.

To those who sustained me—I am more grateful than
I can ever express.

To those who have appeared or re-appeared along the
way—Welcome to my world!

FURTHER READING

The following is a by-no-means exhaustive listing of some of the works I consulted in writing *High on the Hog*. A more complete listing is posted on my Web site www.africooks.com.

Abrahams, Roger D. *Singing the Master: The Emergence of African American Culture in the Plantation South*. New York: Pantheon, 1992.

Banks, Katherine Bell, with Robert C. Hayden. *William E.B. Du Bois: Family and Friendship: Another Side of the Man*. Littleton, MA: Tapestry Press, 2004.

Bascom, Lionel, ed. *A Renaissance in Harlem: Lost Essays of the WPA, by Ralph Ellison, Dorothy West, and Other Voices of a Generation*. Cambridge, MA: Bascom, 2007.

Beckles, Hilary McD., and Verene A. Shepherd. *Trading Souls: Europe's Transatlantic Trade in Africans*. Kingston: Ian Randle, 2007.

Berlin, Ira, et al. *Free at Last: A Documentary History of Slavery, Freedom, and the Civil War*. NewYork: New Press, 1992.

Berlin, Ira, and Leslie M. Harris, eds. *Slavery in New York*. New York: New Press, 2005.

Berzok, Linda Murray. *American Indian Food*. Westport, CT: Greenwood, 2005.

Blassingame, John W. *The Slave Community: Plantation Life in the Antebellum South*. New York: Oxford University Press, 1979.

Boilat, Abbé David. *Esquisses Sénégalaises*. 1853. Dakar: Karthala, 1984.

Bolster, W. Jeffrey. *Black Jacks: African American Seamen in the Age of Sail*. Cambridge, MA: Harvard University Press, 1997.

Bower, Anne L. *African American Foodways: Explorations of History and Culture*. Urbana: University of Illinois Press, 2007.

Boyd, Herb, ed. *The Harlem Reader: A Celebration of New York's Most*

Famous Neighborhood from the Renaissance Years to the 21st Century. New York: Three Rivers Press, 2003.

Buckingham, J. S. *A Journey Through the Slave States of North America*. 1842. Charleston, SC: History Press, 2006.

Burnside, Madeline, and Rosemarie Robotham. *Spirits of the Passage: The Transatlantic Slave Trade in the Seventeenth Century*. New York: Simon & Schuster, 1997.

Campbell, Edward D. C. Jr., and Kym S. Rice, eds. *Before Freedom Came: African-American Life in the Antebellum South*. Richmond and Charlottesville, VA: Museum of the Confederacy and the University Press of Virginia, 1991.

Carney, Judith. *Black Rice: The African Origins of Rice Cultivation in the Americas*. Cambridge: Harvard University Press, 2001.

Carney, Judith, and Richard Nicholas Rosomoff. *In the Shadow of Slavery: Africa's Botanical Legacy in the Atlantic World*. Berkeley: University of California Press, 2009.

Carretta, Vincent. *Equiano the African: Biography of a Self-made Man*. Athens: University of Georgia Press, 2005.

Chesnais, Robert. Introduction. In *Louis XIV: Le Code Noir*. Paris: L'Esprit Frappeur, 1998.

Clinton, Catherine. *Tara Revisited: Women, War and the Plantation Legend*. New York: Abbeville, 1995.

Confederate Receipt Book: A Compilation of Over One Hundred Receipts, Adapted to the Times. Athens: University of Georgia Press, 1960.

Conneau, Theophilus. *A Slaver's Log Book; Or, 20 Years Residence in Africa*. Introduction by Mabel M. Smythe. 1853. Englewood Cliffs, NJ: Prentice Hall, 1976.

Coules, Victoria. *The Trade: Bristol and the Transatlantic Slave Trade*. Edinburgh: Birlinn, 2007.

Covey, Cyclone, ed. *Cabeza de Vaca's Adventures in the Unknown Interior*. Translated by Cyclone Covey. Albuquerque: University of New Mexico Press, 1983.

Crew, Spencer, and Cynthia Goodman. Introduction. In *Unchained Memories: Readings from the Slave Narratives*. New York: Bullfinch, 2002.

Curtin, Philip D. *The Atlantic Slave Trade: A Census*. Madison: University of Wisconsin Press, 1969.

Davis, William C. *A Taste for War: The Culinary History of the Blue and the Gray*. Mechanicsburg, PA: Stackpole, 2003.

Delcourt, Jean. *La turbulente histoire de Gorée*. Dakar: Clairafrique, 1982.

Dodson, Howard, and Sylviane Dioup. *In Motion: The African American Experience*. Washington, D.C.: National Geographic, 2004.

Dow, George Francis. *Slave Ships and Slaving*. 1927. Mineola, NY: Dover, 2002.

Du Bois, W. E. B. *The Philadelphia Negro: A Social Study*. 1899. Introduction by Elijah Anderson. Philadelphia: University of Pennsylvania Press, 1996.

Eden, Trudy. *The Early American Table: Food and Society in the New World*. DeKalb: Northern Illinois University Press, 2008.

Ellison, Ralph. *Invisible Man*. 1947. New York: Modern Library, 1994.

Eltis, David. *The Rise of African Slavery in the Americas*. Cambridge: Cambridge University Press, 2000.

Equiano, Olaudah. *The Interesting Narrative of the Life of Olaudah Equiano; or, Gustavus Vassa, the African, Written by Himself*. Edited by Paul Edwards. Harlow, Essex: Longman, 1988.

Estes, Rufus. *Good Things to Eat as Suggested by Rufus*. Chicago, 1911. Reprinted as *Rufus Estes' Good Things to Eat: The First Cookbook by an African American Chef*. Mineola, NY: Dover, 2004.

Feest, Christian F. *The Cultures of Native North America*. Cologne: Konemann, 2000.

Ferloni, Julia. *Marchands d'esclaves de la traite à l'abolition*. Paris: Editions de Conti, 2005.

Fowler, Damon Lee, ed. *Dining at Monticello: In Good Taste and Abundance*. Monticello, VA: Thomas Jefferson Foundation, 2005.

Frank, Andrew K., ed. *The Routledge Historical Atlas of the American South*. New York: Routledge, 1999.

Gallay, Alan. *The Indian Slave Trade: The Rise of Empire in the American South, 1670–1717*. New Haven, CT: Yale University Press, 2002.

Gates, Henry Louis, and Nellie Y. McKay, eds. *The Norton Anthology: African American Literature*. New York: W. W. Norton, 1997.

Gatewood, Willard B. *Aristocrats of Color: The Black Elite, 1880–1920*. Bloomington: Indiana University Press, 1993.

Genovese, Eugene. *Roll, Jordan, Roll: The World the Slaves Made*. New York: Vintage, 1976.

Gomez, Michael. *Exchanging Our Country Marks: The Transformation of African Identities in the Colonial and Antebellum South*. Chapel Hill: University of North Carolina Press, 1998.

———. *Reversing Sail: A History of the African Diaspora*. Cambridge: Cambridge University Press, 2005.

Goings, Kenneth W. *Mammy and Uncle Mose: Black Collectibles and American Stereotyping*. Bloomington: Indiana University Press, 1994.

Gordon-Reed, Annette. *The Hemingses of Monticello: An American Family*. New York: W. W. Norton, 2008.

Greene, Harlan, Harry S. Hutchins Jr., and Brian E. Hutchins. *Slave Badges and the Slave-Hire System in Charleston, South Carolina, 1783–1865*. Jefferson, NC: McFarland, 2004.

Hall, Martin. *African Archaeology*. Cape Town: David Phillip, 1996.

Harris, Jessica B. *The Africa Cookbook: Tastes of a Continent*. New York: Simon & Schuster, 1998.

———. *Iron Pots and Wooden Spoons: Africa's Gifts to New World Cooking*. New York: Atheneum, 1989.

———. *A Kwanzaa Keepsake*. New York: Simon & Schuster, 1995.

———. *The Welcome Table*. New York: Simon & Schuster, 1995.

Hashaw, Tim. *The Birth of Black America: The First Africans and the Pursuit of Freedom at Jamestown*. New York: Carroll & Graf, 2007.

Hess, Karen. *The Carolina Rice Kitchen: The African Connection*. Columbia: University of South Carolina Press, 1992.

Hilliard, Sam Bowers. *Hog Meat and Hoecake: Food Supply in the Old South, 1840–1860*. Carbondale: Southern Illinois University Press, 1972.

Hine, Darlene Clark, William C. Hine, and Stanley Harrold. *The African American Odyssey*. 3rd ed. Upper Saddle River, NJ: Pearson, Prentice Hall, 2006.

Holdredge, Helen O'Donnell. *Mammy Pleasant*. New York: G. P. Putnam's Sons, 1953.

Horton, James Oliver, and Lois E. Horton. *Slavery and the Making of America*. New York: Oxford University Press, 2005.

Hudson, Lynn M. *The Making of "Mammy Pleasant": A Black Entrepreneur in Nineteenth-Century San Francisco*. Urbana: University of Illinois Press, 2003.

Hughes, Langston. *The Langston Hughes Reader: The Selected Writings of Langston Hughes*. New York: Braziller, 1958.

Hurmence, Belinda. *Before Freedom, When I Just Can Remember*. Winston-Salem, NC: John Blair, 1989.

Johnson, Charles, Patricia Smith, and the WGBH Series Research Team. *Africans in America: America's Journey Through Slavery*. New York: Harcourt Brace, 1998.

Jones, Evan. *American Food: The Gastronomic Story*. New York: Dutton, 1975.

Joyner, Charles. *Down by the Riverside: A South Carolina Slave Community*. Urbana: University of Illinois Press, 1984.

Katz, William Loren. *The Black West: A Documentary and Pictorial History*. Garden City, NJ: Anchor, 1973.

———*The Black West*. 3rd ed. Seattle: Open Hand, 1987.

Kemble, Frances Anne. *Journal of a Residence on a Georgian Plantation in 1838–1839*. Edited by John A. Scott. Athens, GA: Brown Thrasher, 1984.

Kimball, Marie. *Thomas Jefferson's Cook Book*. Charlottesville: University Press of Virginia, 1976.

King, David. *First People*. London: Dorling Kindersley, 2008.

Klapthor, Margaret, et al. *The First Ladies Cook Book: Favorite Recipes of All the Presidents of the United States*. New York: Parents' Magazine, 1969.

Latrobe, Benjamin Henry Boneval. *Impressions Respecting New Orleans: Diary and Sketches, 1818–1820*. Edited by Samuel Wilson. New York: Columbia University Press, 1951.

Latrobe, John H. B. *Southern Travels: Journal of John H. B. Latrobe*. Edited by Samuel Wilson Jr. New Orleans: Historic New Orleans Collection, 1986.

Leckie, William H. *The Buffalo Soldiers: A Narrative of the Negro Cavalry in the West*. Norman: University of Oklahoma Press, 1967.

Linck, Ernestine Sewell, and Joyce Gibson Roach. *Eats: A Folk History of Texas Foods*. Fort Worth: Texas Christian University Press, 1989.

Littlefield, Daniel C. *Rice and Slaves: Ethnicity and the Slave Trade in Colonial South Carolina*. Urbana: University of Illinois Press, 1981.

Luchetti, Emily. *Home on the Range: A Culinary History of the American West*. New York: Villard, 1993.

Mannix, Daniel P., in collaboration with Malcolm Cowley. *Black Cargoes: A History of the Atlantic Slave Trade*. New York: Viking, 1962.

Marseille, Jacques, and Dominique Margairaz, eds. *1789: Au jour le jour*. Paris: Albin Michel, 1988.

Martin, Judith. *Star-Spangled Manners: In Which Miss Manners Defends American Etiquette (For a Change)*. New York: W. W. Norton, 2003.

McInnis, Maurie D. *The Politics of Taste in Antebellum Charleston*. Chapel Hill: University of North Carolina Press, 2005.

McMillin, James A. *The Final Victims: Foreign Slave Trade to North America, 1783–1810*. Columbia: University of South Carolina Press, 2004.

Newman, James L. *The Peopling of Africa: A Geographic Interpretation*. New Haven, CT: Yale University Press, 1995.

Oliver, Sandra. *Food in Colonial and Federal America*. Westport, CT: Greenwood, 2005.

Phillipson, David W. *African Archaeology*. 2nd ed. Cambridge: Cambridge University Press, 1995.

Phipps, Frances. *Colonial Kitchens, Their Furnishings, and Their Gardens*. New York: Hawthorn, 1972.

Plasse, Jean Pierre. *Journal de bord d'un négrier: Adapté du français du XVIIIe par Bernard Plasse*. 1762. Marseilles: Le Mot et le Reste, 2005.

Randolph, Mary. *The Virginia House-wife*. 1824. Washington, D.C. Reprinted as *The Virginia House-wife with Historical Notes and Commentaries by Karen Hess*. Columbia: University of South Carolina Press, 1984.

Rawley, James A. *The Trans-Atlantic Slave Trade*. New York: W. W. Norton, 1981.

Rediker, Marcus. *The Slave Ship: A Human History*. New York: Viking, 2007.

Rowley, Anthony, ed. *Les Français à table: Atlas historique de la gastronomie française*. Paris: Hachette, 1997.

Schenone, Laura. *A Thousand Years over a Hot Stove: A History of American Women Told Through Food, Recipes, and Remembrances*. New York: W. W. Norton, 2003.

Schneider, Dorothy, and Carl J. Schneider. *Slavery in America: An Eyewitness History*. New York: Checkmark, 2007.

Schwarz, Philip J. *Slavery at the Home of George Washington*. Mount Vernon, VA: Mount Vernon Ladies Association, 2001.

Shaw, Thurstan, et al. *The Archaeology of Africa: Food, Metals and Towns*. London: Routledge, 1993.

Sloan. Kim. *A New World: England's First View of America*. Chapel Hill: University of North Carolina Press, 2007.

Stanton, Lucia. *Free Some Day: The African American Families of Monticello*. Monticello, VA: Thomas Jefferson Memorial Foundation, 2000.

———. *Slavery at Monticello*. Monticello, VA: Thomas Jefferson Memorial Foundation, 1996.

Stoney, Mrs. Samuel G. *The Carolina Rice Cook Book*. N.p., n.p., 1901. Reprinted in 1992 in *The Carolina Rice Kitchen* by the University of South Carolina Press with an introduction by Karen Hess.

Survey Graphic: Harlem, Mecca of the New Negro. March 1925. Reprint by Black Classic Press, Baltimore, MD.

Svalesen, Leif. *The Slave Ship Fredensborg*. Kingston: Ian Randle, 2000.

Swanton, John R. *The Indians of the Southeastern United States*. Smithsonian Institution Bureau of American Ethnology Bulletin 137. Washington, D.C.: U.S. Government Printing Office, 1946.

Taylor, Susie King. *Reminiscences of My Life in Camp with the 33rd U.S. Colored Troops, Late 1st South Carolina Volunteers*. Boston, 1902. Reprinted as *Reminiscences of My Life: A Black Woman's Civil War Memoirs*. Edited by Patricia W. Romero. New York: Markus Wiener, 1988.

Taylor, Yuval, ed. *I Was Born a Slave: An Anthology of Classic Slave Narratives*. Vol. 2. Edinburgh: Payback, 1999.

Thomas, Hugh. *The Slave Trade: The Story of the Atlantic Slave Trade, 1440–1870*. New York: Simon & Schuster, 1997.

Thornton, John. *Africa and Africans in the Making of the Atlantic World, 1400–1800*. 2nd ed. Cambridge: Cambridge University Press, 1998.

Thoronborough, Emma Lou. *The Negro in Indiana Before 1900: A Study of a Minority*. Bloomington: Indiana University Press, 1985.

Tibbles, Anthony, ed. *Transatlantic Slavery: Against Human Dignity*. London: Her Majesty's Stationery Office, 1995.

Vlach, John Michael. *Back of the Big House: The Architecture of Plantation Slavery*. Chapel Hill: University of North Carolina Press, 1993.

Ward, Andrew. *The Slaves' War: The Civil War in the Words of Former Slaves*. Boston: Houghton Mifflin, 2008.

White, Deborah Gray. *Ar'n't I a Woman: Female Slaves in the Plantation South*. New York: W. W. Norton, 1985.

Wilson, Charles Regan, ed. *The New Encyclopedia of Southern Culture*. 12 vols. Chapel Hill: University of North Carolina Press, 1989, 2006.

Wood, Peter H. *Strange New Land: Africans in Colonial America*. New York: Oxford University Press, 2003.

Wright, Louis B. *The Cultural Life of the American Colonies*. 1957. Edited by Henry Steele Commager and Richard Brandon Morris. New York: Dover, 2002.

Yetman, Norman R., ed. *Voices from Slavery: 100 Authentic Slave Narratives*. 1970.

Life Under the "Peculiar Institution": Selections from the Slave Narrative Collection. Mineola, NY: Dover, 2000.

Zimmerman, Larry J. *American Indians: The First Nations—Native North American Life, Myth and Art*. London: Duncan Baird, 2003.

SELECTED AFRICAN AMERICAN COOKBOOKS
(*IN CHRONOLOGICAL ORDER*)

Roberts, Robert. *The House Servant's Directory; or, A Monitor for Private Families: Comprising Hints on the Arrangement and Performance of Servants' Work . . . and Upwards of 100 Various and Useful Recipes, Chiefly Compiled for the Use of House Servants.* Boston: Munroe and Francis, 1827.

This is the first work by an African American author that includes recipes. It is fascinating in its advice to young men who wanted to go into the profession of butler.

Russell, Malinda. *A Domestic Cook Book: Containing a Careful Selection of Useful Receipts for the Kitchen by Malinda Russell a Free Woman of Color.* Paw Paw, MI, 1866.

This is the first cookbook by an African American author. It is notable not only for its early date but also for the variety of recipes included.

Fisher, Abby. *What Mrs. Fisher Knows About Old Southern Cooking, Soups, Pickles, Preserves, Etc.* San Francisco: Women's Cooperative Printing Office, 1881.

Long thought to be the first African American cookbook, this work offers recipes for some classic Southern dishes as well as an extensive array of condiments. A facsimile edition with extensive notes by the late culinary historian Karen Hess is available.

Estes, Rufus. *Rufus Estes' Good Things to Eat, As Suggested by Rufus: A Collection of Practical Recipes for Preparing Meats, Game, Fowl, Fish, Puddings, Pastries, Etc.* Chicago: Franklin, 1911.

The first cookbook written by an African American chef offers a sophisticated range of recipes as well as advice for kitchen maids and a brief sketch of Estes's life.

Hayes, Mrs. W. T. *Kentucky Cook Book: Easy and Simple for Any Cook, by a Colored Woman.* St. Louis: Tomkins, 1912.

The work offers recipes for a variety of Southern classics as well as fascinating photographs of some of the cooks.

Carver, George Washington. *105 Different Ways to Prepare the Peanut for the Table.* N.p., n.p., n.d.

The title tells all about this pamphlet, which is also found as an appendix in Carver's biography.

Richard, Lena. *Lena Richard's Cook Book*. New Orleans: Rogers, 1939.
    This work, by the first black woman to have a television show, offers creole recipes from southern Louisiana as well as more traditional culinary classics.

DeKnight, Freda. *A Date with a Dish: A Cookbook of American Negro Recipes*. New York: Hermitage, 1948.
    The book, by *Ebony* magazine's first food editor, contains mid-twentieth-century versions of African American classics. It has been re-edited several times and is still in print as the *Ebony Cookbook*.

Muhammad, Elijah. *How to Eat to Live*. Chicago: Muhammad Mosque of Islam No. 2, 1967.
    The leader of the Nation of Islam offers his views on nutrition and health. A second volume was published in 1972.

Princess Pamela. *Princess Pamela's Soul Food Cookbook*. New York: Signet-NAL, 1969.
    This paperback work by the New York owner of a popular East Village soul food eatery epitomizes the era.

The Tuesday Soul Food Cookbook. Tuesday Magazine. New York: Bantam, 1969.
    This compilation was assembled by the editors of a Sunday supplement for black readers.

Grosvenor, Verta Mae Smart. *Vibration Cooking; or, The Travel Notes of a Geechee Girl*. Garden City, NY: Doubleday, 1970.
    There have been three editions of the NPR commentator's work on her travels around the African Diaspora and the foods that she encountered.

Mendes, Helen. *The African Heritage Cookbook*. New York: Macmillan, 1971.
    This is one of the first works to connect the foods of Africa, the Caribbean, and the American South.

Lewis, Edna, and Evangeline Peterson. *The Edna Lewis Cookbook*. N.p., n.p., 1972.
    "Miss Edna's" first cookbook begins to present her theories on fresh and seasonal foods.

Darden, Norma Jean, and Carole Darden. *Spoonbread and Strawberry Wine: Recipes and Reminiscences of a Family*. New York: Doubleday, 1978.
    The story of the Darden family is told with anecdotes, photographs, and food.

Edwards, Gary, and John Mason. *Onj E Fun Ori Sa* (Food for the Gods). New York: Yoruba Theological Archministry, 1981.

The privately published work looks at the ritual offerings made to the orisha of the Yoruba religion and the loa of Vodun and is the first to examine the foods of the New World African religions that many African American artists are becoming involved with.

Bulter, Cleora. *Cleora's Kitchens: The Memoir of a Cook and Eight Decades of Great American Food*. Tulsa, OK: Council Oak, 1985.

The changing food trends of the twentieth century are told by a domestic cook in this book that is memoir and recipe.

Paige, Howard. *Aspects of Afro-American Cookery*. Southfield, MI: Aspects, 1987.

This is an early and often overlooked work of African American culinary history.

Kondo, Nia, and Zack Kondo. *Vegetarianism Made Simple and Easy: A Primer for Black People*. Washington, D.C.: Nubia, 1989.

Self-explanatory.

Chase, Leah. *The Dooky Chase Cookbook*. Gretna, LA: Pelican, 1990.

The empress of creole cooking offers up the favorite dishes from her restaurant along with photographs of the art for which it is noted.

National Council of Negro Women. *The Black Family Reunion Cookbook: Recipes and Food Memories*. Memphis: Tradery, 1991.

The umbrella organization for many African American women's clubs banded together and made this the bestselling African American cookbook of all time.

Copage, Eric. *Kwanzaa: An African American Celebration of Culture and Cooking*. New York: Quill–William Morrow, 1991.

This is one of the first works to celebrate the increasing popularity of the African American holiday Kwanzaa.

Smith, Barbara. *B. Smith's Entertaining and Cooking for Friends*. With Kathleen Cromwell. New York: Artisan, 1995.

The former model and current restaurateur and entrepreneur par excellence authored this entertaining and lifestyle book, which is lavishly illustrated with four-color photos featuring African Americans in idealized settings.

Shange, Ntozake. *If I Can Cook/You Know God Can*. Boston: Beacon, 1998.

Author of the popular play *For Colored Girls Who Have Considered Suicide When the Rainbow Is Enuf*.

Terry, Bryant. *Vegan Soul Kitchen: Fresh, Healthy, and Creative African-American Cuisine*. Cambridge, MA: Da Capo Press, 2009.

The title says it all, this self-proclaimed eco-chef and food justice activist leads the way toward the future.

ILLUSTRATIONS

INDEX

Africa
  African American visits to, 214–215
  cattle herding knowledge from,
    145–146
  chefs from, 239–240
  European colonialism in, 24–25
  independence movements, 212
  manners in, 108–109
  pottery forms from, 100
  slave trade and slave depots, 24–27
African American museums, 91, 141–143
African food
  arrival of, in Western hemisphere,
    30–31
  cereals, rice, and yams crucibles, 9–10
  chuck wagon cooks and, 149–150
  cooking techniques, 11
  Equiano on, 39
  full circle, 243
  fusion cuisine, colonial, 25–26
  Islamic and Christian influences, 15
  markets of, 7–8
  New World plants, influence of, 11
  one-pot meals, 100
  plant foods brought to New World
    from, 16–19
  prehistory, 9
  rice dishes in Big House from Africa,
    71
  rituals and traditional holidays, 14–15
  on slave ships, 30–33, 34–35
  street food originating from, 129–130
  traveler accounts, 10–15
Albir, Victoria, 25
Allen, Richard, 72
Anderson, Merendy, 3

Atlanta, 199–201
Atlantic Creoles, 25, 33
Augustin family, 119–120

Baker, Ella, 205
barbecue, 102, 169–170
bean pie, 211, 218, 260
Bedford Stuyvesant, 223–226
Bell, Thomas, 151
Bellamy, Frank, 209
Benin, 7–8
Bernoon, Emmanuel Manna, 116–117
Biddle, Nicholas, 118–119
Big House, 67–69, 73–84, 102–106
black-eyed peas, 18, 32, 214
Black Power movement, 206–207
black studies, 211
Blair, Ezell, Jr., 204, 206
Bogle, Robert, 118–119
Boone Hall (Charleston), 89
Boré, Etienne de, 129
British colonies, 51–57, 212
Brown, John, 98, 151
Brown v. Board of Education (1954),
  202–203, 212
Buchanan, William, 158–159
Buckingham, J. S., 70, 94
Buffalo Soldiers, 158–159
Burgess, Mary Keyes, 215
butlers, public, 118
Byran, Letice, 105
Byrd, Frank, 175–176, 177

Cabeza de Vaca, Álvar Núñez, 46–47
Caillé, René, 13
cala (rice fritter), 129

A NOTE ON THE AUTHOR

JESSICA B. HARRIS is the author of eleven cookbooks documenting the foods and foodways of the African Diaspora. She has written extensively about the culture of Africa in the Americas, lectured widely, and made numerous television appearances. She is a professor at Queens College, CUNY, and consults at Dillard University in New Orleans, where she founded the Institute for the Study of Culinary Cultures. She was recently inducted into the James Beard Foundation's prestigious Who's Who of Food and Beverage in America. She lives in New York City, New Orleans, and on Martha's Vineyard.